THE CROWNING PRIVILEGE

OTHER WORKS BY ROBERT GRAVES INCLUDE:

Poems, 1914–1926, Heinemann; Doubleday, 1927
Collected Poems 1938, Cassell, 1938; Random House, 1939
Collected Poems 1914–1947, Cassell, 1948
Poems and Satires 1951, Cassell; Creative Age Press, 1951
Poems 1953, Cassell; Creative Age Press, 1953
Collected Poems 1955, Doubleday, 1955

The English Ballad, Benn, 1926
Lawrence and the Arabian Adventure (*Lawrence and the Arabs*)
Goodbye to All That, Cape; Smith, 1929
The Real David Copperfield
I, Claudius, Barker; Smith, 1934
Claudius the God, etc., Barker; Smith, 1935
Antigua, Penny, Puce (*The Antigua Stamp*), Constable; Random House, 1938
Count Belisarius, Cassell, 1939; Random House, 1938
T. E. Lawrence to His Biographer, Faber; Doubleday, 1939
Sergeant Lamb's America (*Sergeant Lamb of the Ninth*), Random House,
    Methuen, 1940
(with Hodge, Alan) *The Long Weekend,* Faber; Macmillan (U.S.A.), 1940
Proceed, Sergeant Lamb, Random House; Methuen, 1941
(with Hodge, Alan) *The Reader Over Your Shoulder: A Handbook for Writers
    of English Prose,* Cape; Macmillan (U.S.A.), 1943
Wife to Mr. Milton, Cassell; Creative Age, 1943
King Jesus, Cassell; Creative Age, 1946
Hercules, My Shipmate (*The Golden Fleece*), Cassell; Creative Age, 1945
The White Goddess: An Historical Grammar of Poetic Myth, Faber; Creative
    Age, 1948
The Common Asphodel: Collected Essays on Poetry, 1922–49, Hamilton, 1949
The Islands of Unwisdom, Cassell, 1950; Doubleday, 1949
Seven Days in New Crete (*Watch the Northwind Rise*), Cassell; Creative
    Age, 1949
The Golden Ass (*translation*), Penguin, 1950
Occupation: Writer, Cassell; Farrar Straus, 1950
(with Podro, Joshua) *The Nazarene Gospel Restored,* Cassell, 1953; Double-
    day, 1954
Homer's Daughter, Cassell; Doubleday, 1955
The Greek Myths, Penguin (England and U.S.A.), 1955
Cross and Sword (*translation from Spanish*), University of Indiana Press, 1955
The Infant with the Globe (*translation from Spanish*), Faber (Trianon Press),
    1955
Adam's Rib, Faber (Trianon Press), 1955
The Crowning Privilege, Cassell, 1955
Winter in Majorca

The
Crowning
Privilege

COLLECTED ESSAYS ON POETRY

by ROBERT GRAVES

DOUBLEDAY & COMPANY, INC., GARDEN CITY, NEW YORK, 1956

Library of Congress Catalog Card Number 56–6542

First published 1956 in the United States
Copyright 1955 by Robert Graves. All Rights Reserved
Printed in the United States at
The Country Life Press, Garden City, New York
Designed by Patricia Walsh
First Edition

*To the Masters and Fellows
of Trinity College, Cambridge; in gratitude*

FOREWORD

It is doubtful whether lectures intended for delivery to a largely undergraduate audience, and therefore addressed in the first place to the passions, should be published as though they were closely argued critical essays. But such is the custom with the annual Clark Lectures sponsored by Trinity College, Cambridge; and so I have done no more with this year's batch than to check my facts and restore a few passages extemporaneously omitted after an anxious glance at the lecture-room clock. Professor F. W. Bateson, who was up at Oxford with me just after the First World War, has been good enough to read proofs.

My subject was: 'Professional Standards in English Poetry', but I am using the title of the first lecture for this book, since it is enlarged with several essays on poetry or related topics, and a broadcast piece. The 'crowning privilege' of the English poet is, as I explain, his membership of a wholly anarchic profession. No craft-school grants him diplomas; no Royal Academy grades his technical capacities; no General Council disciplines him. His responsibility must be to the Muse alone, a stern taskmistress never satisfied with any performance offered her. He will speak his mind about poetry without polite qualification (short of committing treason or obscene libel), but remains always in a minority of one, unless he breaks with poetic tradition by organizing a clique, pleiad or movement in Continental style.

Deyá, Majorca, Spain   R. G.

CONTENTS

THE COMMON ASPHODEL

THE CLARK LECTURES
1954–1955

THE CROWNING PRIVILEGE

My gratitude to the Trinity College authorities for having thought of me when they chose this year's Clark Lecturer, is tinged with a certain surprise. I have been domiciled in Spain for nearly twenty-five years, and not lectured at an English University since the First World War. In 1917, I was quartered at Wadham College, Oxford, where my audience consisted of officer cadets, mostly from oversea, and my subjects were tactics, leadership, morale, the use and maintenance of weapons, military law, map-reading, and the conduct expected of an officer and gentleman. An ideal audience, because whoever yawned or doodled in his notebook, or argued the toss, or dared to look at me with what we called ' dumb insolence ', was liable to be returned to his unit: which, in 1917, usually meant the trenches. While giving these cadets a three months' intensive course in professional military standards, I had to be practical, and also downright. And also humble: most of them were older than I, and had a better general education. Today I am equally humble, with all the awkwardness of a grey-headed backwoodsman (toting my billy, frying-pan, and axe); but intend to be equally practical and downright.

Before discussing professional standards in English poetry, which are the general topic of these lectures, let me emphasize an important point. Unlike stockbrokers, soldiers, sailors, doctors, lawyers, and parsons, English poets do not form a closely integrated guild. A poet may put up his brass plate, so to speak, without the tedious preliminaries of attending a university, reading the required books and satisfying examiners. Also, a poet, being responsible to no General Council, and acknowledging no personal superior, can never be unfrocked, cashiered, disbarred, struck off the register, hammered on 'Change, or flogged round the fleet, if he is judged guilty of unpoetic conduct.

The only limits legally set on his activities are the acts relating to libel, pornography, treason, and the endangerment of public order. And if he earns the scorn of his colleagues, what effective sanctions can they take against him? None at all.

This difference between the poetic profession and others may seem platitudinous, but I shall insist on it all the more strongly; because what English poets have always been free to enjoy, if they please, is the privilege of not being formally enrolled as such. Where is there any official roll of poets, analogous to the Army and Navy Lists, the Medical Register, or *Crockford?* This general privilege, as I understand it, implies individual responsibility: the desire to deserve well of the Muse, their divine patroness, from whom they receive their unwritten commissions, to whom they eat their solitary dinners, who confers her silent benediction on them, to whom they swear their secret Hippocratic oath, to whose moods they are as attentive as the stockbroker is to his market.

I do not, of course, suggest that every English poet has always been sensible of this crowning privilege, or even aware that the Muse has a real existence—as real, for her devotees, as Karl Marx's existence, or Freud's, or Aquinas's, to theirs. Indeed, when a few years ago I published a book in the Muse's honour, *The White Goddess,* several self-styled poets mistook her for an improvisation of my own. They patronizingly called her ' Mr Graves's *White Goddess* ', although she had already been publicly acknowledged by an English poet at the beginning of the Tudor period. John Skelton wrote a poem called:

Why were ye Calliope *embrawdred with letters of golde?*

SKELTON LAUREATE ORATOR REG. MAKETH THIS
AUNSWERE, ETC.

> *Calliope,*
> *As ye may se,*
> *Regent is she*
>   *Of poetes al,*
> *Whiche gaue to me*
> *The high degre*
> *Laureat to be*
>   *Of fame royall;*

> *Whose name enrolde*
> *With silke and golde*
> *I dare be bolde*
>   *Thus for to were,*
> *Of her I holde*
> *And her housholde;*
> *Though I waxe olde*
>   *And somdele sere,*
> *Yet is she fayne,*
> *Voyde of disdayn,*
> *Me to retayne*
>   *Her seruiture:*
> *With her certayne*
> *I wyll remayne,*
> *As my souerayne*
>   *Moost of pleasure,*
> Maulgre touz malheureux.

It may be asked what right I have to formulate the principles governing the professional conduct of poetry. I have no prescriptive right at all; and it must be clearly understood that I am not speaking *ex cathedra*. A guest lectureship is not a Chair, and nobody is obliged to agree with me. My function, as I understand it, is merely provocative. Besides, gratitude for not being enrolled in any organized society of poets prevents me from suggesting that I may voice the opinion of even a minority of my fellows. What I have to offer for your scrutiny are personal principles, deduced for my own guidance from a long study of poems and poets. Whoever finds them too subjective may correct them to suit himself; or, if he likes, may formulate others.

First, then, to consider the economics of the poetic profession: an interesting theme, because it should not really arise, and yet has become a stock subject of debate in Bloomsbury pubs, the more cultured weeklies, and certain philo-philanthropic cultural uplift organizations. When I was twelve or thirteen years old my father asked me: ' What are you going to be, my boy? ' I answered: ' A poet.' His inevitable reaction was: ' Splendid, but what will you do for your bread and butter? ' Fresh from my history class on the French Revolution, I found myself answering improvidently: ' I shall eat cake.' ' Oatcake? ' asked my father in a kindly voice.

Yes: I ate oatcake for some years, and liked it—I had a Scottish grandmother.

A soldier or sailor draws his pay; a parson draws his stipend, eked out with Sunday collections ' for church expenses '; a doctor or lawyer draws his fees; and I who was once young and am now old have never seen a stockbroker forsaken, or his seed begging bread. But, as my father pointed out, one well-known peculiarity of the poetic profession is that the poet cannot expect to support himself by it. My father, himself a poet, earned his bread and butter as one of Her Majesty's Inspectors of Schools.

In most professions the size of a man's income is a fairly reliable criterion of worth: no inefficient soldier or sailor can hope to draw the pay of a Field-Marshal or Admiral of the Fleet. It is seldom either by chance or by favour that a particular Q.C. or Harley Street surgeon earns a thousand guineas a year more than his fellows. And, as for parsons, such high intellectual and executive qualifications are demanded nowadays from Bishops, Deans, and Canons, however saintly, that the extra loaves and fishes accruing to them need no apology. Among poets, however, the income test works in reverse: make a comfortable living by writing poems and you risk being treated with derision. The argument runs: ' Poetry does not pay, consequently what you sell is not poetry.' And I agree that there seem to be few exceptions to this rule.

The terms of the Clark bequest forbid me to deal with English literature before Chaucer; yet a few flash-backs would probably be in order, to provide the necessary historical data for the post-Chaucerian scene. In Anglo-Saxon times, grants of land, or money-presents in lieu of land, were given to poets by kings and princelings. These gifts were made, it seems, because the presence of a poet at Court was an ancient tradition of royalty (like the healing of diseases by the laying on of hands) that had lasted over from earlier times. And although no written records survive, anthropologists will, I think, allow me to assume an original situation, back in the neolithic age, when the king enjoyed no executive power, being merely a sacred consort of the queen and under her magic tutelage. The queen appointed druids, or oakmen, skilled in magical charms, to stand constantly by the king's side

and ensure that no accidental breach of royal taboo on his part—by
eating beans, touching a dog, wearing a knot in his clothes, and so on
—could endanger the safety or fertility of the realm. King and druid
owed allegiance to the sovereign goddess incarnate in the queen—the
goddess who was still nostalgically invoked in Classical Greece by the
Homeridae, as the Muse—meaning the Mountain-goddess.

The revolutionary usurpation by the All-Father Wotan, or Odin,
or Gwydion, of the throne occupied by the variously-named Northern
All-Mother, parallels the triumph of All-Father Zeus over the variously-named Mediterranean All-Mother. In the course of the second
millennium B.C. the sacred king, after first being occasionally permitted to deputize for the queen and wear her robes, broke the
shackles of taboos—how strong they were can be judged from ancient
Welsh, Irish, Roman, and more recent African analogies—and in-
stituted armed patriarchalism. He became the most powerful individual of his tribe rather than the sacred ritual leader; and, thereafter,
instead of persuading his people to the right behaviour which his own
sacrificial example exemplified, he sustained the social order by giving summary commands to his henchmen. Thus the druids became
court bards, whose function was no longer to guide, protect, and cher-
ish the king, but merely to celebrate his temporal power.

The earlier system continued in Ireland until historical times, having there been modified rather than superseded when the king turned
warrior. His *ollamhs,* or druids, continued to enjoy a prolonged and
intense training in the magical and poetic arts at a forest college. The
arch-ollamh ranked in dignity next to the queen and acted as a vizier;
his profession was endowed, his person was sacrosanct, and a gift for
killing by satire made him the terror of the warrior class and even of
the king. If the Church was slow to undermine his power, this was because Christianity had been introduced by eloquent and tactful missionaries, not (as elsewhere) at the point of the sword; and because
the colleges of *ollamhs* accepted Jesus and his Mother as completing,
rather than discrediting, their ancient theology. The Irish bishops, appointed at first by the kings, not by the Pope, were expected to sing
low, and did sing low. They Christianized the Triple-goddess Brigit,
patroness of poets, as St Bridget, and her immemorial altar-fire at
Kinsale was still alight under Henry VIII.

In Wales, where the Goddess was called Cerridwen, the change from paganism to Christianity came suddenly and violently: the North British Brythons, who entered North Wales with the fifth-century King Cunedda, were Christians.[1] The pagan Goidelic *ollamhs* whom they turned out, and who seem to have been educated and organized in the Irish style, became wandering minstrels. At the Welsh Courts they were superseded by their own apprentices, young men who had not yet been initiated into the supreme religious mysteries. These low-grade bards (*bard* was a word of contempt in Ireland) were willing to embrace Christianity and accept the restrictions imposed on their art by the bishops; so that the Chief Bard eventually won a respectable place at the king's board—though below that of the royal chaplain, the chief falconer, and the steward of the table. A bard's task now was to honour God, praise the king, refrain from untruth (meaning any poetic reference to Cerridwen) and from hurtful satire.

The Anglo-Saxon invaders of England, on the other hand, had no organized colleges of *ollamhs,* nor even (so far as is known) any guild of saga-singers, like the Greek *Homeridae* who claimed the sole right of performing in public. Anyone might compose poems to the harp, if he could; and (this is the point that I want to make) it has fortunately been the same ever since among the English-speaking peoples. An Anglo-Saxon *scop* might inherit his father's stool and harp and repertoire; but his position at Court depended on the king's indisputable pleasure, and should he fail to hold it, he must turn wandering gleeman, to combine recitation with tumbling and mime in the country market places. His standing was far from high: *scop* (versifier) being a polite synonym for the pejorative word *scald,* which meant a ' scold '—one who talks too loud and long. The *Deor,* an Early English fragment of about the year 600, preserved in the *Exeter Book,* witnesses to his social insecurity. It is a coda, attached to the Geatish saga-cycle (of which *Beowulf* also formed part) and summarizing the sufferings of the principal characters in the cycle. The refrain runs:

> *Thaes ofereōde, thisses swā maeg.*
> [*That overpassing, this also may.*]

---

[1] See *The Old Black Cow,* p. 156.

The last verse, suddenly becoming personal, runs:

> *Then I of myself / will this make known:*
> *That awhile I was held / the Heodenings' scop.*
>
> *To my duke most dear; / and Deor was my name,*
> *I performed many winters, / a worthy office*
> *For a handsome lord, / until Heorrenda,*
> *Being skilled in lays, / my land-right usurped*
> *Which the kingdom's strength / of old assigned me.*
> *That overpassing, / this also may.*

Deor attempts no harmful satire on the handsome lord who had preferred another *scop* to himself. He merely registers disappointment
and hopes that one day the loss will be remedied.

The Norman Conquest scotched the Anglo-Saxon tradition of the
court-*scop*, and though Richard Coeur de Lion and Henry III employed a *Versificator Regis*—I suppose for rhymed chronicles, epitaphs and suchlike—at their Norman-French Courts, the office lapsed
about a century before Chaucer's day. Chaucer did not revive it, nor
did he even make poetry a wholetime profession. He was a valuable
public servant with an entrée at Court secured by his marriage into
the family of John of Gaunt, Richard II's uncle. Slavish commendations of royalty had not yet become fashionable. The *envoys* to
Chaucer's shorter poems are dignified; he even dares lecture Richard
II on what kingly conduct should be. Nor did he sue for royal bounty
until late in life; and even then the humorous *Compleint to his Empty
Purse* pays a most restrained court to Henry IV. He simply recognizes Henry as the rightful sovereign of the realm:

> *To you, my purse, and to non other wight*
> *Compleyne I, for ye be my lady dere!*
> *I am so sory, now that ye be light;*
> *For certës, but ye make me hevy chere,*
> *Me were as leef be leyd up on my bere;*
> *For whiche un-to your mercy thus I crye:*
> *Beth hevy ageyn, or ellës mot I dye!*
>
> *Now voucheth sauf this day, or hit be night,*
> *That I of you the blisful soun may here,*

Or see your colour lyk the sonnë bright,
That of yelównesse haddë never pere.
Ye be my lyf, ye be myn hertës stere,
Quene of comfort and of good companye:
Beth hevy ageyn, or ellës mot I dye!

Now purs, that be to me my lyvës light,
And saveour, as doun in this worlde here,
Out of this tounë help me through your might,
Sin that ye wole nat been my tresorere;
For I am shave as nye as any frere.
But yit I pray un-to your curtesye:
Beth hevy ageyn, or ellës mot I dye!

Lenvoy de Chaucer
O conquerour of Brutës Albioun!
Which that by lyne and free eleccioun
Ben verray king, this song to you I sende;
And ye, that mowen al our harm amende,
Have minde up-on my supplicacioun!

Henry filled the purse at once, but in recognition of Chaucer's non-poetical services: as Clerk of Works, Comptroller of the Wool and Petty Customs, diplomat, and secret-service agent.

Gower, Chaucer's contemporary, also had close relations with the King, and did not depend on him for money; he seems to have preferred Court pleasures and honours to the dull routine of a Kentish landowner's life. But, his social position being perhaps less secure than Chaucer's, he wrote courtly praises of Richard II in his *Confessio Amantis* (the subject of which was set him by Richard himself); and, his spirit being less noble than Chaucer's, recast these in Henry IV's favour when Richard abdicated.

Lydgate's case is instructive and exceptional. Though Chaucer wrote solely for his own pleasure, and Gower had been glad to adopt Richard's suggestion of a poetic theme, Lydgate was forced (apparently against his will) to become a sort of scholarly *Versificator Regis*. The rules of his Order compelled every monk to unthinking obedience; so Henry V commissioned Lydgate, through his superior, to translate Giovanni delle Colonne's 30,000-line *Historia Trojana*, which took eight years; then the Earl of Warwick called him to Paris in 1426 to turn into English a French poetical pedigree proving Henry VI to be the rightful King of France. In the same year the Earl of Salisbury set him another translating task: the 20,000-line *Pélérinage de la Vie Humaine*—an allegory by de Guileville. Next, the Duke of Gloucester commanded him to translate Boccaccio's 36,000-line *De Casibus Illustrium Virorum,* an even more formidable commission. Lydgate records how unwelcome it was:

> *Thus my self remembyring on this boke*
> *It to translate how I had undertake,*
> *Ful pale of chere, astonied in my loke,*
> *Myn hand gan tremble, my penne I feltë quake.*
>
> .   .   .   .   .
>
> *I stode chekmate for feare when I gan see*
> *In my way how littel I had runne.*

But he could not refuse the task, though it obliged him to resign his position at Hatfield Priory, where he had been educating young noblemen in the humane arts. A small yearly stipend was then granted him, by way of compensation, and he carried on with his hack duties until he died, pen in hand; though seven years earlier he had complained that his wits were long ' foredulled '.

John Skelton, a horse of a very different colour, tutored Prince Henry, afterwards Henry VIII, and they continued on friendly and even joking terms for many years. Henry's mother had given Skelton the cure of Diss in Norfolk to reward his conscientious tutorship and good influence on the unruly boy, and protected him while she lived. Skelton consented, as ' Royal Orator ', to write a Latin epitaph for her husband, Henry VII, ending this with a loyal address to her son. One of his earliest poems, the elegy *On the Death of the Noble Prince Edward the Fourth,* her father, is sincerely felt, extremely moving, and contains no single word of flattery:

> Miseremini mei, *ye that be my frendis!*
> *This world hath forméd me downe to fall:*
> *How may I endure, when that eueri thyng endis?*
> *What creature is borne to be eternall?*

Now there is no more but pray for me all:
Thus say I Edward, that late was youre kynge,
And twenty two yeres ruled this imperyall,
Some vnto pleasure, and some to no lykynge:
Mercy I askë of my mysdoynge;
What auayleth it, frendes, to be my foo,
Sith I can not resyst, nor amend your complaining?
Quia, ecce, nunc in pulvere dormio! . . .

Where was in my lyfe such one as I,
Whyle lady Fortune with me had continuaunce?
Graunted not she me to haue victory,
*   In England to rayne, and to contribute Fraunce?*
She took me by the hand and led me a daunce,
And with her sugred lyppës on me she smyled;
*   But, what for her dissembled countenaunce,*
I coud not beware tyl I was begyled:
Now from this world she hath me excyled,
*   When I was lothyst hens for to go,*
And I am in age but, as who sayth, a chylde,
Et, ecce, nunc in pulvere dormio! . . .

Skelton, despite the contempt of Pope and Milton, showed a
stronger sense of poetic calling than almost any of his successors. It
was as a poet, not as a priest, that he dared openly defy Cardinal
Wolsey, Henry's right-hand man; for which bravado he spent the last
six years of his life in confinement. The following *Merrie Tale of
Skelton* reads authentically enough. He had ridiculed Wolsey for his
lack of learning and presumption, and called him ' cur and butcher's
dog ':

> On a tyme Skelton did meete with certain frendes of hys at Char-
> yng crosse, after that he was in prison at my lord cardynals com-
> maundment: & his frende sayd, I am glad you bee abrode amonge
> your frendes, for you haue ben long pent in. Skelton sayd, By the
> masse, I am glad I am out indeede, for I haue been pent in, like a
> roche or fissh, at Westminster in prison. The cardinal, hearing of
> those words, sent for him agayne. Skelton, kneeling of hys knees
> before hym, after long communication to Skelton had, desyred the
> cardinall to graunte hym a boun. Thou shalt haue none, sayd the
> cardynall. Thassistence desirid that he might haue it graunted, for
> they thought it should be some merye pastime that he wyll shewe

your grace. Say on, thou hore head, sayd the cardynall to Skelton. I
pray your grace to let me lye doune and wallow, for I can kneele
no longer.

The medieval English court-poet, then, was not engaged as such
by the king; but just as there is a fat boy in every school (even if he
is not really very fat), and a funny man in every barrack-room (even
if he is not really very funny), so there was always a Court-poet at
Court, even if he was not much of a poet. Between Gower and
Skelton came the undistinguished John Kay and Andrew Bernard.
But not until the reign of Elizabeth could a talent for verse-writing
support an application for a place of trust. Then Spenser—through
Leicester's influence—secured a secretaryship in Ireland, a country
which he hated, hoping that if he could please Elizabeth by his praises
of her in the *Faerie Queene,* he would be called to London. Unfortunately, before he had finished his task, the rebellious O'Neils, unaware that he was a poet, turned Spenser out of his castle. He returned, broken in health and purse, and died soon after.

James I, who regarded himself as a critic of poetry, and wrote an
elementary handbook of prosody, recognized Samuel Daniel's talent
for verse by appointing him gentleman-in-ordinary. This encouraged
Michael Drayton to panegyrize James, and even write a sonnet commending his Royal Muse—a breach of professional dignity; but, as it
happened, room could not be found for Drayton at Court, so he
crossly revoked the sonnet. In the next reign, pique at being denied
positions in the King's gift turned at least two poets into the Puritan
camp: Milton, because of the Royal Fellowship at Christ's which he
thought should be his but which was conferred on the original of
' Lycidas '; and May, who was vexed at not being appointed Jonson's
successor as Poet Laureate.

Since poets still had no guild, nor any traditional economic status,
nothing—let me repeat—prevented noblemen or royalty itself from
writing poetry. James IV of Scotland would be remembered as author
of *The Gaberlunzie man,* even if Flodden had never been fought. And
Henry VIII would be remembered for his love song *As the Holly
Groweth Green,* even if there had been no breach with Rome. Wyatt,
Surrey, Sidney, Oxford, Raleigh, and Queen Elizabeth herself were all
poets.

It is an ancient tradition of the European feudal system that the lord does not demean himself by taking wages, under any circumstances; or by going into trade. He may march to war, sack towns, and hold fellow-knights to ransom, or he may stay at home and live on his rents; but he must never openly infringe the function of the merchant or artisan. In Greece, the poet ranked as an artisan, which is (I suppose) why Agamemnon, Odysseus, and Achilles never deigned to call for a lyre; and why Peisistratus, the tyrant of Athens, contented himself with patronizing the *Homeridae* rather than being adopted a member of their guild. In England, until the invention of printing, the poet—if we except the wandering minstrel, who went round the country ale-houses with his store of ballads, and an orphan (*vide* Sir Walter Scott) to carry the harp—did not expect to earn a living by his poems. There was as yet no publishing system to make this possible, and when finally the stationer (a publisher-cum-bookseller) set up shop, no copyright law at first protected the author. A poem was not a physical object of agreed value, liable to be stolen in the usual sense. Unless the author could prove theft of a manuscript book of poems (an obvious felony, because vellum had value, and copyists' fees were high), he had no cause for complaint if someone memorized and printed his poems.

Thus, to be a poet agreed with the code of nobility. When Tottell set the fashion of poetic anthologies, it was the stationer, not the poet, who profited; and after the Charter given in 1566 to the Stationers' Company (as a means for facilitating censorship) it was the stationer, not the poet, who held the copyright. Stationers, by the way, were so called because, unlike the book-peddlers, they kept stationary. Once Thomas Thorp had secured copies of Shakespeare's sonnets from the enigmatic Mr W. H., and entered them at Stationers' Hall, Shakespeare was powerless in law either to prevent, or to profit from, their sale. It is possible that Shakespeare (shrewd businessman though he was in malt, hides, and real-estate) had sold the copyright of *Venus and Adonis* to the publisher who entered the volume at Stationers' Hall; but if so, he would not have advertised the fact. He was bound to keep his distance from the professional ballad-writers: low-born scoundrels who supplied the great public with the brief equivalent of Sunday newspapers, who seldom signed even their initials to what they wrote, and who did not dare claim poet's rank. Shakespeare satirized their patter in a well-known passage of his *Winter's Tale*.

If small poets of the day starved in garrets, that was because they had no patron and tried to live on hack-writing jobs at the playhouse, or among the stationers of St Paul's Churchyard. Davenant in his *Long Vacation* records:

> *Now man that trusts, with weary thighs,*
> *Seeks garret where small poet lies:*
> *He comes to Lane, finds garret shut;*
> *Then, not with knuckle, but with foot,*
> *He rudely thrusts, would enter dores;*
> *Though poet sleeps not, yet he snores:*
> *Cit chafes like beast of Libia; then*
> *Sweares, he'l not come or send agen.*
> *From little lump triangular*
> *Poor poet's sighs are heard afar.*
> *Quoth he, ' Do noble numbers chuse*
> *To walk on feet, that have no shoose? '*
> *Then he does wish with fervent breath,*
> *And as his last request ere death,*
> *Each ode a bond, each madrigal,*
> *A lease from Haberdashers Hall,*
> *Or that he had protected bin*
> *At court, in list of chamberlain;*
> *For wights near thrones care not an ace*
> *For Woodstreet friend, that wieldeth mace. . . .*
>
> .   .   .   .   .
>
> *In stockings blew who marcheth on,*
> *With velvet cape his cloack upon;*
> *In girdle, scrowles, where names of some,*
> *Are written down, whom touch of thumbe,*
> *On shoulder left must safe convoy,*
> *Anoying wights with name of roy.*
>
> .   .   .   .   .
>
> *Courts pay no scores but when they list,*
> *And treasurer still has cramp in fist. . . .*

Davenant concludes with:

> *But stay, my frighted pen is fled;*
> *My self through fear creep under bed;*

> *For just as Muse would scribble more,*
> *Fierce City dunne did rap at door.*

This is a joke on himself. Davenant was comfortably off, though he may have been overspending his income. And poetry as a gainful profession was not yet respectable. . . . Why did Elizabethan and Jacobean noblemen leave drama alone, apart from Masques and Interludes written for Court use, or for performance in their own courtly mansions? Because a peer might not engage in trade: and the Elizabethan theatre was a money-making concern.

This brings me to the subject of dedications. When Shakespeare, Drayton, Daniel, Donne, Chapman, and Jonson published their poems —though not their plays, which did not count as poetry, even if they were—the stationer expected them to supply a formal dedication, sanctioned by some person of honour and influence, as a means of selling the book. The buyer would read the dedication and say: ' Hm ! This is no bookseller's hack writing for profit. This is a true poet, a gentleman of breeding and substance, and on easy terms of friendship with the Earl of So-and-so.' (Or with the Lord Chamberlain; or with the Countess of Such-and-such.) ' The Queen herself would not disdain to cast her eyes on it. Here's my shilling.' The buyer was satisfied, the bookseller delighted, the dedicatee flattered, and the dedicator did not think ill of himself.

Similarly, in Elizabethan times, when the feudal system still went creaking on, a poet who happened to be *sine nobilitate* (a phrase which, shortened to *s.nob* has, some say, given English the valuable word ' snob') was obliged to secure a patron: much as a private soldier today cannot address an officer unless escorted by an N.C.O. Moreover, to gain recognition by the right people—unless he were a *nob,* without the preliminary *s*—the poet had to be either in holy orders or a gentleman. The courtesy of gentlemanly rank (eventually stabilized by the title *Esquire*) was accorded to all masters of art at Oxford and Cambridge, or members of the Inns of Court; which helped several leading dramatists in their social climb, though not Shakespeare. Shakespeare's position was equivocal, despite his eminence on the stage and his friendship with Southampton, Pembroke, and Essex. But he managed to secure a coat-of-arms for his father— which drew derisive hoots from the rival theatre—and thus became presentable at Court and even (as appears in a sonnet) eligible as a canopy-bearer on some State occasion.

One great difference between now and then is that to rank as a poet in the Elizabethan or Jacobean sense, a man must have published a longish work—such as *Venus and Adonis* and *The Rape of Lucrece.* With a few dozen sonnets he could also qualify. But a verse play, even one containing so many detachable poems as *The Tempest,* or *Hamlet,* or *Anthony and Cleopatra,* was considered irrelevant. And, whereas the poetry written today consists almost wholly of ' lyrics '— lyrics without music—in Elizabethan times, every lyric had its music, but lyrics did not count as poems. Shakespeare wrote the lyrics for his plays; probably also the incidental songs required while properties were being shifted and the change of scene announced. (In my *Common Asphodel* I give evidence for supposing that the strange and beautiful poem *Loving Mad Tom* was Shakespeare's adaptation of a Bedlamite ballad, sung by Edgar in *King Lear* after his ' Edgar I nothing am.') No dramatist felt obliged to be his own lyricist; any more than the matador at a Spanish bull-fight feels obliged to plant his own *banderilleras;* though a few of the better matadors do so, and thereby improve the afternoon's performance. Shakespeare would have disdained to advertise: ' *King Lear,* a tragedy by Mr Wm Shakespeare, with lyrics by the same hand.' Nearly all the lyrics from the Elizabethan song books, among them some of the truest poems written in English, are anonymous. The musicians who arranged with the stationers to have their songs published gave the author of the words no printed credit. It is unknown who supplied Captain Tobias Hume with his:

> *Fain would I change this note,*
> *To which false love hath charmed me.*

Or Thomas Ford with:

> *There is a lady sweet and kind,*
> *Was never face so pleased my mind.*

Or Robert Jones with:

> *And is it night? Are they thine eyes that shine?*
> *Are we alone, and here? And here, alone?*

Or John Dowland with:

> *Deare if you change, I'll never choose again;*
> *Sweet if you shrink, I'll never think of love.*

—though it now seems likely that Dowland, like Campion, wrote his own lyrics. Even Henry Vaughan's authorship of *Yet if His Majesty, our Sovereign Lord,* in the manuscript collection of early music books at Christ Church, Oxford, must remain a surmise.

Yet these poems were the work of highly educated men, not stationers' hacks. One of them, written for Thomas Weelkes:

> *A sparrow hawk proud did hold in wicked jail*
> *Music's sweet chorister, the nightingale. . . .*

is a literal translation from Hesiod; and the language of the Song Books never fails to be courtly. We may be certain that the lyricist asked no money for such ' idle toys and trifles '; though the musician may have invited him to a venison pasty and a bottle of good wine, which would not compromise his amateur status. It had been the same with the medieval carols—a form originally introduced by Franciscan friars: to find an author's name attached to them is rare.

I have mentioned the laureateship. Skelton had been appointed ' Royal Orator '; and he was also ' Laureate ' in the sense that he had won distinction for his Classical scholarship at Oxford, Cambridge, and Louvain. Ben Jonson had been similarly laureated: and the Crown did not venture to award its own laurel garland to a poet until 1638, when Charles I bestowed it on Davenant. Jonson's pension was a charitable one. Hearing that he had lost his library by fire, had suffered two paralytic strokes, and had seen his *New Inn* hissed off the stage, Charles increased the pension awarded by James I: in recognition not of Jonson's general poetic fame, but of his services to the Crown in the writing of Court Masques. It is noteworthy that Jonson refused the honour of knighthood offered him as a reward for his Masque *Gipsies Metamorphosed;* presumably because he thought that though a knight might become a poet, poetry was not honoured by the irrelevant accolade. He dismissed titles as ' birdlime for fools '; and called poetry ' The Queen of Arts, which had her original from Heaven '.

Indeed, the only rewards in which a poet is properly entitled to rejoice are three. First, the sense that what he has written not only stands on all four feet, but has sufficient animation to walk away by itself, and perhaps go on walking long years after his death. Second, he rejoices if his worthy poetic contemporaries acknowledge this creative event—though the Elizabethan practice of writing ' commendations ' to the works of a fellow-poet, and even dropping them into his grave, has now lapsed. Last, and above all, he rejoices in the approval shown by the personal Muse for whom he has written the poem, however grudgingly her praise may be couched.

Ben Jonson, the first poet who lectured to his fellows on the subject of professional standards, died in 1637, just before the Puritan Revolution. The vacating of his chair in the *Apollo* room at the Old Devil's Tavern, the closing of the theatres, and the extinction of Merry England on the field of Naseby make a sharp break in this story. As an anonymous Cavalier wrote in a ballad called *The World Turned Upside Down:*

> *To conclude, I'll tell you news that's right:*
> *Christmas was kil'd at* Nasebie *fight,*
> *Charity was slain at that same time,*
> Jack Tell troth, *too, a friend of mine.*

Poetry, also, had received a deep wound, from which the recovery was long delayed. 1645 is a convenient date for me to call a halt; but I trust I have made my point, which is that professional tradition, since Chaucer, prevents the English poet from letting any hopes of gain or of social advancement influence his work. This is not to say that he should refrain from offering his poems for sale as a means of circulating them, or that he should refuse assistance offered him for that purpose by friends or acquaintances. Only, he must not allow a private patron, or a publisher, the right to call the tune: by which I mean the right to decide how he shall write or what he shall write. To call the tune is the function of the Muse alone. Her demands are unforeseeable and ungainsayable; and her hand cannot be forced.

Let me enlarge on this. The legitimacy of accepting official honours for poetry may seem a moot point, but in my opinion, as in Ben Jonson's, they should be politely declined. It is not as though the Sovereign personally chose beneficiaries of Birthday or New Year honours. Both lists are prepared, under orders of the Cabinet, by a committee of political officials; and these have no more right to decide who is a true poet than the poet has to intervene in Cabinet meetings. The situation is made worse by the invidious sliding-scale of official honours conferred. Just as the Distinguished Conduct Medal was devised to enhance the dignity of the Victoria Cross (and, incidentally, to save the Crown the 6d. a day pension which went with it), and the Military Medal to enhance the dignity of the Distinguished Conduct Medal, so the Companionship of Honour was first devised to enhance the dignity of the Order of Merit; and inferior awards now enhance the dignity of the Companionship of Honour. Bestowal of a greater or lesser Order on a man for his supposed services to poetry—as opposed to scientific, military, or political services, which are more easily assessable and in the public domain—that is an act of criticism which no politician nor permanent civil servant has any right to make. Granted, Thomas Hardy, one of the most moral of poets, accepted the Order of Merit. But he knew that the award was conferred on him for his novels, which the Cabinet's advisers had read, rather than for his poems, which they had not; and, on the whole, Civil Servants are as likely to know a good novel from a bad as are professional reviewers or publishers' readers.

Thomas Hardy told me himself, when I stayed with him in August 1920, that he was not interested in the fate of his poems once he had written them.

(By the way, an amusing example of social distinction in the painting world is the certificate of merit awarded to an Associate of the Royal Academy: it is made out to, say, Timothy Dauber, Gent. When Dauber is elected a Member he goes up in rank: he is Timothy Dauber, Esq. I inquired into this, and was told that the ' Gentleman ' was originally a certificate of good conduct: that, if commissioned to paint a portrait, he could at any rate be trusted not to steal the silver or insult the chambermaids. The ' Esquire ', a certificate of elegant manners, gave him access to the drawing room.)

Professional standards in poetry, then, are founded upon the sense enjoyed by every English poet since the time of Chaucer, that he forms part of a long and honourable tradition. Usually he has contemporaries whom he can love and respect; thus it has meant a great deal to me that I once lived on terms of friendship with my elders Thomas Hardy and William Davies, and with men of my own age like Wilfred Owen and Norman Cameron—to name only the dead. It meant much to Keats and Darley that Coleridge had been kind to them, and to Swinburne that Landor had given him the poetic blessing he demanded. A sense of kinship with poets of an earlier age can be as strong as any contemporary bond; and I realize now how deep a professional influence my favourites have had upon me. Not only by the opinions they expressed, but by their behaviour and character; for who has ever successfully disguised his character in what he wrote?

I have never been able to understand the contention that a poet's life is irrelevant to his work—unless this means merely, as it did in the 1870's, that acceptance of the Thirty-nine Articles, or membership of a reputable club, or an orthodox love-life, are not a *sine qua non* of literary eminence. If it means that a poet may be heartless or insincere or grasping in his personal relations and yet write true poems, I disagree wholeheartedly.

Nearly all poets make out a critical list of their favourites, convinced that they alone represent the authentic English tradition. Skelton's list occurs in *Philip Sparow,* fathered on Jane Scroop (the pretended authoress):

> *Gowers Englysh is olde,*
> *And of no value told;*
> *His mater is worth gold,*
> *And worthy to be enrold.*
> * In Chauser I am sped,*
> *His tales I haue red:*
> *His mater is delectable,*
> *Solacious and commendable,*
> *His Englysh well alowed,*
> *So as it is enprowed . . .*
> *At those days moch commended,*
> *And now men wold haue amended*
> *His Englysh, whereat they barke,*
> *And mar all they warke:*
> *Chaucer, that famous clerke,*
> *His termes were not darke,*
> *But pleasaunt, easy, and playne;*
> *No worde he wrote in vayne.*

Also John Lydgate
Wryteth after an hyer rate;
It is dyffuse to fynde
The sentence of his mynde,
Yet wryteth he in his kind . . .
But some men fynde a faute,
And say he wryteth to haute. . . .

And in his *Garland of Laurel* these three poets, in beautiful apparel adorned with diamonds and rubies, lead Skelton to the Goddess's Temple. His only criticism of their works is that they all lacked sound Classical learning.

Ben Jonson's preferences occur in *The Return from Parnassus* (1601), and in his undated *Discoveries*. He lists:

Chaucer,
Wyatt,
Surrey,
Spenser,
Raleigh,
Daniel,
Drayton,
Davies,
Marlowe,
Shakespeare,

and, of course, Jonson himself. But he had changed his mind about some of these by 1619, when Drummond of Hawthornden records of him:

> . . . His Censure of English Poets was this, that Sidney did not keep a Decorum in making every one speak as well as himself.
> Spencer's stanzaes pleased him not, nor his matter, the meaning of which Allegorie he had delivered in Papers to Sir Walter Raughlie.
> Samuel Daniel was a good honest man, had no children, bot no poet.
> that Michael Drayton's Polyolbion (if had performed what he promised to writte the deeds of all ye worthies) had been excellent. His long verses pleased him not.
> that Silvesters translation of Du Bartas was not well done. . . .

William Browne, Jonson's contemporary, but rather more of a modernist, praises Sidney, Drayton, Ben Jonson, Daniel, Brook, Davies, and Wither. Milton as a young man wrote marginal comments on *The Pastorals*, apparently approving Browne's choice. He might have added to the list, with a certain disdain: ' Sweetest Shakespeare, fancy's child, warbling his native wood notes wild.' But probably not Chaucer, and certainly not Skelton, whom he later mentioned in his *Areopagitica* among the authors who deserved total suppression:

> I name him not for posterity sake, whom Henry the 8th named in merriment his vicar of hell.

Milton called Skelton:

> One of the worst of men, who are both most able and most diligent to instil the poison they suck into the courts of princes, acquainting them with the choicest delights and criticisms of sin;

and refused to see the point of Henry's boyish joke: namely that Skelton was Rector of Diss in Norfolk and that ' Dis ' is the Latin for Hell.

Pope persuaded his contemporaries that nothing of consequence had happened in English poetry until Denham and Waller introduced the French style—all before was rusty, rude, and low, or at the best, quaint in the Spenserian style; just as (according to the contemporary French theory) all French poetry, including Villon's, had been until Malherbe. This apostasy caused a serious break in English poetic education. The threads were eventually gathered up again by Hazlitt and Coleridge, when it once more became possible to read Chaucer, Skelton, and Shakespeare in the original, without condescension, and realize that ' Chauser, that famous clerke, His termes were not darke, But pleasaunt, easy and playne, No worde he wrote in vayne.'

Today we are threatened by a new apostasy from tradition; which has been my main reason for accepting the College's generous invitation. I am not a born lecturer, nor even a very willing one; but it seems to me that someone has to speak out, and nobody else seems prepared to do so. My own preferences among the poets, and my reasons for making them, will be clearly given.

If, in the course of this lecture, I have said anything out of order, pray forgive me. I am a stranger here.

THE AGE OF OBSEQUIOUSNESS

To resume my rambling commentary from 1645, when the English world got turned upside down at Naseby: four years later, King Charles was beheaded. This monstrous event silenced some honest poets for ever, among them Herrick, though he lived another quarter of a century and at the Restoration won back the benefice from which his Royalism had excluded him during the Commonwealth. For when the Restoration came, no poet could follow the central English tradition of Chaucer, Skelton, and Ben Jonson. Hitherto professional standards had been approved at Court, and on the Court's return it was found to have gone all French. Charles and his boon-companions ruled that the age of poetical independence was over ('independence' having secured an evil name in the politico-religious context); and that the age of correctness, which in practice meant the Age of Obsequiousness, had begun.

Usually the European power with the strongest army sets the fashion in literary forms, as in clothes and domestic furniture. Spain had done so throughout the sixteenth century, and the Spanish *alto estilo* (advertised by Lyly and his colleagues as 'Euphuistic wit') persisted in English prose until the early seventeenth century, when the Spanish Empire began to crack from overstrain. Then came the turn of the French. A brief intermediate phase of so-called 'Metaphysical' poetry took Euphuistic wit one degree farther into nonsense, and so prepared the way for clean-cut French Classicism, which any commonsensical gentleman could understand and imitate. The metaphysicals were led by Abraham Cowley, a literary careerist who specialized in what Dr Johnson afterwards called 'enormous and disgusting hyperboles':

By every wind that comes this way,
Send me at least a sigh or two:
Such and so many I'll repay
As shall themselves make winds to get to you.

It had all been very well for Ovid, Cowley's mentor, to cut Latin poodle-fashion and put it through the circus hoops. Ovid cultivated a Hellenistic modernism, acceptable in Imperial Rome only because the dignified republican tradition had long lapsed. ' Rome had now become a jack-daw's nest of promiscuousness and imprudent spoliation,' —Gibbon might have written, but didn't—' strange rites were celebrated in temples raised to enigmatic Eastern deities, and barbarian chieftains paraded Romulus's Forum equivocally wrapped in snowy togas.' Cowley had no such excuse for his frivolities: London was not yet a metropolis of Empire. Despite Cromwell's military and naval successes, England remained a cool, green island off the north-western coast of Europe, frequented by few strutting Continentals, and with a vigorous native tradition of honour, decency, and straight speaking. Why then *meta*physicality? Why this rejection of the physical? Had Marlow, Shakespeare, Ben Jonson, and Webster written in vain? Far-fetched rhetorical tropes are not acceptable among the English, except for purposes of burlesque, or to overawe the simple—as Touchstone used them on clownish William in the Forest of Arden (quoting that ' most capricious poet, honest Ovid '); or as, more recently, Dylan Thomas used them on gaping listeners to the Third Programme. Cowley's excuse was that he modelled himself on Donne, whom Ben Jonson had called ' the first poet in the World in some things ', and who had written the oddly tortured *Elegy on the Untimely Death of Prince Henry*. Cowley was perhaps unaware that Donne (according to Ben Jonson) confessed to having written it as a jest: ' to match Sir Edward Herbert in obscureness '.

Cowley's successor, Dryden, who consolidated Denham and Waller's so-called reforms in the simplifying of metres and diction, was a vigorous time-server, the first of a gifted line of poets who made Israel to sin. He earned the doubtful glory of having found English poetry brick and left it marble—native brick, imported marble. Dryden had begun his literary career as a metaphysical. His *Collected Poems* start with the *Epitaph on Lord Hastings,* which he had not

troubled, in later life, either to suppress or to smuggle in among his
facetiae:

> *Must noble Hastings immaturely die,*
> *The honour of his ancient family,*
> *Beauty and learning thus together meet,*
> *To bring a winding for a wedding sheet?*
>
> .   .   .   .   .
>
> *Was there no milder way but the small-pox,*
> *The very filthiness of Pandora's box?*
> *So many spots, like naeves o'er Venus' soil,*
> *One jewel set off with so many a foil;*
> *Blisters with pride swell'd, which through's flesh did sprout*
> *Like rose-buds, stuck i' th' lily-skin about.*
> *Each little pimple had a tear in it,*
> *To wail the fault its rising did commit:*
> *Which, rebel-like, with its own lord at strife,*
> *Thus made an insurrection 'gainst his life.*
> *Or were these gems sent to adorn his skin,*
> *The cab'net of a richer soul within?*

This is so well-known that I quote it only to fix attention on one particular couplet, which is less grotesque than downright shocking:

> *So many spots, live naeves o'er Venus' soil,*
> *One jewel set off with so many a foil. . . .*

The filthy pustules rising on the peer's diseased body are compared
to the halo, or ring of rosy dots, which enhanced the fresh beauty of
Venus's breast.

Can a man who has once sinned so grossly against the Muse hope
to redeem himself in her eyes by however spectacular a conversion?
'Homage to Dryden' indeed! And Dryden's conversion from meta-
physicality was not to the poetic faith of his English predecessors, but
to current French theory—an axiom of which was that English poetry
reflected confusion and barbarity. Louis XIV's consolidation of power
made this theory almost irresistible, because Charles, who trusted in a
French alliance, favoured only those English writers who looked to
France for their salvation. Paris, in the imagination of the French
Court poets (and therefore of Dryden's), was ancient Rome renewed;

and London consequently became a Trans-Tiberine extension of Rome. Charles's leading courtiers modelled their licentious behaviour on the heroes of Petronius's *Satyricon* (first published in Padua and Paris, 1664) and on hints found in Suetonius's *Twelve Cæsars*. Sedley, Buckingham, Rochester, and the rest cultivated a cynical, sycophantic, most un-English elegance, mocked at religion, faith, virtue, and humanity, as outmoded relics of Puritanism, and became adepts in the ' mannerly obscene '.

Charles rewarded Cowley with friendship for his long, grovelling *Ode upon His Majesty's Restoration and Return.* He also forgave Dryden, Waller, and Denham their panegyrics on his father's murderer. But it was the egregious Sedley whom he held up as a literary model. Charles's only dealings with Milton (whom I shall discuss later) were indirect: royal emissaries came secretly to Milton's modest house in Bunhill Fields, asking for legal information that would help them to steer the Lord Roos Divorce Bill safely through Parliament—for Charles wanted to divorce his barren Queen, as Milton had wanted to divorce poor Marie Powell.

There remains, of course, Andrew Marvell. Though finding it impossible at the Restoration to continue a poet in the romantic, sheltered, Appleton House vein, Marvell did not go French. He rejected Court fashions, made the still English city of Hull his spiritual home, not London, and thereafter confined himself to satire. His wit, as in the *Coy Mistress,* was sometimes fantastical, but always robustly humorous. Though Marvell bore no grudge against kings as such, he regarded Charles II as a disaster, and his nostalgia for the Commonwealth derived principally from the great name that England had enjoyed in Europe while it lasted. His parody of a Speech from the Throne (1675—two years before he died) shows by its very moderation, and its closeness to the original, that he was still poetically sound in heart and head. This is Charles himself speaking, not a character of mock-heroic fiction:

> . . . My Lords and Gentlemen,
> . . . I can beare my own straits with Patience, but my Ld. Treasurer protests that the Revenue, as it now stands, is too little for us both; one of us must pinch for it, if you do not help us out. I must speak freely to you: I am under Incumbrances, for besides my Harlots in service my Reformado ones lye hard upon me. I have

a pretty good Estate I confess, but Godfish, I have a great Charge upon it. Here is my Ld. Treasurer can tell you that all the Mony designed for the Summer Guards must of necessity be employed to the next Yeare's Cradles and Swaddling-Clothes. What then shall we do for ships?

I only hint this to you, it is Your Business, not mine. I know by Experience I can live without them, I lived ten years without them abroad and was never in better health in my life. But how will you live without them you had best say; and therefor I do not intend to insist upon it. There is another thing which I must press more earnestly, which is, it seems a good part of my Revenue will fail in two or three Yeares, except you will be pleased to continue it. Now I have this to say for it, Pray why did you give me as much except you resolved to go on? The Nation hates you already, for giving me so much, and I will hate you now if you doe not give me more. So that now your interest obliges you to stick to me or you will not have a friend left in England.

The severance of poetry from the Court, emphasized by the sorry farce of the eighteenth-century Laureateship with its obligatory Birthday and New Year Odes, soon tempted noblemen to expect even more fulsome praise from their protegés than the Sovereign had once earned. Dryden's *Dedicatory Address to the Duke of Ormonde* (1699) is remarkable only because it was written by so firm a hand as his:

My Lord,

God Almighty has endued you with a softness, a beneficence, an attractive behaviour, winning on the hearts of others, and so sensible of their misery, that the wounds of fortune seem not inflicted on them, but on yourself. You are so ready to redress, that you almost prevent their wishes, and always exceed their expectations: as if what was yours, was not your own, and not given you to possess, but to bestow on wanting merit. But this is a topic which I must cast in shades, lest I offend your modesty, which is so far from being ostentatious of the good you do, that it blushes even to have it known: and therefore I must leave you to the satisfaction and testimony of your own conscience, which, though it be a silent panegyric, is yet the best. . . .

There are pages more of this. Dr Johnson explains Dryden's case as follows:

The inevitable consequence of poverty is dependence. Dryden had probably no recourse in his exigencies but to his bookseller [Tonson]. The particular character of Tonson I do not know; but the general conduct of traders was much less liberal in those times than in our own; their views were narrower, and their manners grosser. To the mercantile ruggedness of that race, the delicacy of the poet was sometimes exposed. Lord Bolingbroke, who in his youth had cultivated poetry, related to Dr. King of Oxford, that one day, when he visited Dryden, they heard as they were conversing, another person entering the house. 'This,' said Dryden, 'is Tonson. You will take care not to depart before he goes away: for I have not completed the sheet which I promised him; and if you leave me unprotected, I must suffer all the rudeness to which his resentment can prompt his tongue.'

What rewards Dryden obtained for his poems, besides the payment of the bookseller, cannot be known. Mr. Derrick, who consulted some of his relations, was informed that his Fables obtained five hundred pounds from the duchess of Ormond; a present not unsuitable to the magnificence of that splendid family. . . .

'The inevitable consequence of poverty is dependence.' Perhaps. But is the inevitable consequence of poverty obsequiousness? That seems to have been the general theory in Dryden's day. A poet, to secure support and preferment from a nobleman, had to be both a gentleman and a party-man, responsive to the whip. And whether he chose to be Whig or Tory, it was presently ruled that he might not write anything ' low '—as Chaucer had done in his *Miller's Tale,* Skelton in his *Elinor Rumming,* and Ben Jonson in his *Bartholomew Fair* —or offend against *decorum,* a magical word meaning any thought or expression unacceptable to contemporary French taste. What the reformed poets lacked was not exactly a schoolmaster (for Ben Jonson, from his chair in the *Apollo* room at the Old Devil's Tavern, had put his scholars through the poetic rudiments); it was a posture-master. Dryden, who now assumed this office, gave his classes at Will's, a fashionable coffee-house. He acted as referee in all literary matters, deciding what might (or might not) be considered graceful, elegant, sublime, smooth, just, correct, or modish. He rehabilitated Chaucer by tricking him up in buckled shoes, silk stockings, and a wig. Yet Dryden had learned his critical trade too late, and could himself be accused of inelegancies by the posture-masters of a later generation.

Thus Dr Johnson again:

He had a vanity, unworthy of his abilities, to show, as may be suspected, the rank of the company with whom he lived, by the use

of French words, which had then crept into conversation. . . .
His faults of negligence are beyond recital. Such is the uneven-
ness of his composition, that ten lines are seldom found together
without something of which the reader is ashamed. Dryden was no
rigid judge of his own pages; he seldom struggled after supreme excellence, but snatched in haste what was within his reach; and when
he could content others, was himself contented. He had more music
than Waller, more vigour than Denham, and more nature than
Cowley; and from his contemporaries he was in no danger. Standing
therefore in the highest place, he had no care to rise by contending
with himself; but while there was no name above his own, was willing to enjoy fame on the easiest terms.

At the turn of the century, a delicate and precocious boy, named
Alexander Pope, persuaded some friends to take him to Will's and
introduce him to Dryden. Pope seems to have decided at once that
Dryden's position would suit him well and that he would gain it by
hook or crook. He had escaped regular schooling since early childhood, and now set himself a course in modern English literature, paying special attention to Dryden and to translations from Italian,
French, Greek, and Latin poetry. William Walsh, a critic of repute,
told young Pope:

> . . . that there was one way left of excelling: for though we had
> several great poets, we never had one great poet that was correct,
> and desired me to make that my study and aim.

A neighbour then introduced Pope to the French critics, René le
Bossu, René Rapin, and Boileau, whom he mugged up in the original.
At the age of seventeen, being prevented by his Catholicism from conquering either of the Universities, he set out to conquer Town, and
headed straight for Will's.

When I read English Literature at Oxford, my moral tutor re-
proached me for a report sent in by one of his colleagues: ' It is suggested, Mr Graves, that you prefer some authors to others.' Well, I
still hold that the whole period between, say, Marvell and Blake was
poetically barren, except for a few resolute blades of green grass showing up here and there between the marble paving stones. By all means
let historians of English literature consider *The Age of Dryden* and
The Age of Pope. As Nature abhors a vacuum, so does literary history; and Dryden and Pope were certainly the dominant figures of
their days. But (and this *but* is introduced by a great A, little a, bounc-

ing B), English poets do not wear wigs; they wear their own hair—
while it lasts. And the force inspiring them is love, controlled by
reason; not rhetoric controlled by timidity; not correctness controlled
by cynicism.

My father gave me a strictly Classical education, which meant that
for several years I composed Latin verses once a week throughout
term-time. Latin being a dead language, I could dissociate this classroom activity from the private writing of poems in my cubicle by the
light of a pocket torch. I came of a large Victorian family and, at home,
excelled in parlour games. This game of Latin Verse Composition
challenged my wits. I had to be meticulous about quantity—I well remember the big *Male* I won, when I first started, for carelessly ending
a hexameter composition on the diving-bell with the words *Bona
Machina*.[1] And I had to make Virgil or Ovid my exemplars in metrical
correctness. But more important still was the poetic vocabulary. If
asked to versify: ' Aeneas's fleet sailed north-east from Mt Eryx to
Italy ', I learned to wrap it up like this, with the help of Smith's
Classical dictionary: ' Daedalus's tasteless honey-offering to the Dar-
danian leader's smiling grandmother having been left behind on the
heathered couch of the Argonaut, the prows of destiny cleft the
caerulean plain of Cronos's trident-armed son, slantingly impelled to
the Ausonian shore by kindly bulging Favonian cheeks.' The *Gradus
ad Parnassum* suggested minor evasions of the difficulties provoked by
an originally foreign metre—the natural Latin metre was the Satur-
nian; and if I doubted whether a word might be legitimate in poetry
of the ironically named *Golden Age,* I could consult my *Lewis and
Short.* So I learned exactly in what a *Gradus ad Parnassum* spirit
eighteenth-century odes and pastorals were written; and how easy it
was to compose mock-heroic satires on the Charterhouse Masters,
from sheer boredom with the literary epic.

Here is Dr Johnson on Pope:

> Alexander Pope was born in London, May 22, 1688, of parents
> whose rank or station was never ascertained: we are informed that
> they were of ' gentle blood '; that his father was of a family of
> which the Earl of Downe was the head; and that his mother was the

---

[1] When I gave this lecture, my audience looked puzzled, and I had to explain
that the proper scansion of these words was not *bŏnă măchīnă,* but *bŏnă
māchĭnă.*

daughter of William Turner, Esquire, of York, who had likewise three sons, one of whom had the honour of being killed, and the other of dying, in the service of Charles the First; the third was made a general officer in Spain, from whom the sister inherited what sequestrations and forfeitures had left in the family. This, and this only, is told by Pope; who is more willing, as I have heard observed, to show what his father was not, than what he was. It is allowed that he grew rich by trade; but whether in a shop or on the Exchange was never discovered, till Mr. Tyers told, on the authority of Mrs. Racket, that he was a linen-draper in the Strand. Both parents were Papists.

Dr Johnson then mentions Pope's deformed body, his rigorous self-education and his megalomania: ' as he confesses, he thought himself the greatest genius that ever was.' The schemes and shifts by which Pope made himself not merely a posture-master, but a dictator, are common knowledge. He began by disclaiming any originality—his *Windsor Forest* was an avowed imitation of Denham's *Cooper's Hill;* and by inspiring pity and making full use of his one physical asset, a beautifully modulated voice, to secure introductions to the nobility and the chief literary figures in London: Wycherley, Congreve, Addison, and the rest. As Dr Johnson notes: ' Pope was through his whole life ambitious of splendid acquaintance.' And the more splendid it became, the cooler grew his relations with the less splendid.

Up the ladder went this sedulous ape, continually turning about to bite and scratch those below him. He reached the top triumphantly with *The Dunciad,* which he flattered Sir Robert Walpole into laying before the King and Queen—though he later changed the hero-victim from Lewis Theobald to the King's own Laureate, Colley Cibber. A new departure: hitherto poets had felt themselves bound by a sacred tie, despite occasional ' flyting ' matches, staged as a tournament of wit. Ben Jonson had voluntarily jailed himself in the company of colleagues who expected to be docked of their ears for treason; and showed himself as generous in his praise of contemporaries as just in his censure. Nobody had ever thought of securing the Prime Minister's support for a general libel on humbler colleagues.

Pope, not having a University degree, solved his social problems by claiming gentle birth, on however doubtful grounds, and then bestowing his patrician praise on men like ' low-born Allen ' of Bath, who had achieved fame despite their plebeian origins. He solved his economic problems by the subscription list—persuading friends to rope in subscribers for a translation of the *Iliad* (though he knew practically no Greek), and later for a translation of the *Odyssey* (which he used ill-paid hacks to help him complete). With the large sums of money that accrued he bought annuities, representing a high rate of interest on the capital, and could thereafter afford to despise the ' unabashed Defoe ' and other low hand-to-mouth writers. To set a good moral example he complained:

> *Chaucer's worst ribaldries are learned by rote*
> *And beastly Skelton Heads of Houses quote . . .*

But to show that he himself was beyond criticism, he published a smutty—' smutty ' is the exact word—*Imitation of Chaucer*, ' done by the author in his youth '. And the extraordinary thing is that, as a technician even in the limited field to which he confined himself, Pope was an extremely poor one.

If I had time, I should be charmed to take you line by line through any long poem of Pope's you pleased, demonstrating its technical in-competency when judged by the standards of his predecessors and successors. Pope has no control of his *s's*, he does not sufficiently vary his vowel sounds, his antitheses are forced, his poetic vocabulary in-exact, his inversions of syntax are not only un-English but misleading. As a test of my opinion, while preparing this lecture, I opened *Pope's Works* at random, and came across this six-line passage from his *Imitations of Horace*. It should have been carried through three more drafts at least.

> *Let Envy howl, while Heaven's whole chorus sings,*
> *And bark at honour not conferred by Kings . . .*

Envy and *Heaven*, like *howl, while,* and *whole,* are too close in sound to occur decently in the same line. *Howl, Heaven,* and *whole* are over-alliterative. *Chorus sings* is not as tuneful as the sense requires. The suggested antithesis between the Heavenly Chorus and royal honours can hardly be intended.

> *Let Flattery sickening see the incense rise*
> *Sweet to the world and grateful to the skies. . . .*

Pope's *s's* are quite out of hand here. And does he mean that Flattery sickens others, or that Flattery itself falls sick? And if the latter, was this sickness antecedent to the sight of rising incense, or due to it?

Do ' the skies ' mean merely the sky, to which the fumes ascend, as opposed to the earth; or do they mean God's Heaven, as opposed to this world of men? And is the incense a flattering incense, or is it an incense which all devout Catholics, like Pope, are required to burn?

> *Truth guards the poet, sanctifies the line*
> *And makes immortal, verse so mean as mine.*

The incense, *the* world, *the* skies, *the* poet, *the* line! Five *the's* in nineteen words. Pope could never control his definite article. And does ' the line ' stand for the lines of a poet's verse, or the line of succession —as he uses it three couplets later. *-fies the line* is ugly. *Makes immortal, verse so mean as mine* is over-alliterative again, and the inversion of ' makes verse so mean as mine immortal ' calls for an awkward comma to separate *immortal* from *verse*—otherwise the sense would be: ' And makes even immortal verse as mean as mine '.

The Dunciad (its revision provoked by a fancied slight from Cibber in the matter of a stage-crocodile) was supposedly aimed at dullness. But is anything duller in the world than the ideal of correctness, even if not seriously framed?

One result of Pope's largely successful attempt to put contemporary verse into a strait-jacket of which he held the key (and buried this in his coffin at Twickenham), was the virtual disappearance of personal Muses. Skelton had honoured his Jane Scroop; Donne his Anne More—though he never mentioned her by name, and laid a curse on anyone who thought he knew it; Ben Jonson his Lady Venetia Digby, of whom he wrote at her death:

> *'Twere time that I dy'd too, now she is dead,*
> *Who was my Muse, and life of all I sey'd.*
> *The spirit that I wrote with, and conceiv'd,*
> *All that was good, or great in me she weav'd,*
> *And set it forth; the rest were cobwebs fine,*
> *Spun out in name of some of the old Nine,*
> *To hang a window or make darke the roome,*
> *Till swept away, th' were cancell'd with a broome!*

By the rules of Ben Jonson's *Apollo Room,* 'chosen women'
(*lectae feminae*) might not be debarred from entry; but what woman
of reputation would have been admitted to Will's Coffee House sixty
years later? Romantic love, forbidden by the Puritans as a seduction
and snare, was disavowed at the Restoration in favour of a rakish
carnality. It is a long way from Dowland's—if it was Dowland's—
'*Deare, if you change, I'll never choose again*', to Rochester's modish lines:

> *All my past life is mine no more,*
> *The flying hours are gone,*
> *Like transitory dreams given o'er,*
> *Whose images are kept in store*
> *By memory alone.*
>
> *The time that is to come, is not;*
> *How can it then be mine?*
> *The present moment's all my lot,*
> *And that, as fast as it is got,*
> *Phillis, is only thine.*
>
> *Then talk not of inconstancy,*
> *False hearts, and broken vows:*
> *If I by miracle can be*
> *This live-long minute true to thee,*
> *'Tis all that heaven allows.*

The true lover was unmasked, as he has been unmasked again
today by Doctors Freud and Kinsey; and Pope's rider, that

> *Every woman is at heart a rake* . . .

was tacitly accepted for the next hundred years to excuse men for
treating women as, at best, an amusing, if irksome, sexual convenience. Martha Blount may have been Pope's mistress, or even his wife
(though this is only a surmise), and became his residuary legatee;
but she does not figure in his poems and is not even implied by them,
however shadowily.

So, although the age abounded in impersonal Chloes, Amandas,
and Belindas, the only personal Muse I can recall was Swift's Stella.

Swift may seem to be joking in his *To Stella Visiting Me in My Sick-*
ness (1720), when he writes:

> *Pallas, observing Stella's wit*
> *Was more than for her sex was fit,*
> *And that her beauty, soon or late,*
> *Might breed confusion in the state,*
> *In high concern for human-kind,*
> *Fix'd* honour *in her infant mind.* . . .
>
> *And lest we should for honour take*
> *The drunken quarrels of a rake;*
> *Or think it seated in a scar,*
> *Or on a proud triumphal car,*
> *Or in the payment of a debt*
> *We lose with sharpers at picquet;*
> *Or when a whore in her vocation*
> *Keeps punctual to an assignation* . . .
> *Let Stella's fair example preach*
> *A lesson she alone can teach* . . .
> *Ten thousand oaths upon record*
> *Are not so sacred as her word:*
> *The world shall in its atoms end,*
> *Ere Stella can deceive a friend.*

But Swift is in earnest. My old friend Richard Ashe King once remarked:

> I do not envy the man who is untouched by the infantile prattle
> of Swift's *Journal to Stella*—written in the intervals of his dictating
> the policy of England at home and abroad—or who is unmoved by
> the white-hot agony of his anxiety during her illness, or of his
> anguish after her death.

Dryden had told Swift at Will's: ' Cousin Jonathan, you will never
be a poet! ' And indeed, Swift never did become a poet of the Age
of Obsequiousness. Like Defoe, Fielding, Dr Johnson and other
writers known for their generous hearts and incorruptible character,[2]

---

[2] Defoe's intelligence work first for the Tories, then for the Whigs (after 1714)
while the Tories thought him still their man, proves a sense of humour rather
than a failure in integrity.

he renounced poetry in favour of prose: except for the composition of trifles. But these trifles, though darkened by a morbid horror of man's physical circumstances, demonstrate the proper use of English: they are clear, simple, inventive, pungent, unaffected, original, generous, utterly outspoken.

A plea can be made on Pope's behalf that Swift counted him in the first rank of his friends. But even this plea, I think, fails. Pope seems to have exerted all his charm on Swift; knowing how cruelly Swift's pen would have scorched him up if it had come to a quarrel, but how readily he could be won over as a loyal and industrious ally by a pretence of sincere friendship. It was only when Swift's wits began to fail that Pope showed the true quality of his friendship. He routed out Swift's early letters to himself and amended them in his own favour, as he had done with Wycherley's.

No, I am not altogether ungrateful to the eighteenth century. I pay the tribute of a sentimental sigh to such pleasant simplicities as John Newton's:

> *There is a land of pure delight*
> *Where saints immortal reign;*
> *Infinite day excludes the night*
> *And pleasures banish pain.*
>
> *There everlasting Spring abides*
> *And never-withering flowers.*
> *Death like a narrow stream divides*
> *That heavenly land from ours.*

and Richard Graves's:

> *Upon the bridge's coping-stone*
> *The loitering boy doth lean alone,*
> *And watches with a steadfast look*
> *The falling waters of the brook. . . .*

as I remember certain pleasant eighteenth-century wallpapers, and formal gardens, and silk handkerchiefs, and magnificent chairs and sets of table silver. Also, one would have to be hard-hearted indeed to dislike either Gray or Collins. But for any sense of personal poetry (except in Swift who was, of course, educated at Kilkenny School and Trinity College, Dublin; and Goldsmith, another Irishman) one must adventure among scribblers and dunces. Goldsmith is exceptional because he had roved about in low company through several countries, rambling and gambling his money away, and would no sooner have thought of buying an annuity than of committing murder. Besides, *The Deserted Village,* despite its air of formality, is a true poem; because, like Swift, Goldsmith was in earnest. He was offering, disguised as an essay on the break-up of English village society, a lament for the ills of Ireland, modelled on contemporary Irish minstrel songs—walk, description, meditation, moral vision, invocation of the Goddess; even the distressful crone is there, and the damsel who tears out her hair in handfuls. Auburn really lies in County Roscommon; the poem is full of personal recollections, and glows with sorrowful anger.

Eighteenth-century scribblers and dunces wrote such splendid drinking-songs as:

> *Here's a health to the King and a lasting peace,*
> *To faction an end and to wealth increase,*
> *O come let us drink it while we have breath,*
> *For there's no drinking after Death;*
> *And he who will this health deny*
> *Down among the dead men let him lie!*

And there were low-life ballads, such as *Wednesbury Cocking,* to set your hair on end; I should like to recite the whole of the *Cocking,* because I have it by heart, but have time only for the serene opening verses:

> *At Wednesbury there was a cocking,*
> *A match between Newton and Scroggins;*
> *The colliers and nailers left work,*
> *And all to old Spittle's went jogging.*
> *To see this noble sport,*
> *Many noblemen resorted;*
> *And though they had but little money,*
> *Yet that little they freely sported.*
>
> *There was Jeffery and Colborn from Hampton,*
> *And Dusty from Bilston was there;*

> *Flummery he came from Darlaston,*
> *And he was as rude as a bear.*
> *There was old Will from Walsall,*
> *And Smacker from Westbromwich come;*
> *Blind Robin he came from Rowley,*
> *And staggering he went home.*

And there was Defoe's *True Born Englishman:*

> *The* Royal Refugee *our Breed restores,*
> *With* Foreign Courtiers, *and with* Foreign Whores:
> *And carefully repeoples us again,*
> *Throughout his Lazy, Long, Lascivious Reign;*
> *With such a blest and True-born* English *Fry,*
> *As much Illustrates our Nobility . . .*
> French *Cooks,* Scotch *Pedlars, and* Italian *Whores,*
> *Were all made Lords, or Lords' progenitors.*
> *Beggars and Bastards by his new Creation,*
> *Much multiply'd the Peerage of the Nation;*
> *Who will be all, e'er one short Age runs o'er,*
> *As* True-Born *Lords as those we had before.*

This brings me to the problem of satire. Poetry has always had two hands, the left and the right; the left for cursing and the right for blessing, as there is a right-handed and a left-handed worship of the Goddess Khali in India; and as, among the Mohammedans, the left hand undertakes certain tasks from which the right shrinks. Yet it is axiomatic that the right hand must be used to bless only what deserves blessing, and that the left may curse only what deserves cursing. Marvell's satire was legitimate, because generous. Samuel Butler's satire in *Hudibras* was legitimate, because he had served under the Puritan colonel whom he ridicules, and been forced for years to swallow back his Royalist spittle. Defoe's satire was legitimate: he had been abused as a foreigner by 'True-Born Englishmen'. And though he may be blamed for indicting a whole nation with:

> *. . . France,*
> *Where mankind lives in haste, and thrives by chance,*
> *A dancing nation fickle and untrue*
> *Have oft undone themselves and others too. . . .*

the times required that this should be jokingly said. But Pope's satire was patently illegitimate, because neither provoked nor generous. Professional standards in English, as opposed to Continental, poetry, have for centuries insisted that satire should not reflect private rancour or hope of personal gain. Swift understood this well enough, perhaps because the principle was first formulated in Ireland.

I shall now leave Twickenham and Grub Street—eventually disinfected of its associations by being renamed ' Milton Street '—and take you over to ancient Connaught. My excuse will be the elucidation of Rosalind's phrase in *As You Like It:* ' I have never been so berhymed since I was an Irish rat.' Rosalind was referring to a seventh-century satire, *The Proceedings of the Grand Bardic Academy,* which was not translated into English until some ninety years ago. I have no notion by what chance she, or Shakespeare, came to hear of it.

The satire describes how three hundred professors and students of the Grand Bardic Academy, led by the Chief Bard Seanchan son of Torpest, abused the munificent hospitality of Guaire, King of Connaught, with the threat of satire if he refused them anything; until one Marvan, the Royal Swineherd, took vengeance on them for this blackmail, and for their murder of his own gifted white pig. Marvan's pig was no ordinary pig, but had been at once his physician, his music-maker and his messenger; and the murder lay at the door of the professor's greedy old foster-mother, who would not be satisfied until Guaire presented her with a great collar of its lard.

Eumaeus the swineherd of the *Odyssey* is addressed as ' god-like ', an adjective which Classical scholars ignorantly translate either ' honest ' or ' worthy '. In Odysseus's Ithaca, as in ancient Ireland and Wales, the swineherd served the sow-headed Phorcis, Goddess of Death and Poetic Inspiration; Eumaeus might therefore be called ' Chief Prophet of Heaven and Earth ', like his colleague Marvan. The death of Marvan's pig is a mythographic way of recording the murder of inspired poetry by a new-fangled academicism. At first, the bards despised Marvan as an interloper, and asked him to prove his right to converse with them on equal terms. But his poetic passport was a mantle of prophetic wind; and though these professors were skilled in astronomy, mathematics, cosmology, law, cyphers, counterpoint, and all the latest prosodic fashions, they could not stand up against a Royal Swineherd when it came to a battle of wits.

Seanchan asked Marvan pompously: ' Tell me, peasant, what was the antecedent of the First Cause? ' Marvan did not cite the metaphysical arguments of the Early Fathers, or Aristotle, or Epicurus, or Heraclitus, but answered simply and accurately: ' Blind nuts! '— which, for me, remains the only possible answer to such a stupid question, though it might not go down very well nowadays in a D.Phil. *viva*. The hazel was the ancient Irish and Welsh symbol of Divine Wisdom, and the First Cause must therefore be the nut from whose kernel grew the Sacred Hazel which, according to tradition, overshadowed the Salmon-pool of Enlightenment. So what, in poetical terms, could the antecedent of the First Cause be, but a blind nut—a nut without a kernel?

Marvan answered magisterially every one of the professors' questions, and in return humbled them with problems beyond their power to solve—for instance, they could not even guess at the true origin of the poet's harp, or of poetic metre. Incidentally, he treated them to inspired but sorry revelations of what their wives were doing at home. When the three hundred had failed on all counts, he put a bond on them, which debarred them from ever again abusing a patron's hospitality, or from interfering with the affairs of others—' thenceforth to the womb of Judgement '.

Seanchan's end came when, after rhyming ten rats to death for stealing his dinner scraps, he turned his petulant rage on the united cats of Ireland. He announced that they had neglected their job, and satirized Irusan, their King, by calling him ' Otter's leavings, clumsy claws, with a dandyish drooping tail like a cow's '.

The storyteller continues:

> It was told to Seanchan that Irusan was on his way coming to kill him; and he requested Guaire to come with the nobility of Connaught to protect him against Irusan. They all came around him, and had not been long there when they heard a vibrating, impetuous and impressive sound, similar to that produced by a tremendously raging fiery furnace in full blaze; and it appeared to them that there was not in Connaught a plough bullock larger than Irusan.
>
> His appearance was as follows: blunt-snouted, rapacious, panting, determined, jagged-eared, broad-breasted, prominent-jointed, sharp and smooth-clawed, split-nosed, sharp and rough-toothed, thick-snouted, nimble, powerful, deep-flanked, terror-striking, angry, ex-

tremely vindictive, quick, purring, glare-eyed; and he came towards
them in that similitude. He passed amongst them generally, but did
not stop till he reached to the place where Seanchan was. He took
hold of him by one arm, jerked him on his back, and returned with
him by the same way as he had come, for he had no other object in
view but to fetch away Seanchan. Seanchan now had recourse to
flattery of Irusan, praising his leap, his progress in his running, his
power, strength and activity. . . .

But it was too late. The rats were avenged.

The professional moral of all this is that when a natural urge in
poets to resort and debate together—as Shakespeare, Ben Jonson,
Drayton, and the rest did at the *Mermaid*—is exploited by literary
politicians, and cabals are formed, poetry is in danger. And that arch-
poets who petulantly rhyme a few rats to death—meaning the ignorant poetasters—should take care not to satirize the King Cat, the
emissary of the Cat-goddess. They must remember that the source of
all poetry is not reason, but the wind of inspiration. Only swine can
see the wind. And, since I must not hold anything back from you, the
origin of the poet's harp was the wind which blew on the sinews of
a whale's skeleton in the days of Macuel son of Miduel; and metre
originated in the days of Lamiach from the sound of two hammers of
different weight beaten alternately on an anvil. However, the kennings
of these riddles—like the kennings of Seanchan's satire on Irusan—
are not to be found in Boileau. I reserve them for my fifth lecture,
when I shall deal with the technical side of poetry.

THE ROAD TO RYDAL MOUNT

The Seven Years' War shook the absolutist régime set up by Louis XIV, inherited by Louis XV, and either copied or envied by their royal contemporaries throughout Europe. Eventually the revolt of the American colonies, brought to a successful finish by French intervention, touched off the French Revolution. Since absolutism had been extended from the political field to that of philosophy, the arts, and literature, this general collapse in France, which now threatened England too, sent the more inquisitive English poets searching back in history to find out where a false step had been taken. They decided that Dryden, Pope, Addison, and other poets of the Age of Obsequiousness were mistaken: that poetry had not always been a drawing-room product, but had at one time implied a warm relationship between all classes—the early English kings, for instance, had ' dear comrades ' not subjects. From which they deduced that a man was a man for a' that, and for a' that, and for a' that; and that the current poetic technique was artificial and constrictive. As Romantic Revivalists they dismounted from what Keats irreverently called ' the rocking horse ' of the heroic couplet; they cultivated the Elizabethans, ceased to court the peerage, avoided public life, and did not feel obliged to live in Town. Most of them were avowed, if ineffective, revolutionaries. Blake walked the streets of London in a red cap of Liberty; Wordsworth carried the British flag in a Jacobin procession and attracted the notice of Pitt's secret police; Shelley sealed a letter to the Duke of Norfolk with a revolutionary wafer. As Hazlitt wrote, they scorned ' degrees, priority, place, and the distinctions of birth ', and ' were surrounded, in company with the Muses, by a rabble of idle apprentices and Botany Bay convicts, female vagrants, gipsies, meek daughters in the family of Christ, of idiot boys and mad mothers, and after them "owls and night-ravens flew " '.

Others, of course, like Keats, loved the Gothic past more than they welcomed the democratic or the pantisocratic future. ' O Chatterton, how very sad thy fate! ' wrote Keats. For Chatterton's failure to secure Horace Walpole's patronage by means of his Rowley forgeries had reduced him to writing shilling-a-line satires on the Duke of Grafton, the Earl of Bute, and the Princess of Wales, until he expired in poverty. Keats himself felt the lack of a patron; his publisher's lure, *Cap and Bells,* if not his diploma pieces *Hyperion* and *Endymion,* prove that he would have attempted any poetical subject within reason suggested to him by a coroneted patron. But fate had attached him to Leigh Hunt's party; and to court the Tories would have been disloyal. Moreover, as a result of the wonderful profits made by Moore and Byron, who gave the large romantically-inclined public what it wanted, individual patronage waned. ' Why shouldn't other poets do the same? ' the peers began to ask. This was all very well for Samuel Rogers, a rich banker; and for Crabbe, a country parson; and for Shelley, who had private means; and for Lamb, with his not very demanding clerkship in the India Office. But it seemed mighty hard on John Clare.

I can best explain my feelings about professional standards by contrasting the careers of two early nineteenth-century poets: Clare and Wordsworth—Clare, who began as a servant of the public, but ended as a devotee of the Goddess; Wordsworth, who reversed the process —Clare, with his growing sense of what poetry demanded; Wordsworth, with his growing sense of what the public demanded.

Clare, a labourer's son, was mouse-poor, and quite without influence or connexions. Though his first book of poems (1820) proved immediately successful, it sold well only because poetry happened to come all at once into fashion, for dubious reasons. Since Taylor, his publisher, who had seen his work by accident, was billing him truthfully enough as an ' English peasant poet ', Clare became a nine days' wonder. He had clay on his boots, hay-seed in his hair, genius in his eye, spoke as charmingly odd a dialect as Burns, yet was able to forge a neat, melodious pastoral rhyme that would not have disgraced Robert Bloomfield, William Cowper, or even the self-elected High Priest of Nature, Wordsworth. Visitors came in coaches from London

to the remote village of Helpstone, where they gaped at this miracu-
lous son of toil, a rival sideshow to his contemporary, the legless and
armless Miss Biffin, who threaded needles and worked samplers with
her lips and teeth alone (poor creature!). Clare (poor creature!)
similarly transcended the disadvantages of birth, environment and
education, and though his biographers suggest that he disliked the
label of ' Peasant Poet ', this is not altogether true. He wrote an autobiographical poem under that title, and in his *Village Minstrel* roman-
ticized himself as a Spenserian ' Lubin ':

> *Young Lubin was a peasant from his birth;*
> *His sire a hind born to the flail and plough,*
> *To thump the corn out and to till the earth,*
> *The coarsest chance which nature's laws allow—*
> *To earn his living by a sweating brow;*
> *Thus Lubin's early days did rugged roll,*
> *And mixt in timely toil—but e'en as now,*
> *Ambitious prospects fired his little soul,*
> *And fancy soared and sung, 'bove poverty's control.*

The Village Minstrel appeared in his second volume, which sold
badly. The third and fourth volume (1827 and 1835) were dismal
failures, but not because Clare refused to cater for popular taste. He
pleased the large ' Keepsake ' public by imitations of elder poets and,
oddly enough, these are far closer to the originals than Pope's, as can
be seen by comparing their rival imitations of Sir John Harington.
And here Clare is making obeisance to the aristocratic Augustan
tradition, which had reasserted its sway at the defeat of Revolutionary
France:

> To My Oaten Reed
>
> *Thou warble wild, of rough, rude melody,*
> *How oft I've woo'd thee, often thrown thee by!*
> *In many a doubtful rapture touching thee,*
> *Waking thy rural notes in many a sigh:*
> *Fearing the wise, the wealthy, proud and high,*
> *Would scorn as vain thy lowly ecstasy,*
> *Deeming presumptuous thy uncultur'd themes.*
> *Thus vainly courting Taste's unblemish'd eye,*
> *To list a simple labourer's artless dreams. . . .*

In the 1820's, unless a poet could take his place naturally and gracefully at a gentleman's table, cut or keep out of sight his plebian connexions, and move to Town, he still might not hope for advancement. Then what was to be done with Clare, however untainted by Jacobinism and however obligingly he tuned his oaten reed? He had married Patty Turner, a poor illiterate fellow-villager, merely to make an honest woman of her; now lived in an insanitary cottage full of ragged, ailing brats; worked as a day labourer; and never hankered for city life. The fashionable sightseers who visited Helpstone paid no shilling entrance-fee for the privilege of wasting Clare's time; they scattered a few compliments, wrinkled their noses at the sour smell of poverty, and drove away again. Their visits, like his week-long rhyming fits, merely discouraged the local farmers from giving him steady employment. A general slump occurred in the sales of poetry, and Clare slowly went to pieces under the strain.

A fund was, indeed, raised to keep him afloat, but this proved insufficient to feed and clothe his family of seven children. And though it is true that an adequate income might have kept him from sinking so deep into the trough of melancholy, it would not have assuaged his loneliness. The only cure for his disease would have been the society of his fellow-poets. Yet it was not until about the year 1830, when he grew weary of courting ' Taste's unblemish'd eye ', that he graduated as a true poet. He had by now been favoured with a dream vision of the White Goddess of Poetry, and henceforth his companions should have been those who bore her seal on their brows. He wrote:

> These dreams of a beautiful presence, a woman deity, gave the sublimest conceptions of beauty to my imagination; and being last night with the same presence, the lady divinity left such a vivid picture of her visits in my sleep, dreaming of dreams, that I could no longer doubt her existence. So I wrote them down to prolong the happiness of my faith in believing her my guardian genius.

But where, then, were his fellow-poets? In 1820 there had been talk of a friendly exchange of poetic opinions between Clare and Keats, who knew the Goddess as *La Belle Dame sans Merci,* and such a meeting might have done both of them a deal of good. Keats, born a Cockney, criticized an early nature poem of Clare's by saying that ' the Description too much prevailed over the sentiment '; whereas

Clare wrote of Keats: 'He often described Nature as she appeared to his fancies and not as he would have described her had he witnessed the things he described.' However, this meeting had never come off; and now Keats was dead, and so was Shelley; and Clare's friendships with Darley, Lamb, and Cary, limited to letters and very occasional visits, died away.

Clare seems to have stumbled accidentally upon the solution to his dilemma; perhaps he found it in the *Book of Samuel,* where David escaped from the Philistines by feigning madness. The best way to discourage unwelcome visitors was casually to identify himself with Lord Byron or with Tom Cribb, the prizefighter; such deceitful fictions soon scattered them. But being already cut off from village society by presuming above his station, he found that the loneliness increased. He wrote in a letter:

> I live here among the ignorant like a lost man in fact like one whom the rest seems careless of having anything to do with—they hardly dare talk in my company for fear I should mention them in my writings & I find more pleasure in wandering the fields than in mixing among my silent neighbours who are insensible of everything but toiling & talking of it & that to no purpose.

The distressed Patty was not his equal, either in intellect or sensibility, and as an anodyne he took to deceiving himself with another sort of fiction. He contrived to believe that he was really married to Mary Joyce, a farmer's daughter four years younger than himself, with whom he had been passionately in love as a boy, but whom he had never aspired to marry. She became his pastoral Muse, the perpetual Other Woman. After the failure of his fourth book of poems in 1835, he turned his back on reality and lived more and more in the lost world of his boyhood, peopled only by beasts, birds, and Mary. In 1837, his London friends sent him to a private mental home in Epping Forest, from which he ran away in 1841; but six months later, by order of the local gentry whom he had libellously lampooned in *The Parish,* was confined to Northampton General Lunatic Asylum, where he remained until his death in 1864. The charge was: ' years addicted to poetical prosings '.

Clare's lunacy, being self-inflicted, was only partial—as when recruits shoot off their trigger fingers rather than put bullets through their heads. It did not affect his poetic capacity—if, as it seems, he wrote and talked certifiable nonsense merely to discourage visitors. Though he ceased from satire or such low-life ballads as *The Help-stone Statutes,* he broke quite new ground in *The Dying Child:*

> *He could not die when trees were green,*
> *For he loved the time too well.*
> *His little hands, when flowers were seen,*
> *Were held for the bluebell,*
> *As he was carried o'er the green.*
>
> *His eye glanced at the white-nosed bee;*
> *He knew those children of the Spring:*
> *When he was well and on the lea*
> *He held one in his hands to sing*
> *Which filled his heart with glee.*
>
> *Infants, the children of the Spring!*
> *How can an infant die*
> *When butterflies are on the wing,*
> *Green grass, and such a sky?*
> *How can they die at Spring?*

And his ' I am, but what I am who cares or knows? ' and ' I lost the love of Heaven ' are already among the recognized glories of English poetry. Since in those days warders had officially stopped flogging lunatics, and doctors had not yet developed drastic therapeutic training or shock treatment, he had a less unhappy time than might be supposed—at any rate, until the governors decided to deny even harmless inmates leave to wander freely about the town, and so turned an asylum into a prison.

How good was Clare? At his best he was very good indeed, with a natural simplicity supported by a remarkable sense of language; he meant what he said, considered it well before he wrote it down and wrote with love. Most of his poems were about Nature because, after all, he had never been anything but a countryman and described only what he knew. By comparison, Wordsworth had a very cursory knowledge of wild life; he did not get up early enough in the morning. (Wordsworth on Nature is like Virgil on boxing; I prefer Theocritus, who had obviously been a bit of a bruiser himself, as his account of the Amycus-Pollux match shows.) Clare wrote a great deal of descriptive verse on the nesting habits of particular birds, and the queer ways of wild animals and insects, and on country people as part of the landscape. But Clare never bores, being always precise and economical and relying on patient observation; besides, he had somehow acquired the rare faculty of knowing how and when to end a poem. His obsession with Nature made him think of a poem as a living thing, rather than a slice cut from the cake of literature, and his poems are still alive. I find myself repeating some of them without having made a conscious effort at memorization. And though it was taken as a symptom of madness that he one day confided in a visitor: ' I know Gray—I know him well ', I shall risk saying here, with equal affection: ' I know Clare; I know him well. We have often wept together.'

There was no Age of Clare, as there was no Age of Smart, the magnificence of whose *Song to David* (1763) makes all other poems of the day look sick and sorry. Smart had also vainly and too long courted Taste's unblemish'd eye—going so far as to translate Pope's *Ode on St Cecilia's Day,* an imitation of Dryden's on the same subject, into Latin! He wrote *A Song to David* in a lunatic asylum, and when his collected poems were published in 1791, it was omitted as ' not acceptable to the reader '. This poem is formally addressed to David —Smart knew that he was no madder than King David had been, and a tradition survives that he scrabbled the verses with a key on the walls of his cell; but the deity whom he really celebrated was the central figure of the Muse Triad, the *Lady of Wild Things:*

> *Strong is the horse upon his speed;*
> *Strong in pursuit the rapid glede,*
>   *Which makes at once his game;*
> *Strong the tall ostrich on the ground;*
> *Strong through the turbulent profound*
>   *Shoots xiphias to his aim.*
>
> *Strong is the lion—like a coal*
> *His eyeball—like a bastion's mole*
>   *His chest against the foes:*
> *Strong the gier-eagle on his sail,*
> *Strong against tide, th' enormous whale*
>   *Emerges, as he goes.*

But even Dr Johnson, who liked Smart personally and did all he could to help him, had no use at all for *A Song to David,* and once ended an argument as to who was the better poet—Smart or a dullard called Derrick—by saying: 'Sir, there is no settling the point of precedency between a louse and a flea.'

So as I was saying, there was no Age of Clare, and no Age of Smart, but there was an Age of Wordsworth. You will find it in all the literary histories. 'The Age of' is a political term. One may legitimately talk of the Age of Pericles, because Pericles was the most energetic and gifted statesman of fifth-century Athens; and Athens was the most energetic and gifted city-state in Greece, as Greece was the most energetic and gifted country in Europe or Asia. One can similarly talk of the Age of Augustus, or the Age of Louis XIV. But the 'Age of' is a non-poetic concept, and when applied to English poets is either a misnomer—for instance *The Age of Shakespeare* wrongly suggests that Shakespeare was the most influential and esteemed poet of his day—or it means that the poet selected to name the age was a politician rather than a poet.

Wordsworth came of comfortable family and got stung, during an adventurous visit to France in 1791–2, by the gadfly of Republicanism. His intention of presenting himself as a leader of the Girondists was thwarted when an uncle shook the family purse-strings at him; whereupon he came to his senses, and deserted not only his revolutionary friends but his Muse, 'Julia'—Annette Vallon—whom he had got with child. And when the 'stings of viperous remorse' no longer pricked him, and he could even congratulate himself on his providential escape, that was the end of Wordsworth the poet. He virtuously led his companions back to the eighteenth-century ecclesiastical Tory fold from which he had strayed. Byron, who also came home, though on his own initiative, wrote to Murray the publisher in 1820:

> *All* of us—Scott, Southey, Wordsworth, Moore, Campbell, I—are all in the wrong . . . that we are upon a wrong revolutionary poetical system, or systems, not worth a damn in itself . . . and that the present and next generations will finally be of this opinion. . . . I took Moore's poems and my own, and some others, and went over them side by side with Pope's, and I was really astonished (I ought not to have been) and mortified at the ineffable distance in point of sense, harmony, effect, and even *Imagination,* passion and

Invention, between the little Queen Anne's Man, and us of the Lower Empire.

Though Wordsworth (as Matthew Arnold records) did not earn enough money by poetry to keep him in shoestrings, he managed to live frugally on a £900 legacy bequeathed him in 1795, which saved him from going to London and undertaking journalism. Seven years later the then Lord Lonsdale died, and his successor paid the Wordsworths a long-standing debt owed to their father. After another ten years Wordsworth wheedled his stamp-distributorship out of Lord Lonsdale—soon worth an annual £1,000. De Quincey commented enviously: 'Money always fell in' to Wordsworth, enabling him to pursue his poetic career without distraction. In 1842 he gave up the post, and Sir Robert Peel rewarded him for having done so with a £300 Civil List pension, and the Laureateship, which Wordsworth stipulated must be a sinecure. 'All for a handful of silver he left us . . . !'

As a birthday present, when I was young, my father sent me without explanation a letter in an old man's hand, undated and signed with the initials W.W. The paper and ink looked ancient, but since the addressee was plainly 'Robert Graves, Esq.', I began reading what seemed a personal message rather than a historical document. It began abruptly:

> Mr. Graves will bear in mind what I said against the phrase of making a Tour in Switzerland as generally understood to relate to Alpine Switzerland—the best thing to be done is to cross the Alps by as many passes as you conveniently can; descending into Italy and back again—to and fro.

On turning to the end of the letter again, I discovered the words 'Rydal Mt.' in the margin. The writer was none other than William Wordsworth, a 'sincere friend' of my grand-uncle Robert Graves, the physician. I had not yet read Wordsworth with attention, and was prepared to modify my unfavourable first impressions, for my father's sake, if this letter gave me honest cause. A hasty perusal showed that it referred mostly to a tour of the Continent which he had made twenty years previously, in 1820, with his wife and his sister Dorothy. So I reached for my Oxford edition of the *Poems,* borrowed a *Wordsworth Concordance,* and settled down to study him in earnest.

> Taking you up at Berne is in some respects inconvenient—as it
> leaves the Lakes of Zurich and Wallenstadt and the noble pass of
> the Via-Mala, and over the Splugen, and so down upon Chiavenna
> and the Lake of Como etc., upon your left hand. But as you must
> start from Berne it would probably be best as *we* did in 1820, to
> go to Thun—at T. (if you have an hour to spare) is a pleasant walk
> in the grounds of . . .

Here it seems, Wordsworth, unable to recall the name of the place,
consulted his *Memorials of a Tour on the Continent;* but the relevant
poem, *Memorial Near the Outlet of the Lake of Thun,* gave him no
information. So he wrote:

> . . . near the outlet of the lake

but then scratched the words out, and abandoned the problem.

> where is a small Tablet to the memory of Alois Reding. The views
> from the Ch:yd and Castle are also very interesting—up the Lake
> to Unterbeer and Interlacken.

I found that he had immortalized Reding's tablet as follows:

> *Around a wild and woody hill*
> *A gravelled pathway treading,*
> *We reached a votive Stone that bears*
> *The name of Aloys Reding.*
>
> *Well judged the friend who placed it there*
> *For silence and protection;*
> *And haply with a finer care*
> *Of dutiful affection.*
>
> *The Sun regards it from the West*
> *And, while in summer glory*
> *He sets, his sinking yields a type*
> *Of that pathetic story. . . .*

Raising my eyebrows a little, I read on:

> The Lake of Brientz—the falls near it which we did not visit—
> are worth seeing, if you have time, but we preferred going to Lauter-
> brunnen.

What poetic harvest had Wordsworth brought back from Brienz? He
watched certain ' harvest-damsels float, Homeward in their rugged

boat. . . . The rustic maidens, every hand, Upon a Sister's shoulder laid ': and heard them ' chant as glides the boat along, A simple, but a touching song; To chant as Angels do above, The melodies of Peace in love.'

> And over the Wengern Alp to Grindelwald—thence over the Schidec to Meyringham— Observe on your descent upon M. look for the celebrated fall of Reichenbach. From M. we gave a day to the Oberhasli Vall, and the famous falls of Handec—whence we *might* have proceeded over the Grimsel Pass to Unteren etc.,—but we preferred returning to M.—thence by side of the Lake of Lungern and Sarnan on to Lucerne.

At Lucerne the Wordsworths had met a twenty-year-old Bostonian, Frederick Goddard, and were delighted to hear English spoken again, ' while festive mirth ran wild '. Three days later, Goddard was drowned in the late near Zurich and Wordsworth mourned his fate:

> *Beloved by every gentle muse*
> *He left his Transatlantic home.*
> *Europe, a realised romance,*
> *Had opened on his eager glance.*
> *What present bliss! what golden views!*
> *What stores for years to come!*
>
> *Fetch, sympathising Powers of air,*
> *Fetch, ye that post o'er seas and lands,*
> *Herbs moistened by Virginian dew*
> *A most untimely grave to strew*
> *Whose turf may never know the care*
> *Of* kindred *human hands!*

Since Goddard hailed from Massachusetts, ' herbs moistened by Virginian dew ' is perhaps a festive synonym for tobacco; though this seems a little out of key in an elegiac context.

> From Lucerne to the top of Riga—

He means the Rigi. The Rigi ascent he celebrated in *Our Lady of the Snows,* from which a short passage may be quoted for the eighteenth-century ingenuity of the second line:

> *Even for the Man who stops not here*
> *But down the irriguous valley hies,*

> *Thy very name, O Lady! flings,*
> *O'er blooming fields and gushing springs,*
> *A tender sense of shadowy fears*
> *And chasing sympathies.*

Coleridge, by the way, held that love of mountain scenery was a purely literary emotion, found among mountaineers only when they had enjoyed a liberal education. ' Where this is not the case, as among the peasantry of North Wales, the ancient mountains, with all their terrors and all their glories, are pictures to the blind, and music to the deaf.'

So on to the Rigi and:

> . . . thence, by the Town of Switz to Brunnen on the Uri branch of the Lake of the 4 Cantons. So on, by Boat to Tell's Chapel and Fluellen. Then to Altorf, Amstag, to the valley of Urseren. Here let me observe you might cross over the Difenti, on one of the branches of the Rhine and thence up the Viamala to Splugen and over to Chiavenna, and so down the Lake of Como. This I did 50 years ago, only reversing it.

By ' 50 years ago ' he means 1790 when, as an undergraduate at the end of his third year, he and Robert Jones went on a Long Vacation walking tour. Their itinerary is recorded in his *Descriptive Sketches taken during a pedestrian tour among the Alps.* Tell's Chapel had then greatly impressed him:

> *But lo! the boatman overawed, before*
> *The pictured fane of Tell suspends his oar. . . .*

It remains a nice question whether rowing was merely suspended when the chapel hove into view, or whether the boatman disembarked and hung up his oar as a votive offering. The passage ends heroically:

> *Where bleeding Sidney from the cup retired*
> *And glad Dundee in ' faint huzzas' expired.*

While I appreciated Wordsworth's delicacy in disclaiming the authorship of ' faint huzzas ', it seemed a pity that metrical exigency had changed ' Bonnie ' to ' Glad '.

> —or from Urseren as we did in 1820 over the St Gotard down by *Airola, Bellingzonn, Locarna,* where embark to Luvina and thence

by Ponte Tresa to Lugana. Here ascend San Salvador—for the views.

In 1821 he had apostrophized the Church of San Salvador in a few well-turned verses beginning:

Thou sacred Pile . . .

This contained a stanza which my father occasionally quoted:

Glory and patriotic Love
And all the Pomps of this frail ' spot
Which men call Earth ' have yearned to seek,
Associate with the simply meek,
Religion in the sainted grove
And in the hallowed grot.

Then take boat for *Porlezza* and over the hill to *Managgio*—thence to *Cannabbia* thence across the lake to the promontory of *Bellagio* and from the Alcove in the Duke's grounds you see parts of the 3 reaches of the Lake of Como—magnificent prospect—here if you find our names, pray refresh them—[he was that sort of traveller].

It was at Cannabbia (or Cadenabbia) that Wordsworth had fallen in with an ' Italian Itinerant ' who was planning to hawk clay busts of Shakespeare and Milton round the English countryside, and penned the following affectionate lines:

What stirring wonders wilt thou see
In the proud Isle of Liberty!
Yet will the Wanderer sometimes pine
With thoughts which no delights can chase,
Recall a Sister's last embrace,
His mother's neck-entwine;
Nor shall forget the Maiden coy
That would have loved the bright-haired boy.

And therefore wished him ' safe return. To Como's steeps—his happy bourne!, In garden glade to prop the twig, That ill supports the luscious fig.' I have seen the branches of apricot, apple, and plum propped to support the weight of fruit; but never the twigs of figs. ' Twig ', however, undoubtedly rhymes with ' fig '.

Here you must determine whether you will go to Como and Milan —and so by Varesa, Bavann, the Borromean Islands, and over the

Simplon back into Switzerland—or, if time allows on by the Lesca branch to Bergamo a fine situation—Town and Lake of Issea.

His first memories of the Simplon I found in *The Prelude,* Book VI (1850 text): there he was trying to show that poetry can be distilled from the most literally pedestrian experiences, if one *clomb* rather than *climbed:*

>   *we clomb*
> *Along the Simplon's steep and rugged road . . .*
> *The only track now visible was one*
> *That from the torrent's further brink held forth*
> *Conspicuous invitation to ascend*
> *A lofty mountain. After brief delay*
> *Crossing the unbridged stream, that road we took*
> *And clomb with eagerness, till anxious fears*
> *Intruded, for we failed to overtake*
> *Our comrades gone before. By fortunate chance,*
> *While every moment added doubt to doubt,*
> *A peasant met us, from whose mouth we learned*
> *That to the spot which had perplexed us first*
> *We must descend, and there should find the road*
> *Which in the stony channel of the stream*
> *Lay a few steps, and then along its banks. . . .*

Wordsworth was thoroughly scared and it looks as if the mistake was his, not Robert Jones's.

> . . . to Louvera at its head and by Brescia, where are Roman Antiquities, to the Lago di Garda, up to Riva at its head where is magnificent scenery. Hence you might cross over into the Tyrol, but all this would carry you a long way from Switzerland.—So I will suppose you to go by the Lake from Cadenabbia to Como—there, if time allows, to Milan for the sake of the Cathedral.

At Milan, in 1820, he had faithfully recorded an Eclipse of the Sun, in a tribute to Science beginning:

> *High in her speculative tower*
> *Stood Science waiting for the hour*
> *When Sol was destined to endure*
> *That darkening of his radiant face*

> *Which Superstition strove to chase*
> *Erstwhile with rites impure.*

He was being broad-minded. Science, despite Erasmus Darwin, was as yet hardly respectable in English poetry, and this is one of the earliest friendly advances made her by a recognized poet.

> . . . from Milan to *Varesa* to the Borromean Islands and over the Senplin. But I regret much that we did not turn aside for Banen so to take in the Lago di Orta in our way to Domo d'Ossolo—near Domo d'Ossolo, (as also near Varesi, I believe) is one of those shrines to which you ascend by different stations, as they are called, which Chantrey told me was altogether striking. From *Brig,* in the Vallais downwards, we turned up to the Baths of Leuk—so up the noble ascent of the Gemmi returning, after we had looked down into the vale which leads to Thun, to Leuk—thence by *Sion* to *Martigny*.

At Gemmi he heard a dog barking and the sound echoing from the mountain. It made so deep an impression on him that he resorted to a Keatsian use of Classical mythology:

> *As multitudinous a harmony*
> *Of sounds as rang the heights of Latmos over*
> *When from the soft couch of her sleeping lover*
> *Upstarting, Cynthia skimmed the mountain-dew . . .*

Wordsworth was one of the very first Englishmen to explore the Alps, and did so mainly, I think, because of his admiration for Jean Jacques Rousseau, whom George Sand called ' the Christopher Columbus of Alpine poetry ' and whom Chateaubriand called ' the Father of French Romanticism '. When Wordsworth's revolutionary enthusiasm cooled and he reverted to eighteenth-century normal verse-technique, he continued to admire Swiss scenery and was proud of his pioneering fame: had he not ' discovered ' the valley of Chamonix and the Mer de Glace for future generations of British tourists?
He continues:

> From this place you might re-cross into Italy by the Grand St Bernard and here you need directions which I cannot give for coming back from behind Mt Blanc, somewhere into Savoy or Switzerland. *We* went from Martigny over the Col d'Balin into Chamony from which you explore the Mer d'Glace and as much of Mont Blanc as time and strength will allow.

In 1790 he had been disappointed in Mont Blanc (which is, indeed, a smug wedding-cake of a mountain) and:

> . . . *grieved*
> *To have a soulless image on the eye*
> *That had usurped upon a living thought*
> *That never more could be* . . .

but consoled himself with the reflection that:

> . . . *with such a book*
> *Before our eyes, we could not choose but read*
> *Lessons of genuine brotherhood, the plain*
> *And universal reason of mankind,*
> *The truths of young and old.*

' Nobody must mistake *me* for a North Welsh peasant,' he is saying.

> Thence down the vallies to Geneva, on Geneva are steam boats (as are also upon the Lago d'Gardo—and a public boat from Iseo to Riva)—and now supposing you to bear the General direction in mind I have done and will only observe that of the minor Passes, by which I mean from one part of Switzerland to another, that of the Gemmi and above all that from Meynringham to Sarnan—

Here he crossed out the words ' and above all ', and also the phrase: ' the one for grandeur and the other for beauty ', which followed.

> —are far the most interesting—see them all if possible.

I could find no reference in the *Poems* to these particular steam boats, though he probably immortalized them somewhere. He had, as a matter of fact, written a piece about ' a steam boat seen off St Bees Head ' in 1833, and though ' depressed ', as he admits, by its steady progress ' indifferent to breeze or gale ', he made amends for his emotional lapse in his sonnet *Steamboats, Viaducts and Railways,* written the same year:

> *Motions and Means, on land and sea at war*
> *With old poetic feeling, not for this,*
> *Shall ye, by Poets even, be judged amiss!*
> *Nor shall your presence, howsoe'er it mar*
> *The loveliness of Nature, prove a bar*

To the Mind's gaining that prophetic sense
Of future change, that point of vision, whence
May be discovered what in soul ye are.
In spite of all that beauty may disown
In your harsh features, Nature doth embrace
How lawful offspring in Man's art; and Time,
Pleased with your Triumphs o'er his brother Space,
Accepts from your bold hands the proffered crown
Of hope, and smiles on you with cheer sublime.

This was quoted with telling effect in Court (1950) by my brother-in-law E. J. Neep, Q.C., when Wordsworth lovers brought an injunction against the Electricity Board for threatening to destroy Lakeland amenities with a line of pylons. The case collapsed at once.

Wordsworth had persuaded himself that no subjects were so novel, so mean, or so prosaic but that a lofty style could extract poetry from them. To seal his Tory convictions, he wrote a spirited protest against the Secret Ballot, beginning:

Forth rushed from Envy sprung and self-conceit
A power misnamed the Spirit of Reform
. . . now stoops she to entreat
Licence to hide at intervals her head
Where she may work, safe, undisquieted
In a close box!

He even deigned to apostrophize a spade. He had been lending a hand in a neighbour's potato patch; but though he called a spade a spade he could not bring himself to call a labourer a labourer, or a potato patch a potato patch. The title is: *To the Spade of a Friend (an agriculturist). Composed while we were labouring together in his Pleasure Ground.*

Well, the Wordsworths felt greatly relieved to get home safely from their Swiss tour (as who does not?); yet it is one thing to be able to feel and another to be able to express in graceful verse the sentiments that are common to all returned travellers. Wordsworth, whom my father had once described to me as a 'shrewd philosopher of the natural emotions', managed this very creditably in two Thomas

Mooreish stanzas, designed for singing to a tall, gilt drawing-room harp:

> *Though the toil of the way with dear Friends we divide,*
> *Though by the same zephyr our temples be fanned*
> *As we rest in the cool orange-bower side by side,*
> *A yearning survives which few hearts shall withstand:*
>
> *Each step hath its value while homeward we move;—*
> *O joy when the girdle of England appears!*
> *What moment in life is so conscious of love,*
> *Of love in the heart made more happy by tears?*

The letter ended:

> . . . One word more by way of correction—[in 1837] Mr [Crabbe] Robinson and I were encumbered with a carriage, so that we were obliged to go back from Louvera to the Town of Isean whereas pedestrians no doubt might cross from Louvera to Resa— and so save space and time. With the best of good wishes
> I remain faithfully yours
> W.W.
> Rydal Mt.
> N.B. Every foot of ground spoken of that I have seen myself is interesting.

Wordsworth never visited Clare at Northampton, of course; but throngs of Wordsworthians visited Rydal Mount to be entertained by his sportive sister Dorothy—until she went feebleminded about 1833 —and to be able to say that they had seen the great man. My father was only ten years old when Wordsworth died, but his Uncle Robert took him to the auction of surplus Wordsworthiana at Rydal Mount, an experience which set him up for the rest of his life.

The moral of all this is, perhaps, that poets should not be ' encumbered with a carriage ', especially if they owe this luxury to a political patron. And I haven't the heart to take you on a conducted tour into the Age of Tennyson, which ended (as they say in Spain) only yesterday morning. Tennyson's career resembled Wordsworth's: the early escapade in 1830, when he lived and loved in the Pyrenees as a Spanish revolutionary under Torrijos; the romantic poems— *Lady of Shalott, Lotos Eaters, Mariana, Oenone,* and so on; the parsimonious and retired life; rescue from indigence and melancholy by Sir Robert Peel's bounty; the Laureateship; a tour in Switzerland;

the rise to fame and respectability; the suitably unromantic marriage; the urge to write major works; self-dedication and post-graduate self-improvement as the mouthpiece of his fellow-citizens; poems dictated by popular patriotism; the increasing sweetness and purity of his style.

But no Muse! Wordsworth had disowned and betrayed his Muse. Tennyson never had one, except Arthur Hallam, and a Muse does not wear whiskers. The Lady of Shalott floating down to Camelot, Oenone deserted by Paris, Mariana among her caked flower pots in the moated grange—'he cometh not' she said—are all Tennyson's pathetic self-inversions. And the *Princess* is his good-humoured, patronizing admission that woman is capable of a certain intellectual and artistic advancement on male lines—a view as repellent in its way as Dr Johnson's downright view of her general inferiority to man. W. H. Auden recently tried to rehabilitate Tennyson in a modern edition; I cannot say why.

Edmund Gosse wrote:

> Between the years 1866–1870 the heightened reputation of Browning and still more the sudden vogue of Swinburne, Morris and Rossetti considerably disturbed the minds of Tennyson's most ardent readers. He went on quite calmly, however, sure of his mission and his music. In 1889 the death of Browning left him a solitary figure indeed in poetic literature. He soon wonderfully recovered the high spirits of youth, and even a remarkable portion of physical strength.

Gosse notes:

> No living poet has ever held England quite so long under his unbroken sway as Tennyson.

This may be true, because Pope died fairly young, and until his declining years Wordsworth had rivals in Byron, Moore, Rogers, Southey, and Mrs Hemans. But for a living poet to hold England under his sway, even for a brief period, runs counter to English poetical morality. Pope had won his supremacy by blackmail; Wordsworth had won his by climbing on the band-wagon at exactly the right moment and sitting tight; Tennyson won his by industry, sweet persuasiveness, and much the same gearing of his poetic intelligence to national progress, or aspirations of progress, as are nowadays so roundly condemned in poets and artists of the Communist *bloc*. Pope had suffered agonies of spleen (according to Dr Johnson) when he read Cibber's vigorous reply to his *Dunciad* libels; Wordsworth's surly defiance of Jeffrey and other adverse critics who ridiculed what he thought his best work ' did not ' (the text-books say) ' prevent a premature depression and a consequent deadening of his powers.' Tennyson's breakfast (according to my father, who knew him personally and persuaded him to versify *The Voyage of Maeldune*) was ruined if the Aldworth postman did not bring him at least two or three fan-letters from impressionable young ladies. Tennyson continued to wear his black cape, but in the same style as those that he and Hallam had worn during the Torrijos campaign, and in the high spirits of his renewed youth devoted his leisure to a different sort of literary composition. It is on record that his family physician, an ardent Tennysonian, coming to call on the great man one mellow rose-scented August afternoon, found him drowsing, pencil in hand, on his chair under the great cedar. A paper of verses fluttered to the ground and the physician stole forward reverently and picked it up, anxious to be the first to eye those immortal lines.

It was a limerick, beginning: ' There once was a Chinaman, drunk. . . .'

I should not refrain from discussing the sad case of Blake, who avoided the pauper asylum by being so skilful a painter and engraver that at the worst he could always become a print-seller's hack. Blake began as a poet; later he lost heart and turned prophet. As Laura Riding has written: ' To each is given what defeat he will.' The prophetic robe with its woof of meekness and its warp of wrath was forced on him by loneliness and his modest station in life: to be a mechanic was even more of a handicap for a late eighteenth-century poet than to be a peasant. Since he had no friends with whom he could converse on equal terms, he went in search of disciples. And though it has hitherto been thought that Blake's prophetic books are original and unprecedented (if only because he claimed angelic inspiration for them, as Milton had done for his *Paradise Lost*), it now appears that the angels tricked him. Instead of a live coal from the altar, they offered a digest of the numerous odd religious and pseudo-historical works current in his day, and he trustfully accepted it. So, despite the magnificence of his language and the splendour of his illustrations, we need not apologize if we find the Prophecies dated, tedious, and perverse.

Blake built up his prophetic corpus as a gigantic compensation for the neglect of his shorter, truer poems. His early *Island in the Moon* —1784, when he was twenty-seven years old—a satire on the dismal literary circle into which he had been drawn, is worth a thousand prophetic books. It contains songs such as:

> *Lo, the Bat on leathern wing,*
> *Winking and blinking,*
> *Winking and blinking,*
> *Winking and blinking,*
> *Like Dr Johnson.*

and:

> *When Old Corruption first began,*
> *Adorned in yellow vest,*
> *He committed on flesh a whoredom—*
> *O what a wicked beast!*

and:

> *I say, you Joe,*
> *Throw us the ball!*
> *We've a good mind to go*
> *And leave you all.*
>
> *I never saw such a bowler*
> *To bowl the ball in a turd*
> *And to clean it with my handkercher*
> *Without saying a word.*

and:

> *Little Phoebus came strutting in*
> *With his fat belly and his round chin.*

and:

> *When the tongues of children are heard on the green*
> *And laughing is heard on the hill,*
> *My heart is at rest within my breast*
> *And everything else is still.*

Most of this playfulness and true inspiration had deserted him by
1804. Blake then wrote in his introduction to *Jerusalem:*

> After my three years slumber on the banks of the ocean, I again
> display my Giant Forms to the Public. . . . I hope the Reader will
> be with me, wholly One in Jesus our Lord, who is the God *of Fire*
> and Lord *of Love* to whom the Ancients look'd and saw his day afar
> off, with trembling & amazement. . . . When this Verse was first
> dictated to me, I consider'd a Monotonous Cadence, like that used
> by Milton & Shakespeare & all writers of English Blank Verse, de-
> livered from the modern bondage of Rhyming, to be a necessary and
> indispensable part of Verse. But I soon found that in the mouth of
> a true Orator such monotony was not only awkward, but as much a
> bondage as rhyme itself. I therefore have produc'd a variety in
> every line, both of cadences & number of syllables. Every word and
> every letter is studied and put into its fit place; the terrific numbers
> are reserved for the terrific parts, the mild & gentle for the mild &
> gentle parts, and the prosaic for inferior parts; all are necessary to
> each other. Poetry Fetter'd Fetters the Human Race. Nations are
> Destroy'd or Flourish in proportion as Their Poetry, Painting and
> Music are Destroy'd or Flourish! The Primeval State of Man was
> Wisdom, Art and Science.

The last sentence is anthropologically indefensible; and the criticism of Shakespeare's blank verse is wilfully obtuse; and Blake has
confused the orator with the poet. An orator might well be ' fettered '
if forced to dress his legal arguments in metre and rhyme; but ' fetter '
implies slavery. Shakespeare, like every true poet, accepted the
Muse's yoke in the spirit of *Ecclesiasticus:*

> *An ornament of gold is her yoke,*
> *And her traces a ribband of purple silk.*

It is not as though anyone had ever been fettered by Blake's own
rhymes—by his *Tyger, Tyger, Burning Bright,* or by his:

> *I wonder whether the girls are mad*
> *And I wonder whether they mean to kill?*
> *And I wonder if William Bond will die?*
> *For assuredly he is very ill.*

No: poetry and prophecy make ill-assorted bedfellows; prophecy,
especially the evangelical sort, will claim sheet, blankets, and both
pillows in God's name, and let poetry die of exposure.

The truth was that Blake had rallied to Milton's standard in a deliberate revolt against the Muse, repudiating her as the evil ' Female Will ' which seduced Adam, caused the Trojan War, and was responsible for the idolatrous concepts of Chivalry. He correctly identified her with Rahab—the Palestinian Love- and Sea-goddess—but saw her, with the baleful eyes of Isaiah and the Author of the Apocalypse, as the Great Whore, enemy of spiritual man. Like Milton, he had apparently been encouraged in this revolt by his wife's stubborn refusal to accept as gospel whatever he said and decided. His account of the Giant Albion's fall and surrender to Vala—another name for Rahab—parallels Milton's account of Adam's fall and surrender to Eve, and of Samson's to Delilah. In *Milton,* Blake has bloated a local and personal quarrel into monstrous epic proportions. A drunken private soldier named Schofield had accidentally broken into his garden at Felpham; Blake had ejected him; and Schofield, who then charged him with the capital crime of High Treason, appeared to Blake's disordered imagination as a villain in the pay of William Hayley, the poet.

Hayley was Blake's patron, a rich and amiable dilettante who had been trying to help him by directing his genius into socially acceptable channels, securing him commissions for painting miniatures and handscreens. Blake had at first found Hayley's friendship providential, but soon saw his personal integrity threatened by Hayley's well-meaning approach to Mrs Blake, who was ill: Hayley had convinced her that Blake ought to postpone his great projected Epic (which would not serve any practical purpose, either religious or poetic), and execute these valuable commissions as a means of earning his bread and butter. Blake now came to the crazy conclusion that Hayley (though Hayley's evidence at the treason trial was instrumental in securing his acquittal) had not only ' acted on my wife ', but ' hired a villain '— Schofield—' to bereave my life '. ' Skofeld ' duly appears among the ' Gigantic Forms ' of Blake's *Milton* beside Satan (who is Hayley), Palamabron (who is Blake), Elynittria, described as ' Palamabron's Emanation ' (who is Mrs Blake), and various unidentifiable friends or relatives of Hayley's. Blake wrote: ' The manner in which I have routed out the nest of villains will be seen in a Poem concerning my Three years' Herculean Labours at Felpham, which I will soon Publish.' He continued to regard Hayley as a member of an organized conspiracy to swindle him, to spread the rumour of his insanity—unfortunately Hayley had also been patron to Cowper, who was later certified as insane—and to exclude his pictures from the Royal Academy.

It is dangerous to fight the Muse. Milton's end should have been a warning to Blake. Richardson had written of Milton's last years:

> Besides what affliction he must have had from his disappointment on the change of times and from his own private losses, he was in perpetual terror of being assassinated. Though he had escaped the talons of the Law, he knew he had made himself enemies in abundance. He was so dejected he would lie awake whole nights . . . and was tormented with headaches, gout, blindness.

These horrors Blake escaped, perhaps because he had a sweeter nature and no frauds or cruelties on his conscience. But despite the nobility of the engravings, which excuse their re-publication, his prophetic books lie under the Muse's curse of permanent unreadability.

HARP, ANVIL, OAR

Last week I spoke about Marvan, the seventh-century poet of Connaught who revealed to the professors of the Great Bardic Academy how the poet's harp originated: namely when the wind played on the dried tendons of a stranded whale's skeleton in the time of Macuel son of Miduel. And how metre originated: namely in the alternate beat of two hammers on the anvil, while Lamiach was still alive. The three hundred professors could not follow Marvan here, having long ceased to think poetically. As historic or scientific statements his revelations are, of course, challengeable: not a grain of evidence can be cited for the existence of the whale, or even for that of Macuel son of Miduel. Nevertheless, as poetic statements they are exact. What is the whale? An emblem of the White Love-goddess Rahab, Ruler of the Sea, who used yearly to destroy her sacred kings in numerous cities from Connaught to the Persian Gulf; until at last the god Enlil, or Marduk (or Jehovah, according to the prophet Isaiah) killed her with the new-fangled weapon called a sword—the Babylonians claimed in a hymn that he sliced her like a flatfish. But the King of Babylon still had to do ritual battle with her every year, be swallowed, and spewed up again on the third day, as Jonah was. And though Jehovah's prophets chanted: ' O ye whales, bless ye Adonai, praise Him and magnify Him for ever! ' they knew that Leviathan was unregenerate, uncontrollable and not to be fished up with any hook let down. Hence the author of the Apocalypse prophesied that one day ' there shall be no more sea '; by this he meant ' no more Rahab, and no more whales '.

The emblems of the Muse Trinity are a white dove in the sky, a white hind in the forest, a whale taking his pastime in the depth of the sea. Where, then, could one find a better figure of death than the white skeleton of a stranded whale? And wind, North Wind, the wind that (proverbially) pigs alone can see, the wind that, as I told you, Marvan carried in his mantle, the wind that fertilized the windswift sacred mares of Trojan Erichthonius and the prophetic vultures of Roman augury—wind (*spiritus, pneuma*) is the emblem of inspiration. The bones of Rahab the Whale may lie stranded on the shore; but, for a poet, there is more truth in her dead sinews than in Marduk's living mouth. When Macuel son of Miduel heard the wind howling tunefully in the Æolian harp of the whale's skeleton, he bethought himself and built a smaller, more manageable one from the same materials. And when he struck his harp and cried: ' Sing to me, Muse! ' this was no formal invitation—Rahab herself sang at his plea.

A close parallel, by the bye, may be found in English popular poetry. The ballad of the *Twa Sisters of Binnorie* tells of a drowned woman whose hair was used for harp-strings:

> *And by there came a harper fine*
> > Edinbro', Edinbro'
> *Such as harp to nobles when they dine.*
> > Stirling for aye
> *He's ta'en twa strands of her yellow hair*
> *And with it strung a harp sae rare*
> > Bonnie St Johnstone stands on Tay.

> *He's done him into her father's hall,*
> > Edinbro', Edinbro'
> *And played the harp before them all,*
> > Stirling for aye
> *And syne the harp spake loud and clear*
> *' Farewell my father and mither dear.'*
> > Bonnie St Johnstone stands on Tay.

> *And syne the harp began to sing*
> > Edinbro', Edinbro'
> *And it's ' Farewell, sweetheart,' sang the string*
> > Stirling for aye
> *And then, as plain as plain could be,*
> *' There sits my sister who drownéd me.'*
> > Bonnie St Johnstone stands on Tay.

The harp is the prophetic voice of the yellow-haired goddess—the Muse-goddess was always yellow-haired—and she sings of love, and grief, and doom. Marvan, moreover, was careful to distinguish the fitful inspirational music of the Æolian harp from the purposeful rhythmic clatter of the smith's anvil.

I am aware that I should here be discussing the English, not the Irish, literary scene. But Irish poetry is to English poetry, as—may I say?—the Pharisaic synagogue is to the Christian Church: an antecedent which historians are tempted to forget or belittle. The English have long despised the Irish; and though generously ready to acknowledge their debt to Anglo-Saxon, French, Italian, Latin and Greek literatures, are loth to admit that the strongest element in English poetic technique (though certainly acquired at second or third hand) is the Irish tradition of craftsmanship.

When two hammers answer each other five times on the anvil— *ti-tum, ti-tum, ti-tum, ti-tum, ti-tum*—five in honour of the five stations of the Celtic year, there you have Chaucer's familiar hendecasyllabic line:

> *A knight ther was, and that a worthy man*
> *That fro the tymë that he first began*
> *To ryden out, he lovéd chivalrye. . . .*

But Anglo-Saxon poetry had been based on the slow pull and push of the oar:

> *Then I of myself / will máke this known*
> *That awhíle I was held / the Héodenings' scop,*
> *To my duke most dear / and Déor was my name.*

The function of the Nordic *scop* seems to have been twofold. Not only was he originally a ' shaper ' of charms, to protect the person of the king and so maintain prosperity in the realm; but he had a subsidiary task, of persuading a ship's crew to pull rhythmically and uncomplainingly on their oars against the rough waves of the North Sea, by singing them ballads in time to the beat. When they returned from a successful foray, and dumped their spoil of gold collars, shields, casques, and monastic chalices on the rush-strewn floor of the beerhall, then the *scop* resumed his song. The drunken earls and churls straddled the benches, and rocked to the tune: ' Over the whale's way, fared we unfearful. . . .'

Anglo-Saxon poetry is unrhymed, because the noise of rowlocks does not suggest rhyme. Rhyme reached England from France. It had been brought there by Irish missionaries who recivilized Western Europe after the Frankish invasions. These missionaries wrote and talked Latin, and *The Rhythm of St Bernard of Cluny,* the first rhymed poem of high literary pretensions written by an Englishman (during the reign of Henry I or II) follows the pure Irish tradition. Its complicated series of internal and end-rhymes, and its faultless finish, leave no doubt about this. Here are four of the three thousand rhymed lines:

> *Urbs Syon aurea, Patria lactea, cive decora,*
> *Omne cor obruis, omnibus obstruis et cor et ora.*
> *Nescio, nescio, quae jubilatio, lux tibi qualis,*
> *Quam socialia gaudia, gloria quam specialis.*

Prosodists have a Latin name for the metre: *Leonini cristati trilices dactylici.* St Bernard's *Rhythm* has been translated into English, pretty well (though with a loss of all the rhyme pairs except the end ones, which have become monosyllables), by the Victorian hymn-writer, J. M. Neale:

> *Jerusalem the Golden,*
> 　*With Milk and Honey Blest,*
> *Beneath Thy Contemplation*
> 　*Sink heart and voice oppressed:*
> *I know not, O I know not,*
> 　*What social joys are there;*
> *What radiancy of Glory,*
> 　*What Light beyond Compare!*

Nordic verse-craft, as I was saying, is linked to the pull of the oar. Greek verse-craft is linked to the ecstatic beat of feet around a rough stone altar, sacred to Dionysus (or Hermes, or Eros, or Zeus Cronides), probably to the sound of the dactylic drum played by a priestess or a priest:

$$-\cup\cup/-\cup\cup/-//\cup\cup/-\cup\cup/-\cup\cup/--$$

The Greeks also admitted the iambic, traditionally named in honour
of lasciviously hobbling Iambe, who (you may remember) tried to
coax a smile from the bereaved Demeter at Eleusis. Iambic metre
may have begun with Helladic totem dances which imitated the hobbling of partridge or quail:

$$\cup - / \cup - / \cup / / - / \cup - / \cup - / \cup -$$

There was also the spondaic measure derived from the gloomy double-
stamp of buskined mourners, arousing some dead hero to drink the
libations (*spondae*) that they poured for him:

$$- - / - - / - / / - / - - / - - / - -$$

A metrical line in Greek poetry represents the turn taken by a
dancer around an altar or tomb, with a cæsura marking the halfway
point: the metre never varies until the dancers have dropped with
fatigue. Similarly in *Beowulf* and other Anglo-Saxon poems, the oars'
pull and push continues mercilessly until harbour is reached, or until
the drunken diners fall off their bench to the floor, unable to rise
again.

The Irish concept of metre is wholly different. All poets owed
allegiance to the Muse-goddess Brigid—who may be decently equated
with the Helladic Moon-goddess Brizo of Delos. Brigid had three
aspects: the Brigid of Poets, the Brigid of Smiths, and the Brigid of
Physicians. A Brigid of Smiths may seem anomalous, because English
smiths have long ranked lower in the social scale than poets and
physicians. In England smithcraft ceased, with the triumph of Christianity, to be an inspired profession; it was wrested by monks from the
hands of the lame Smith Wayland (who served the Goddess Freya)
and registered merely as a useful trade. Even as a trade, it is dying
now: wedding ring, or scythe, or steel helmet is supplied by factories
where not even a superstitious vestige of the Wayland cult has gone
into the making. But the pagan smith, whether goldsmith, whitesmith,
or blacksmith, approached his work with enormous care and magical
precaution.

The religious connexion between poetry, smithcraft, and medicine
is a close one. Medicine presupposes a knowledge of times, seasons,
and the sovereign properties of plants, trees, beasts, birds, fish, earths,
minerals. Poetry presupposes an inspired knowledge of man's sensuous
and spiritual nature. Smithcraft—for the smith was also carpenter,

mason, shipwright and toolmaker—presupposes an inspired knowledge of how to transform lifeless material into active forms. No ancient smith would have dared to proceed without the aids of medicine and poetry. The charcoal used on his forge had been made, with spells, at a certain time of the year from timber of certain sacred trees; and the leather of the forge bellows, from the skin of a sacred animal ritually sacrificed. Before starting a task, he and his assistant were obliged to purify themselves with medicines and lustrations, and to placate the Spites which habitually crowd around forge and anvil. If he happened to be forging a sword, the water in which it was to be tempered must have magical properties—May dew, or spring water in which a virgin princess had washed her hair. The whole work was done to the accompaniment of poetic spells.

Such spells matched the rhythm of the smiths' hammers; and these were of unequal weight. A sledge hammer was swung by the assistant; the smith himself managed the lighter hammer. To beat out hot metal successfully, one must work fast and follow a prearranged scheme. The smith with his tongs lays the glowing lump of iron on the anvil, then touches with his hammer the place where the sledge blow is to fall; next he raps on the anvil the number of blows required. Down comes the sledge; the smith raps again for another blow, or series of blows. Experience teaches him how many can be got in while the iron is still hot. So each stage of every process had its peculiar metre, to which descriptive words became attached; and presently the words found their own tunes. This process explains Marvan's mysterious reference to Lamiach, who appears in the English translations of *Genesis* as ' Lamech '. Lamech was the father of Tubal the first smith, and Jubal the first musician. Nor did the smith (as many archæ-ologists assume) let caprice rule the number and shape of ornaments that he introduced into his work. Whether he was forging a weapon, or a piece of armour, or a tool, or a cauldron, or a jewelled collar, every element in the design had a magical significance.

An Irish poet versified to the ring of hammers; and the fact that rhyme and regular metre had become characteristic of English poetry by Chaucer's time implies that the smithy tradition of careful thought and accurate workmanship, which these call for, had also been to some extent adopted. The metaphor of beating out one's verses on the anvil is now, indeed, a poetical commonplace. But let me put it

this way: though every English poet is a smith for the greater part of
the year, he takes to the sea during the brief sailing season. Chaucer
may seem to be a hammer-and-anvil poet when he writes:

> *A knight ther was, and that a worthy man*
> *That fro the tymë that he first began*
> *To ryden out, he lovéd chivalrye. . . .*

Ti-tum, ti-tum, ti-tum, ti-tum. Then he lays down the hammer and
reaches for the oar. Instead of:

> *Honoùr and freédom, trùth and coúrtesy,*

he writes:

> *Trùth and honoùr / freédom and coúrtesy . . .*

and this has been the English verse-tradition ever since.

Skelton also reconciled the anvil with the oar in a metre which he
used in his early *Lament for Edward IV,* and again at the close of his
life in *Speke Parrot.* Note the Anglo-Saxon alliteration:

> Miseremini mei / *ye that be my frendis!*
> *This world hath forméd me / downë to fall.*
> *How many I endure / when that everi thing endis?*
> *What creäture is bornë / to be eternáll?*

and:

> *The myrrour that I tote in* / quasi diaphanum,
> Vel quasi speculum / in aenigmate,
> Elencticum, *or ells* / enthymematicum,
> *For logicians to loke on* / somewhat sophistice:
> *Retoricyons and oratours / in freshe humanyte,*
> *Support Parrot, I pray you / with your suffrage ornate,*
> Of confuse tantum / auoydynge the chekmate.

The history of Shakespeare's blank verse is a progression from the
careful anvil work of, say, *The Comedy of Errors,* to *The Tempest,*
where the oar is pulling in a very rough sea. *The Comedy of Errors*
begins:

EGEON: *Proceed, Solinus, to procure my fall,*
        And by the doom of death end woes and all.

DUKE OF *Merchant of Syracusa, plead no more.*
EPHESUS: *I am not partial to infringe our laws;*
         The enmity and discord which of late
         Sprung from the rancorous outrage of your Duke
         To merchants, our well-dealing countrymen,
         Who wanting guilders to redeem their lives,
         Have sealed his rigorous statutes with their bloods,
         Excludes all pity from our threatening looks. . . .

But in *The Tempest* the opening exchanges between shipmaster and boatswain are recognized as blank verse only because every now and then a regular line occurs to reassert the norm. (Heming and Condell in their edition of the *First Folio* print them as prose, and all cautious editors follow suit.)

(The BOATSWAIN appears when the MASTER summons him)

THE MASTER: *Good. Speak to the mariners; fall to't yarely.*
            Or we run ourselves aground. Bestir, bestir!
BOATSWAIN: *Heigh my hearts, cheerily, cheerily, my hearts,*
               yare, yare!
            Take in the topsail! Tend to the master's whistle!
(to the MASTER)
            Blow till thou burst thy wind, if room enough!

The rules of prosody apply only to anvil verse, or to sacred-dance verse, in which every syllable is evaluated and counted. Pope, for instance, says that he lisped in numbers for the numbers came; ' numbers ' translates the Latin *numeri,* which imply a careful count of syllables. Pope never escaped from the ' numbers ' theory: which posits an orderly sequence of metrical feet each with the same determined time value, every long syllable being given the value of a crotchet, and every short syllable the value of a quaver; though the Elizabethan critics, headed by George Puttenham, had emphatically rejected this theory. The only fundamental difference between Pope's notion of verse and Virgil's, or Horace's, was that the Latin convention of what made a syllable long or short had lapsed. Now, in Bernard of Cluny's *Rhythm,* for instance, the Latin rules of quantity are maintained: every syllable is regarded as long or short by nature, though a short syllable may become long by position; and a terminal vowel, or vowel plus *m,* will be elided and disappear. This, it must be realized, was a highly artificial convention: ordinary Latin speech, as heard in the home and Forum, seems from the scraps of camp songs penned by Suetonius to have been accentual, and the accent did not necessarily fall on the long vowel.

It amused educated English poets—such as Chaucer, Skelton, Ben Jonson, Milton, Marvell, Dr Johnson, and Coleridge—to compose Latin verses in Classical style; but the freedom to observe natural speech stresses (as opposed to the laws of quantity) not only in vernacular verse but in Latin too, if they pleased, had already been won for them by the hymnologists and carol-makers and Goliardic song-writers of the Middle Ages. The first two lines of the famous medieval students' drinking song:

> *Mihi est propositum in taberna mori;*
> *Vinum sit appositum potatoris ori.* . . .

contain thirteen false quantities, and the first two lines of the equally famous hymn:

> *Dies irae, dies illa*
> *Solvens saecla in favilla.* . . .

contain eight. (Don't bother to count them.) This is not due to ignorance. Who would dare accuse St Thomas Aquinas of ignorance because he rhymes *natus* with *datus?* Aquinas knew well enough that rhyme was a barbarism in Classical Latin poetry—and that Cicero had made a fool of himself with the internal rhyme of:

> *O fortunatam natam, me Consule, Romam!*

But he also knew that these quantities had been justified by Irish metrical example; the Irish did not acknowledge quantity, they relied on accent.

Skelton, in his *Devout Trentale for Old John Clerk, Sometime the Holy Patriarche of Diss,* actually alternated correct hexameters with Goliardic verse:

> *Sequitur trigintale,*
> *Tale quale rationale,*
> *Licet parum curiale,*
> *Tamen satis est formale,*

Joannis Clerc, hominis
Cujusdam multinominis,
Joannes Jayberd qui vocatur,
Clerc cleribus nuncupatur.
Obiit sanctus iste pater
Anno Domini MD, sexto.
In parochia de Dis.
Non erat sibi similis;
In malitia vir insignis,
Duplex corde et bilinguis;
Senio confectus,
Omnibus suspectus,
Nemini dilectus,
Sepultus est amonge the wedes:
God forgeue hym his mysdedes!

> *Dulce melos*[1]
> *Penetrans coelos.*

Carmina cum cannis cantemus festa Joannis:
Clerk obiit vere, Jayberd nomenque dedere;
Dis populo natus, Clerk cleribusque vocatus.

The Elizabethan critics, humanists to a man, were a little uneasy about this divergence from Classical metric theory, but there was clearly no help for it. Samuel Daniel, in his *Defence of Rhyme* (1603), found it necessary to lay down: 'As Greeke and Latine verse consists of the number and quantity of sillables, so doth the English verse of measure and accent.' They admitted, in fact, that the natural accent of current English speech decides whether a syllable should be long or short—even though the same word may change its value in the same line. Thus, for instance, the pentameter:

ōffĕr hĕr / ĭcĕs, ŏr / ā // lōvelў cŏm/fōrtăblĕ / chāir

is quantitatively correct according to Ovidian rule, but does not scan. Moreover, the Virgilian hexameter, as Thomas Nashe forcefully explained in his answer to Gabriel Harvey's recommendation of it, is not natural to English:

---

[1] Mĕlŏs rhyming with cōelōs.

The Hexamiter verse I graunt to be a Gentleman of an auncient house (so is many an english beggar); yet this Clyme of ours hee cannot thriue in. Our speech is too craggy for him to set his plough in; hee goes twitching and hopping in our language like a man running vpon quagmiers, vp the hill in one Syllable, and downe the dale in another, retaining no part of that stately smooth gate which he vaunts himselfe with amongst the Greeks and Latins.

And so a strong sense has grown up among practical English poets that the natural rhythm of speech decides where accents fall; and that, therefore, the less artificial the words, the truer the poem.

Tell a schoolchild that Keats's *Fairy Song* is an iambic poem with three four-foot lines followed by one of five feet, another of four feet, one of two feet, and finally a five-footer, rhyming AB, AB, C, C, B—and he will read it like this:

> *Ah woe / is me / poor silv/er wing*
> *That I / must chant / thy lad/y's dirge*
> *And death / to this / fair haunt / of spring*
> *And mel/ody / and streams / of flower/y verge.*
> *Poor Silv/erwing / ah woe / is me*
> *That I / must see*
> *These Bloss/oms snow / upon / thy lad/y's pall.*

But if the words are spoken in the manner most natural to their sense and feeling, this is how Keats will have meant it to be said; and you realize that the laws of prosody are, to verse, very much as copperplate models are to handwriting. Keats had a poet's ear for verse; and Shakespeare had; as Donne had; as Coleridge had; as Skelton had. But Keats was easily seduced. When he put on his singing robes and played at being a Classical poet, he became gorbliminess incarnate. In his *Ode to Apollo,* for example:

> *Then, through thy Temple wide, melodious swells*
> *The sweet majestic tone of Maro's lyre:*
> *The soul delighted on each accent dwells,—*
> *Enraptur'd dwells,—not daring to respire,*
> *The while he tells of grief around a funeral pyre.*
>
> *'Tis awful silence then again;*
> *Expectant stand the spheres;*
> *Breathless the laurell'd peers,*

Nor move, till ends the lofty strain,
Nor move till Milton's tuneful thunders cease
And leave once more the ravish'd heaven in peace.

Thou biddest Shakespeare wave his hand,
  And quickly forward spring
The Passions—a terrific band—
  And each vibrates the string
That with its tyrant temper best accords,
While from their Master's lips pour forth the inspiring words.

Keats should have known that to impose an artificial word-order, or an artificial vocabulary, on poems is a lapse in poetic dignity.

There is so much to say about professional standards in verse-technique, that I shall confine myself to generalities. For instance, that though the muscular *str* and *scr* words: *strain, strength, string, strangle, stretch, struggle, strident, extravagant, screw, scrape, scrawny,* and such easy skipping words as *melody, merrily, prettily, harmony, fantasy* match sense with sound, other words are not so onomatopœic. *A strangely striped strip of satin* is far too emphatic in sound for the sense, and *a terribly powerful Florida hurricane* is not nearly emphatic enough. Yet to alter the spirit of an original poetic thought for the sake of metre or euphony is unprofessional conduct. So the art of accommodating sense to sound without impairing the original thought has to be learned by example and experiment. Under-emphasis or over-emphasis in a word can be controlled by playing other words off against it, and carefully choosing its position in a line, and making the necessary adjustments to neighbouring lines until the ear at last feels satisfied. It is an axiom among poets that if one trusts whole-heartedly to poetic magic, one will be sure to solve any merely verbal problem or else discover that the verbal problem is hiding an imprecision in poetic thought.

I say magic, since the act of composition occurs in a sort of trance, distinguishable from dream only because the critical faculties are not dormant, but on the contrary, more acute than normally. Often a rugger player is congratulated on having played the smartest game of his life, but regrets that he cannot remember a single incident after the first five minutes, when he got kicked on the head. It is

much the same with a poet when he completes a true poem. But
often he wakes from the trance too soon and is tempted to solve the
remaining problems intellectually. Few self-styled poets have experienced the trance; but all who have, know that to work out a line
by an exercise of reason, rather than by a deep-seated belief in
miracle, is highly unprofessional conduct. If a trance has been interrupted, it is just too bad. The poem should be left unfinished, in the
hope that suddenly, out of the blue, days or months later, it may
start stirring again at the back of the mind, when the remaining problems will solve themselves without difficulty.

Donne's chief failing as a love-poet was his readiness to continue
the inspired beginning with a witty development. For instance:

> *Goe, and catche a falling starre,*
> *Get with child a mandrake roote . . .*

Here Donne paused, apparently remembered Villon's *neiges d'antan,*
and went on:

> *Tell me, where all past yeares are . . .*

And then consciously searched for a rhyme to *roote*. But he had
not the least idea where the poem was taking him, except into a discussion of impossibility. So he continued in quite a different key:

> *Or who cleft the Divels foot,*
> *Teach me to heare Mermaides singing,*
> *Or to keep off envies stinging . . .*

He paused again and apparently remembered Shakespeare's:

> *Blow, blow thou winter wind,*
> *Thou art not so unkind*
> *As man's ingratitude . . .*

and Dante's remarks about the bitterness of having to seek advancement from haughty patrons. So he ended the verse with the quite
irrelevant:

> *And finde*
> *What winde*
> *Serves to advance an honest minde.*

Again he opened magnificently:

> *I wonder by my troth, what thou, and I*
> *Did, till we lov'd? were we not wean'd till then?*
> *But suck'd on countrey pleasures, childishly?*

Here inspiration faded and he resorted to artifice:

> *Or snorted we in the seaven sleepers' den?*
> *T'was so; But this, all pleasures fancies bee.*
> *If ever any beauty I did see,*
> *Which I desir'd, and got, t'was but a dreame of thee.*

Donne is adept at keeping the ball in the air, but he deceives us here by changing the ball. Coleridge often does the same thing, for example when he fakes a sequel to the inspired opening passage of *Christabel*—but he handles the ball so clumsily that we are seldom deceived.

It is unprofessional conduct to say: ' When next I write a poem I shall use the sonnet form '—because the theme is by definition unforeseeable, and theme chooses metre. A poet should not be conscious of the metrical pattern of a poem he is writing until the first three or four lines have appeared; he may even find himself in the eleventh line of fourteen before realizing that a sonnet is on the way. Besides, metre is only a frame; the atmospheres of two sonnets can be so different that they will not be recognized as having the same form except by a careful count of lines and feet. Theme chooses metre; what is more, theme decides what rhythmic variations should be made on metre. The theory that all poems must be equally rich in sound is an un-English one, borrowed from Virgil. Rainbow-like passages are delightful every now and then, but they match a rare mood of opulence and exaltation which soon fatigues. The riches of *Paradise Lost* fatigue, and even oppress, all but musicians. Rainbows should make their appearances only when the moment has come to disclose the riches of the heart, or soul, or imagination; they testify to passing storms and are short-lived.

Another professional principle is that *mimesis* should be regarded as vulgar. By mimesis I mean such *tours de force* as Virgil's:

> *Quadrupedante putrem sonitu quatit ungula campum,*

and Tennyson's:

> *The moan of doves in immemorial elms,*
> *The murmur of innumerable bees.*

To these I should add the Homeric:

> *Autis epeita pedonde cylindeto laäs anaides,*

the shameless stone of Sisyphus bounding downhill, if I did not
think that this was high-spirited verbal comedy, proclaiming dis-
belief in the whole theory of divine punishment.

Pope's translation of the Sisyphus passage, by the way, runs:

> *With many a weary sigh, and many a groan,*
> *Up the high hill he heaves a huge round stone . . .*

though the corresponding lines in the *Odyssey* do not mimic Sisyphus's breathlessness. And Pope's concluding couplet is wretchedly
incompetent:

> *The huge round stone, resulting with a bound*
> *Thunders impetuous down and smokes along the ground.*

The false internal rhymes of *round* and *bound* and the half-rhymes
down and *ground* effectively act as brakes on the stone's merry
progress. As Blake said in one of his Public Addresses: ' I do not
condemn Pope or Dryden because they did not understand imagination, but because they did not understand verse.'

One of the most difficult problems is how to use natural speech
rhythms as variations on a metrical norm. And here we meet with
the heresy of free verse. Until the time of Blake and his oratorical
cadences, it was generally agreed that the reader should never be
allowed to lose his sense of metrical norm. But Blake, finding the
contemporary technique of poetry too cramping, burst it wide open
and wrote something that was neither poetry nor prose. Whitman
did much the same, though for different reasons: he epitomizes the
restless American habit, first noted in the eighteenth century, of moving adventurously west across the trackless prairie, scratch-farming
as one goes, instead of clinging to some pleasant Pennsylvanian farm,
improving crops and stock by careful husbandry, and building a
homestead for one's children and grand-children. All who, like

Whitman, choose to dispense with a rhythmical norm are welcome
to explore the new country which he opened up, but it now wears
rather a dismal look. Robert Frost's poems, which combine traditional metres with intensely personal rhythms, show the advantage
of staying put and patiently working at the problem.[2]

A dogma has recently been planted in English schools that the
King James version of the Bible is poetry. It is not. The polishing
of the English translation was, of course, admirably done by a team
of capable University scholars, trained in the oratorical art. Sometimes they even included a perfectly metrical line:

How art thou fallen from Heaven, O Lucifer, son of the morning!

And:

Come down and sit in the dust; O virgin daughter of Babylon,
Sit on the ground. . . .

But one might as well call *The Times* leaders poetry, because they
are written by skilled journalists and because they contain a high
proportion of blank-verse lines, sometimes as much as 30 per cent.

Ben Jonson told Drummond of Hawthornden that ' for not keeping of accent '—that is to say, allowing his readers to lose the sense
of metrical norm—' Donne deserved hanging '. Jonson had also said
that Donne was ' the first poet in the world in some things ', and that
he had a few of his early poems by heart. It is difficult to reconcile
these statements. But Jonson seems to be referring to the *Satyres,*
where Donne at times deliberately changes the metre—as when a

----

[2] Mr. Eliot has written about free verse:
>   It is not defined by non-existence of metre, since even the worst verse
>   can be scanned.

This is to beg the question. In so far as verse can be scanned, it is not freed
of metre. He has also written:
>   But the most interesting verse which has yet been written in our lan-
>   guage has been done [*sic*] either by taking a very simple form, like the
>   iambic pentameter, and constantly withdrawing from it, or taking no
>   form at all, and continually approximating to a very simple one. It is this
>   contrast between fixity and flux, this unperceived evasion of monotony,
>   which is the very life of verse.

Interesting to some, embarrassing to others, like a jaunt in a car after mixing
a little water with the petrol to make it go by fits and starts. I was never interested in that sort of experiment; I expect verse to be verse, and prose to be
prose.

competitor in a walking race shamelessly bends his knees and breaks
into a short run:

> . . . *So in immaculate clothes, and Symetrie*
> *Perfect as circles, with such nicetie*
> *As a young Preacher at his first time goes*
> *To preach, he enters, and a Lady, which owes*
> *Him not so much as good will, he arrests,*
> *And unto her protests, protests, protests;*
> *So much as at Rome would serve to have throwne*
> *Ten Cardinalls into the Inquisition;*
> *And whispers by Jesu, so often, that A*
> *Pursevant would have ravish'd him away*
> *For saying of our Ladies psalter. But 'tis fit*
> *That they each other plague, they merit it . . .*

In the same satire, Donne also makes the units of sense play havoc
with the units of metre:

> . . . *No, no, Thou which since yesterday hast beene*
> *Almost about the whole world, hast thou seene,*
> *O Sunne, in all thy journey, Vanitie,*
> *Such as swells the bladder of our court? I*
> *Thinke he which made your waxen garden, and*
> *Transported it from Italy to stand*
> *With us, at London, flouts our Presence, for*
> *Just such gay painted things, which no sappe, nor*
> *Tast have in them, ours are; And naturall*
> *Some of the stocks are, their fruits, bastard all.*

But let me speak up for Donne. There are, of course, certain
familiar proprieties in English poetry. Accent must be kept, which
means, as I have shown, that however the metrical norm may be
varied, it should stay recognizable—one must not write lines that
go off into another metre altogether. Rhyme must be kept within
certain decent limits, and the consonantal part of rhyme must be
regarded as more important than the vowel. It is, for instance, indecent to rhyme *charm* with *calm,* or (*pace* W. H. Auden) *bore*
with *mother-in-law;* though *love* and *prove, all* and *usual, fly* and
extremity are traditionally countenanced. Three-syllable rhymes are

indecent, so are mixed metaphors, and what Corinna called ' sowing with the sack '—namely overornamentation of every kind. Again: an even level of language should be kept: one must decide to what period each poem belongs and not relapse to an earlier, or anticipate a more modern, diction. Thus it is indecent to address *you* and *thee* in the same verse to the same person—even if Pope and Marvell are quoted in justification. And, most important, there should be no discrepancy between the sound and the sense of a poem. It would be difficult, for instance, to quarrel on technical grounds with a simple iambic stanza such as this:

> *Mother is dead; my heart to pieces torn,*
> *I hear my kinsmen weep—*
> *Uncle, niece, nephew, cousin, who convey her*
> *Unto her last long sleep.*

But turn this into dactyls, and the effect is ludicrous:

> *Mother is dead and my heart is in pieces,*
> *Hark how the friends of the family weep!*
> *Cousins and uncles and nephews and nieces*
> *Accompany her to her last long sleep.*

These are elementary rules, a few chosen at random from what I may call the Common Law of English Verse. But, in English satire, all rules can be deliberately broken. Byron's satiric comment on Keats's death, for example:

> *Strange that the soul, that very fiery particle,*
> *Should let itself be snuffed out by an article. . . .*

is emphasized by the deliberate use of the three-syllabled rhyme.

And comically inexact rhyme is the strength of Siegfried Sassoon's squib, written in the palmy days of George V, which he has generously allowed me to resurrect:

> *Because the Duke is Duke of York,*
> *The Duke of York has shot a huge rhinoceros;*
> *Let's hope the Prince of Wales will take a walk*
> *Through Africa, and make the Empire talk*

> *By shooting an enormous hippopotamus,*
> *And let us also hope that Lord Lascelles*
> *Will shoot* all *beasts from gryphons to gazelles*
> *And show the world what sterling stuff we've got in us.*

The word *satire* is not derived, as most people suppose, from the witty, prick-eared satyrs of the early Greek comedy, but from the Latin phrase *satura lanx,* or ' full platter '. Latin satire was a burlesque performance at a harvest festival, in which full-fed countrymen would improvise obscene topical jokes to a recurrent dance tune—as the islanders of Majorca still do to the *copeo,* at their annual pig-killing. The harvest atmosphere was free and easy; anything went. Urban satire, as Horace, or Juvenal, or Persius wrote it, was quite a different affair: Greek in origin, and bound by the same rules as epic or pastoral verse. Samuel Butler's *Hudibras* is fescennine; so are Donne's satires. Donne, in fact, did not deserve hanging if he failed to keep his accent in the satires; he could plead privilege.

Pope, who modelled himself as a satirist on Horace, thought fit to regularize Donne's lines:

> *Thou, who since yesterday hast roll'd o'er all*
> *The busy, idle blockheads of the ball,*
> *Hast thou, oh Sun! beheld an emptier sort,*
> *Than such as swell this bladder of a court?* . . .

> *Thus finish'd and corrected to a hair,*
> *They march, to prate their hour before the fair.*
> *So first to preach a white-glov'd chaplain goes,*
> *With band of lily, and with cheek of rose,*
> *Sweeter than Sharon, in immac'late trim,*
> *Neatness itself impertinent with him.* . . .

The difference between these two versions is that Donne's is readable, and Pope's is not; the regularity of the metre defeats its object after the first fifty couplets. Its readers remain unmoved; they sigh, and fall gently asleep. And this suggests another subject.

The Irish and early Welsh bards had made a discovery, which the Greeks and Romans had never made, and which reached England very late; namely, that regular verse, though a wonderful aid to memory, is soporific unless frequent changes occur in the metre; and that

though, say, Virgil's *Æneid* or Homer's *Iliad* may contain numerous
poems, the verse which links these poems together, because written
in the same metre, robs them of their force. What jeweller would dis-
play a pearl, unless perhaps a black one, in mother-of-pearl setting?
The Irish bards, while vellum was prohibitively dear, recorded their
chronologies, their treatises on geography, husbandry, and so on, in
mnemonic rhyme. Yet their tales (of which they had to know nine
hundred or more) were prose; and these the poet told in his own way,
to keep them fresh, and individual, and up to date; until he reached
a dramatic climax, and this was a traditional poem, which he had to
know by heart.

Mother-of-pearl, though a noble material for cutting and engraving,
is not pearl. The greater part of every long poem, even Spenser's
Faerie Queene, is necessarily mother-of-pearl. Ben Jonson hinted at
this in his *Discoveries.* He wrote:

> Even one alone verse sometimes makes a perfect poem as when
> Aeneas hangs up and consecrates the Armes of *Abas* with this in-
> scription:
>
> *Aeneas haec de Danais victoribus arma . . .*
>
> and calls it a *Poeme* or *Carmen.*

This drawing of attention to the poems included in a long work written in set stanzas—as Dante enthusiasts point to *The Death of Ugo-
lino* and similar pearls—suggests that the rest is not up to sample.
And how can it be, if the same metre is insisted on throughout?

In blank verse drama one can easily mark off the poems from the
roughage. Not only is blank verse capable of almost infinite variations, but prose is allowed to supply comic relief or passages which
further the plot. Shakespeare, for instance, makes Trinculo and
Stephano in *The Tempest* speak familiar quayside prose, which Cali-
ban answers in poems. But it is manifestly impossible that a long narrative poem which contains genealogy, description of scenery, battles,
love-passages, laments, and so on, can be reduced to a single metre
without dilution of the poetic content. Long poems are like old French
or Spanish tapestries: the design and colour and needlework may be
charming but there is no sharpness of detail, no personal characterization, no difference in quality or colour between foreground and background.

Are there any anthropologists present? If so, they may recall the giant yam of Abulam. At Abulam in New Guinea, yams for ordinary eating are planted and tended by the women, but every planting season a tense competition arises among the men: who can grow the yam of the year. This is a purely ritualistic yam, like the Harvest Festival marrow in an English village. The winning exhibit is said to be of approximately the size and shape of a bull-hippopotamus (discounting its head and legs) and perfectly inedible. It provides, in fact, an emblem of the literary epic, which was still being cultivated in Victorian days. With the passing of this Epic, followed by the formal Elegy, and the Ode addressed to heedless nightingales, rocking-chairs, abstractions, and noblemen, of what does poetry now consist? It is reduced, at last, to practical poems, namely the lyrical or dramatic highlights of the poet's experiences with the Goddess in her various disguises. The prose setting is withheld; and, because of this, professional standards demand that it should either explain itself fully, or present a note, as schoolchildren do who arrive late or without some necessary part of their school equipment.

Before closing, I must tell you about a girl who is reading English here under Professor X. I asked her: ' What poems do you enjoy most? ' and she answered with dignity: ' Poems are not meant to be enjoyed; they are meant to be analysed.' I hope you do not think that I subscribe to this heresy.

DAME OCUPACYON

In my last lecture I raised the problem of the poet's public, meaning: How large or small can this be in his lifetime? As large, I should say, as the widest possible extension of his circle of potential friends, or as small as the narrowest number of these potential friends to become aware of his work. Friends: not neighbours, not relatives, not business acquaintances: friends. People with roughly the same background of birth, environment, education, emotional propensities and intellectual prejudices. Friends, because, though they need not know the poet personally, they should feel at their ease with the poem. A poet may use any means that offer to make his work available to them. But if he tries to win a larger public by writing down to it, he is guilty of professional misconduct. I will go further: he should not consider his public at all, until the poem is written.

The medical profession supplies an analogy to this paradox. A true physician, obsessed with his work, will not regard himself as morally bound to any particular practice or hospital; he will readily move to another practice, or another hospital, which offers him more favourable working conditions, even if the pay is smaller. His chief interest lies in the diagnosis and cure (or palliation) of disease; and his chief loyalty is to the Goddess Hygieia, not to a particular group of sick people who need medical attention. The poet's chief interest lies, similarly, in the conception and working out of poems, and his chief loyalty is to the Goddess Calliope, not to his publisher, or to the booksellers on his publisher's mailing list. What the subsequent fate may be of the poems he writes should never influence their conception; as the act of love should be uncomplicated by thoughts of rich godparents for the child to be, perhaps, conceived. Also, the poet's approach to the Goddess is a personal one: he comes as himself, not in fancy-dress or borrowed clothing; and does not rant at her as though she were a public meeting, but speaks gently, clearly, intimately—they are closeted alone together. . . . By the way, I heard an answer today to the platitude: ' There's no money in poetry.' It was: ' There's no poetry in money, either.'

Epitaphs and elegies are a good test of poetic seriousness; because they may tempt the poet to hollow rhetoric. I have already quoted Skelton's *Epitaph on Edward IV*, and Clare's *The Dying Child* and, by contrast, Dryden's fancy-dress *Epitaph on Lord Hastings*. Here are two more poems of the same solemn category from opposite ends of the social scale. What makes Surrey's *Epitaph on Clere of Cleremont* a good poem is that he remains uncompromisingly himself, with all the faults and virtues of his nobility, and that he feels a sincere grief:

> *Norfolk sprang thee, Lambeth holds thee dead;*
> *Clere, of the County of Cleremont, thou hight.*
> *Within the womb of Ormond's race thou bred,*
> *And saw'st thy cousin crownéd in thy sight. . . .*
> *Shelton for love, Surrey for Lord, thou chase;*
> *(Aye me! while life did last that league was tender)*
> *Tracing whose steps thou sawest Kelsall blaze,*
> *Laundersey burnt, and battered Bullen render,*
> *At Mottrel gates, hopeless of all recure,*
> *Thine Earl, half dead, gave in thy hand his will;*
> *Which cause did thee this pining death procure,*
> *Ere summers four times seven thou couldst fulfill.*
> > *Ah! Clere! if love had booted, care, or cost,*
> > *Heaven had not won, nor earth so timely lost.*

What makes *The Night Before Larry Was Stretched,* a late eighteenth-century Dublin street-ballad, a good poem is that the writer, whoever he may have been (and one Harefoot Bill is generally credited with it) also remains uncompromisingly himself, with all the faults and virtues of his villainy, and he too feels a sincere grief:

> *The night before Larry was stretched,*
> > *The boys they all paid him a visit;*
> *A bit in their sacks too they fetched,*
> > *They sweated their duds till they riz it;*

For Larry was always the lad,
  When a friend was condemned to the squeezer,
Would fence all the togs that he had
  Just to help the poor boy to a sneezer,
    And moisten his gob 'fore he died. . . .

The boys they came crowding in fast;
  They drew their stools close round about him,
Six glims round his trap-case they placed;
  He couldn't be well waked without 'em.
When one of us asked, could he die
  Without having truly repented?
Says Larry, ' That's all in my eye,
  And first by the clergy invented
    To get a fat bit for themselves.'

. . . Then the deck being called for, they played
  Till Larry found one of them cheated.
A dart at his napper he made,
  The lad being easily heated.
' So ye chates me because I'm in grief;
  O, is that, by the Holy, the rason?
Soon I'll give you to know, you black thief,
  That you're cracking your jokes out of sason,
    I'll scuttle your nob with my fist.'

. . . When he came to the nubbling chit,
  He was tucked up so neat and so pretty;
The rumbler jogged off from his feet,
  And he died with his face to the city.
He kicked, too, but that was all pride,
  For soon you might see 'twas all over;
And after the noose was untied,
  Then at darky we waked him in clover,
    And sent him to take a ground sweat.

What (by your leave) makes *Lycidas* a bad poem, when judged by
the same standards, is that Milton has put on Theocritan fancy-dress;
and, as Dr Johnson first pointed out, it must ' not be considered the
effusion of real passion '.

Dr Johnson observes:

> Among the flocks, and copses, and flowers, appear the Heathen
> deities; Jove and Phœbus, Neptune and Aeolus, with a long train
> of mythological imagery, such as a college easily supplies. Nothing
> can less display knowledge, or less exercise invention, than to tell
> how a shepherd has lost his companion, and must now feed his
> flocks alone, without any judge of his skill in piping; and how one
> god asks another god what is become of Lycidas, and how neither
> god can tell. He who thus grieves will excite no sympathy; he who
> thus praises will confer no honour.

He might have added that Milton's chief interest while writing *Lycidas*
was an experiment in adapting Welsh verse-theory to English.

About obscurity. Obscurity is often charged against a poem by
readers for whom it was not intended, because they are outside the
poet's natural circle of friends. They feel aggrieved at having wasted
their money or time. This is foolish. Since I am neither scientist nor
philosopher, I should not venture to call any scientific or philosophical treatise obscure. If for some reason or other I find myself bogged
down in a technical passage which someone has pressed into my
hands, I assume that the terms are beyond me, and make no com-
plaints; unless the fault lies clearly in the careless or illogical use of
English prose, which has certain agreed semantic principles.

Unhistorically-minded readers, not at home in a mid-sixteenth-
century English castle, or a late-eighteenth-century Dublin thieves'
kitchen, may find *The Epitaph on Clere* or *The Night Before Larry
Was Stretched* obsure; Calliope, to whom they are directly addressed,
does not. She is no snob about class, or dialect, or a poet's occupa-
tional obsessions. True poems have been written by oyster-dredgers
and gangsters and cricketers. But when casually off-target lines are
addressed to her (as the present fashion is), with an invitation to
get a general atmospheric sense of what the poet means instead of
reading them attentively, she feels insulted. This Impressionistic technique, like most other modernisms in poetry, has been borrowed from
French painting theory. Another kind of Impressionism presents her
with a series of stark images—as it might be natural objects that strike
the week-ender's attention on a country walk—but leaves her to inter-
relate them. And then there is the Expressionist technique, which
relies on the perverse associations that some words have for a par-

ticular poet; he does not trouble to consider whether Calliope will find them acceptable. And by the way, this is the first time in history that poets have been dependent on painters for their inspiration; it used to be the other way about.

Expressionism raises a professional problem: what references are legitimate in a poem? A poet may, of course, thrust a poem in the hands of his personal muse, with: ' Dear love, this is for your eyes only ', and then intimate and far-fetched jokes shared between them are in order. And I must admit that old acquaintance is not always necessary for the understanding of obscure references. One may achieve a surprising rapport with a stranger, whose imaginative processes are similar to one's own—for example while playing ' The Game '—I mean the Hollywood charade game, to which I am partial. The player has to convey a song title, or a book title, or a newspaper headline, or whatever it may be, to members of his team by a rapid use of dumbshow, and is timed for speed. Try it, and you may find that one of your team, of the opposite sex, will divine instantly, against all the accepted rules of semantics, what you are acting for them. For instance, you catch her eye, and paying no attention to the other members of your side, you adopt the stance of a *banderillero,* then pinch your nose, claw the air with purposeful stripes and wave your hand enthusiastically above your head. You have been asked to convey the song-title: ' Three cheers for the Red, White, and Blue '— and *she* knows that in the fish-market at Barcelona, which has the best bull-ring in Spain, fish are classified according to their colour as red, white, and blue. . . . Or *you* know, when she pretends to be a cricketer and goes through the motion of asking for middle-and-leg, and (after a few other gestures) sits on the floor, her head tilted at a certain angle, that she represents Michelangelo's Sybil—the last two syllables of the word ' *possible* ', and you guess that the newspaper headline which she has been asked to convey is *Probables v. Possibles.* A strong, irrelevant love-element may be present on these occasions —an intellectual equivalent of the telepathic signals exchanged by certain insects when they mysteriously summon each other from a dozen miles away for an ecstatic nose-rubbing. It is a very pleasant feeling, because of its intimacy, and because no other player has understood. According to Irish legend, Cuchulain and Emir had this same experience when he wooed her in the presence of her women.

He had never addressed her before, yet she guessed the kennings of all his poetic riddles and answered him in kind. The women sat gaping and nonplussed. But this is private poetry; trespassers are prosecuted.

Now, the Goddess of Fame, according to Skelton's *Garland of Laurell,* employs a registrar called Dame Ocupacyon; when one brings her a poem, it is she who decides whether to enrol it in the public records. Dame Ocupacyon has a good general education, reasonableness, and a sympathetic heart. She takes a shrewd look at your lines, and if they make sense and demand no telepathic knowledge of your more capricious thought-processes, gives them her *imprimatur.* She will pass, for example, a reference to Isabella-coloured satin, because whoever the original Isabella may have been (some say she was the Archduchess who swore not to change her shift until Ostende fell), Isabella is generally recognized as a sort of greyish yellow. But ' dressed in Susan-coloured satin ' will not pass her scrutiny. Dame Ocupacyon knows many Susans, of widely-varying complexions, eyes and hair, and therefore with different tastes in dress; whereas this poet seems to know only one Susan who always wears, perhaps, the same lavender-grey—or is it brown-red?

To the Impressionist, Expressionist, Futurist, and Surrealist techniques, a Byzantine technique has recently been added: let me call it the Lycophronic. In current English this would be called the *quiz* technique, because it makes the reader humbly ashamed of the gaps in his education. But Dame Ocupacyon will have none of it. She rejects all over-erudite references in the poems offered her. For instance, she would be very sticky with these lines:

> *As Hymenoptera jinked by Isaria*
> *(Which are Torrubia's conidia)*
> *So we are kimed and huffed.*

Ocupacyon finds, on examination, that these lines make public sense —they compare the annoying attacks directed by one genus of low life on another, with similar attacks on the writer and his friends by petty enemies. But she holds that a less far-fetched metaphor with a closer and more exact relevance to the personal situation could surely have been hit upon. And that the reader who knows the meaning of ' jinked ', ' kimed ', and ' huffed ' will be unlikely to know what *Isaria* or *conidia* are; and *vice versa*. It is easy for a quiz-poet to acquire a reputation as a polymath by borrowing recondite words and phrases from various specialized books and mixing them up Lycophronically. I am far from being a polymath myself; and, in fact, to knock together the *Hymenoptera* verse just quoted, I was lazy enough to use only the H–K volume of *The Oxford English Dictionary*.

An absorbing subject is the poetry-reader's notion of boredom. Some readers, with theatrical rather than poetic interests, are entranced by tricks of rhetoric, and expect from the poem a wide range of fantasies, irrelevant to its central statement. Personally, I expect poems to say what they mean in the simplest and most economical way; even if the thought they contain is complex. I do not mind exalted language in poetry any more than I mind low language, but rhetoric disgusts me. I confess that I am equally allergic to oratorical prose: I read for information only, and cannot manage even Gibbon's *Decline and Fall* with patience, though it is a book of great interest, its ideas well marshalled, and the language chaste. I don't at all mind what are called dull books, so long as they are factual, accurate, and unpretentious: Brazilian politics, the digestive apparatus of sea-urchins, the art of wig-making—all is reading matter to me.

I don't even mind the so-called dull poems—such as Clare's Nature poems—if they ring true; but at the least touch of rhetoric or insincerity I close the book without marking the page. What duller poem, for example, could you imagine than an early nineteenth-century description in heroic couplets of a retired village grocer and his wife, written by the authoress of *Twinkle, Twinkle, Little Star*? Yet Jane Taylor's *The Mayor and Mayoress* happens to ring true as a poem because the appalling dullness of the theme struck her between the eyes, and she recorded it with devilish female exactness:

> *In yonder red-brick mansion, tight and square,*
> *Just at the town's commencement, lives the mayor.*
> *Some yards of shining gravel, fenc'd with box,*
> *Lead to the painted portal—where one knocks:*
>
> *There, in the left-hand parlour, all in state,*
> *Sit he and she, on either side the grate.*
> *But though their gods and chattels, sound and new,*
> *Bespeak the owners* very well to do,

His worship's wig and morning suit betray
Slight indications of an humbler day. . . .

That long, low shop, where still the name appears,
Some doors below, they kept for forty years:
And there, with various fortunes, smooth and rough,
They sold tobacco, coffee, tea and snuff. . . .

Her thoughts, unused to take a longer flight
Than from the left-hand counter to the right,
With little change are vacillating still
Between his worship's glory and the till.

Rhetoric may be the boast of the theatre—as Christopher Fry's admirers claim—but it is the curse of poetry. This must be emphasized, especially here at Cambridge where rhetoric was at one time the principal subject of study; after all, the Universities owe their existence to the medieval need for trained priests and lawyers. Rhetoric is the art of persuasion by a public speaker. When the primitive Christian Church went Greek, its leaders decided to abandon, as impractical, Jesus's strict injunctions: that his disciples should not premeditate when confronted with the enemies of their faith, but should rely on the inspiration of the Holy Spirit. Gentile Christian priests were then trained in the pagan schools of rhetoric, where the curriculum was based on close observations of the psychology of juries and public meetings—observations which helped the trained orator to make a poor, or even a bad, cause appear good. With the adoption of Christianity as a state religion the schools of rhetoric passed under Church control; but the pagan models were preserved. It is no business of mine to evaluate the damage done to simple faith by the tropes, tricks, and traductions of rhetoric; but I am convinced that poets who rely on rhetoric rather than inspiration are behaving unprofessionally. However, I must be careful not to overstate my case. A University education in rhetoric does, of course, make students properly conscious of logic and syntax and emphasis, and the rhythm and weight of their phrases, and the history and concealed meanings of individual words—all of which are useful in poetic composition. It is the *direction* of these studies which is anti-poetic; the student remains perpetually conscious of an imaginary audience whose resistance to argument he must beat down.

A poem (must I say again?) is addressed to the Goddess. She smilingly forgives clumsiness in the young or uneducated—early poems have a nap, or bloom, not found in later poems. And she appreciates the loving care put into a poem by the more experienced; she dislikes slovens. But she insists on truth, and ridicules the idea of using argument or rhetorical charm to overbear her intuition of truth. Milton fell from grace because he allowed his rhetorical skill, learned at Christ's, to dull his poetic sense. While reading his ' minor poems ' one becomes aware of poetry still struggling against the serpent coils. It is the unhappy flutterings of its wings in *Comus* and the Nativity Ode—I am thinking particularly of *Sabrina Fair* and ' the yellow-skirted fays '—that give these poems their poignant and, on the whole, distasteful character. Earlier, when writing the sixth poem of his Latin *Silvae,* at the age of twenty-three, Milton could energetically argue the cause of the ' Golden Muse ' against his father, on whom he depended for his allowance. Milton's father, a scrivener and a well-known musician, held that poetry was a pleasant relaxation for grave scholars and noblemen in the afternoon of their life, but that his son should choose some other sort of profession. Milton flatters him by saying: ' Apollo made you a musician, and me a poet.' Here is Skeat's translation:

> . . . *Hence it is that as sire and son we win*
> *Dividual lot in his divinity.*
> *To hate my gentle Muse though thou dost feign,*
> *Thou canst not hate her, Father, I maintain:*
> *Since thou hast ne'er bid me to go where lies*
> *The broad highway and easier field of gain,*
> *Where hopes gleam sure of coin in mounded heap;*
> *Not hal'st me to the Bar and laws we keep—*
> *Too often wrench'd; nor with distasteful cries*
> *Mine ears dost peal: but seeking only power*
> *My mind well-stor'd with richer wealth to dower*
> *In deep retirement from the city's roar,*
> *Lettest me thus in jocund leisure stride*
> *As if at Phœbus's side,*
> *With benediction from our Muse's shore.*

The poem ends with Milton's promise to celebrate his father's kindness in immortal verse.

So we come to the Theme of Fame. Skelton raised it; but only in joke. *The Garland of Laurell,* an account of his induction into the Temple of Fame, is a comic fantasy written for the Countess of Surrey, the Ladies Isabel and Miniall Howard, Lady Ann Dakers of the South, and his other women-friends at Court. Fame was no joke for Milton, but an obsession, as appears throughout the *Silvae,* especially in his letter to Manso, and in *Lycidas.* Thirst for fame explains much that is dishonest and ruthless in his life, besides his passionate cultivation of polemical oratory. Milton appears never to have loved anyone, after the death of his friend Charles Diodati, except himself; and certainly had no women-friends with whom he could be on joking terms. Men became the objects of his adulation or execration only as they advanced or impeded his career. While an undergraduate, he wrote two elegies on bishops, and a Fifth of November poem in which he sentenced to ' pains condign ' (though the dupes of Satan) the treasonable wretches who tried to encompass the death of our devout King James; he had his eye, it seems, on a Royal Fellowship. But when the coveted fellowship went elsewhere, and a Bishop, a former tutor with whom he had quarrelled, proved to have been responsible, Milton lost all respect for bishops. In *Eikonoclastes* he justifies the judges who sentenced King James's devouter son Charles to similar ' pains condign ' at the block. His adulation of Queen Christina of Sweden in *The Second Defence of the English People* contrasts so revoltingly with his obscene libels on Charles in *The First Defence,* that nothing which he wrote later when influenced by the Muse ' of Horeb and Sinai ' can persuade me of his poetic sincerity; grapes are not gathered from thistles.

Poets have aimed at two kinds of poetic fame: the first, contemporary fame, is suspect because it is commonly acquired by writing for the public, or for the representatives of the public, rather than for the Muse—that is to say for poetic necessity. The second, posthumous fame, is irrelevant; though, if the poet falls in love and becomes obsessed with terrors of death, he may be forgiven (as we forgive Shakespeare) for contemplating the immortality bestowed on his beloved by means of a poem. Milton was obsessed by thoughts of his own fame. His strongest reaction to the news of Lycidas's drowning was: 'Heavens, it might have been myself! Cut down before my prime, cheated of immortal fame!'

I grant that a poet cannot easily imagine a future in which he is no longer active; and poets do tend to live in a timeless world, where their predecessors are as real to them as their contemporaries. But I find that the predecessors whom I love, and for whom I might thoughtlessly lay a place at the supper table, are not those who, when they wrote, had designs on me as their posterity, but those who lived in the present and trafficked with the past. As I wrote once:

> *To evoke posterity*
> *Is to weep on your own grave. . . .*
>
> *And the punishment is fixed:*
> *To be found fully ancestral,*
> *To be cast in bronze for a city square,*
> *To dribble green in times of rain*
> *And stain the pedestal.*
>
> *Spiders in the spread beard;*
> *A life proverbial*
> *On clergy lips a-cackle;*
> *Eponymous institutes,*
> *Their luckless architecture.*
>
> *Two more dates of life and birth*
> *For the hour of special study*
> *From which all boys and girls of mettle*
> *Twice a week play truant*
> *And worn excuses try. . . .*

Poetic integrity. Of what does it consist? I should not like to think that integrity once lost is, like a maidenhead, irrecoverable. The young may, I believe, become actively engaged in non-poetic activities, and then repent, to re-establish themselves firmly on poetic ground. By non-poetic activities I mean those that prejudice the poet's independence of judgement; such as a religious life which imposes ecclesiastical control on his private thoughts; or politics, which bind him to a party line; or science, if it is old-fashioned enough to deny the importance of magic; or philosophy, if he is expected to generalize about what he knows to be personally unique; or schoolmastering, if he must teach what he considers neither true nor necessary. Ideally, poets should avoid enrolling themselves in any club, society, or guild: for fear they may find themselves committed to group action of which they cannot individually approve.

Many solutions have been found to the problem of how to separate oneself from the non-poetic world without turning anti-social. The fact is, that in this carefully organized country no poet can altogether avoid the responsibilities of citizenship, even if he should be unfit for military service; though to be a poet is a whole-time occupation to which all else must be subordinated. William Davies had solved his problem by becoming a common tramp, until he lost a foot (stealing a ride on an American railway truck)—then wrote his *Autobiography* and lived quietly by his pen in London; nevertheless, he was summoned one day for jury service. He described his experiences in a poem, *The Inquest*, which I have always admired both for its passionate detachment from the matter in hand (namely the assessment of factual evidence about a child's death); and for the troubled ambiguity of the: ' So help me God! I took that oath! '

> *I took my oath I would inquire,*
> *Without affection, hate, or wrath,*
> *Into the death of Ada Wright—*
> *So help me God! I took that oath.*
>
> *When I went out to see the corpse,*
> *The four months' babe that died so young,*
> *I judged it was seven pounds in weight,*
> *And little more than one foot long.*
>
> *One eye, that had a yellow lid,*
> *Was shut—so was the mouth, that smiled;*
> *The left eye open, shining bright—*
> *It seemed a knowing little child.*
>
> *For as I looked at that one eye,*
> *It seemed to laugh and say with glee:*
> *' What caused my death you'll never know—*
> *Perhaps my mother murdered me.'*

When I went into court again,
  To hear the mother's evidence—
It was a love-child, she explained,
  And smiled, for our intelligence.

' Now, Gentlemen of the Jury,' said
  The coroner—' this woman's child
By misadventure met its death.'
  ' Aye, aye,' we said. The mother smiled.

And I could see that child's one eye
  Which seemed to laugh, and say with glee:
' What caused my death you'll never know—
  Perhaps my mother murdered me.'

Davies's main difficulty was that, once he had written his autobiography, little remained to sell but his poems, of which he wrote and published too many; however, this was not a mortal sin—the unnecessary ones drop out, the necessary ones remain.

Once a poet has known the excitement of conceiving a poem and taking it through various drafts, still under the same excitement, the craving will always be with him. When it becomes oppressive, he often puts himself into a receptive posture, keeps pen and paper handy, and waits for the miracle of the Muse Goddess's appearance; then grows impatient, begins doodling with words (as you give the planchette a little push to make it start), and soon finds a promising rhyme or phrase. Thus he contrives a visitation—not of the Goddess but of one of those idle, foolish, earth-bound spirits that hover around the planchette board, or the pillows of sick men. An extraordinary difference in quality can be seen, for example, between Coleridge entranced and Coleridge unentranced—between *Kubla Khan* and *Frost at Midnight* on the one hand, and on the other *Lewti, The Nightingale,* and *The Old Man of the Alp*—all written in the same year (1798). Every poet knows in his heart which are the necessary and which the unnecessary poems. But too often he tries to fool himself that all are necessary. Necessary poems are rare; and poems in which the original necessity has not been blunted by unskilful elaboration are rarer still. Ideally, only these should be published, but flawed gems are none the less gems, and no poem is entirely flawless; so it should be enough in a *Collected Poems* to eliminate at least the glass and synthetic stones. Yet few poets are sufficiently ruthless to make a thorough job even of this.

A poet has certain natural loyalties—say, to a village where he spent his childhood, to a University where he was well treated, to a regiment with which he saw active service, to his family if they have respected his intransigeance. Such ties of affection need not prejudice his critical judgement, and he must take care never to join an organization where he will be expected to condone actions or attitudes of which he disapproves; or be told where he must live, how he must dress, and what sort of friends to avoid. A young poet down from the University is often tempted to go in for broadcasting, or publishing, or literary journalism. Yet he would be well advised to ask the B.B.C. for a job only as messenger or sound-technician, or the publishing house for a job as a packer or vanman, and the literary weekly for a job in the circulation department. Any position that makes him condone the printing or broadcasting of poems which he himself would not choose to print or broadcast is a dangerous one.

It is often said that poetry is unconcerned with morals; but this needs amendment. Of course, François Villon, Harefoot Bill, and Billy Gashade (author of the *Jesse James* ballad) seem to have little in common, morally speaking, with Richard Rolle, Thomas Traherne, and Henry Vaughan. But the first three were at least true to the principles of honour which prevail among thieves, and the remaining three to the principles of sainthood; their poems were honest declarations of personal integrity. Had Harefoot Bill turned stool-pigeon or Methodist preacher, it would have been as shocking as if Traherne had been caught robbing coaches on Hounslow Heath; or if either had tried to imitate the fashionable writers of his day.

And though it may be argued that no acceptable code of sexual morals can be laid down for the poet, I am convinced that deception, cruelty, meanness, or any violation of a woman's dignity are abhorrent to the Goddess; and that she loathes the deliberate sexual perversion which has male self-sufficiency for its object, and which has never been more boldly pursued by would-be poets than today.

It may also be argued that no acceptable religious code can be laid down for the poet. All I propose to say here is that one of the several strands in the Christian Faith, namely the mystery of the ever-Virgin

Mother and her Son—the crucified king whose seasonal birth, initia-
tion, death, and resurrection are celebrated by countryfolk—is wholly
poetic. But other strands—the theological, the ecclesiastical, the
liturgical—I find equally unpoetic. Anonymous carol-makers of pre-
Reformation days did not find it hard to reconcile poetry with faith,
because popular Catholicism was still closely connected with the
pagan cult of ' Our Lady '—the Goddess as Queen of Elphame, who
initiated Thomas the Rimer into her mysteries. Take, for instance, the
sixteenth-century carol *The Fawcon Hath Born my Mak Away:*

> *Lully, lulley; lully, lulley;*
> *The fawcon hath born my mak away.*
>
> *He bare hym vp, he bare hym down;*
> *He bare hym into an orchard brown.*
>
> *In that orchard ther was an hall,*
> *That was hangid with purpill and pall.*
>
> *And in that hall ther was a bede;*
> *Hit was hangid with gold so rede.*
>
> *And yn that bed ther lythe a knyght,*
> *His wowndes bledying day and nyght.*
>
> *By that bedes side ther kneleth a may,*
> *And she wepeth both nyght and day.*
>
> *And by that beddes side ther stondith a ston,*
> *' Corpus Christi ' wretyn theron.*

Though in a North Staffordshire version the lady is described as
the Virgin Mary, an earlier Scottish version calls her, more cautiously,
a *leal maiden:*

> *With silver needle and silken thread.*
> *Stemming the wounds where they did bleed.*

And the knight is not Christ, he is the Queen of Elphame's sacrificed
lover: call him Arthur, or Robin Hood, or the Young Cordwainer, or
what you will.

Skelton could still write a poem on the Passion free of the eccle-
siasticism that later clipped George Herbert's wings, and free of the

asceticism that made Gerard Manley Hopkins bite his nails to the quick:

> *Woffully araid,*
>   *My blode, man,*
>   *For thé ran,*
> *It may not be naid;*
> *My body bloo and wan,*
> *Woffully araid.*
> *. . . Off sharpe thorne I haue worne a crowne on my hede,*
> *So paynyd, so straynyd, so rufull, so red. . . .*
>   *My fete and handes sore*
>   *The sturdy nailis bore;*
>   *What myzt I suffir more*
> *Than I haue don, O man, for thé?*
> *Cum when thou list, wellcum to me,*
>   *Woffully araide.*

I do not know the present attitude of the Roman Church to poetry, but in 1916, when I was recovering from wounds near Quarr Abbey in the Isle of Wight, the good Benedictine monks tried to persuade me to join their Order after the War. One tempting argument was that they had a wonderful library of 20,000 volumes—on every possible subject—agriculture, music, history, mechanics, printing, mathematics. . . . But I asked Father Blanchon-Lasserve, the Guest-master: ' What about poetry? ' ' No, my son,' he answered, ' we have no poetry. It is not necessary.' As for the Protestant Church: a number of English clergymen once wrote most unecclesiastical poems— William Stevenson (' Back and side go bare, go bare '), Herrick and Swift among them—but this merely meant that in their days a priest could be a poet and forget about his priesthood. Since the early nineteenth century such an act of oblivion has been exceedingly difficult to perform. The last poet to do so was the gifted and strange Canon Frederick Langbridge of Limerick, who spent a great deal of his time writing lyrics for Edwardian musical comedies, and whose poems, *The Power of Red Michael,* published more than forty-five years ago, were as impressive as they were heretical.

A poet's integrity, then, consists in his not forming ties that can impair his critical independence, or prevent him from telling the whole truth about anything, or force him to do anything out of character. It consists also in his refusal to pay more respect to persons than decency demands, or their attainments permit. This does not, of course, give him the right to argue with a parson in the pulpit; or fail to rise in a public place when *God Save the Queen* is played; or show contempt of Court by incivility to a magistrate. But he will not permit a parson to lecture him from anywhere else but the pulpit; or the Crown to curtail his traditional liberties; or a magistrate to insult him out of court. He will also stubbornly resist all editorial attempts to alter any line of his poetry, unless the editor clearly has a better sense of the poem's needs than himself; which is possible, though unlikely.

And he will never include in his budget the money he gets from the sale of poems. If poems happen, let them be bought and published by whatever journal asks for them. If they gradually pile up, let them be published in volume form. If reputable anthologies then want to reprint a few, why not? But any money paid for a poem should, I believe, be regarded as if it were an unexpected legacy from a distant relative, whose favour one has not courted and whose death one has not anticipated. It should be spent on things of which the Goddess would approve: such as plain texts of the better poets, or the planting of a mulberry tree. . . . Let prose, or some other activity, pay the grocer and the gas collector.

According to one school of thought, a poet's life should be full of action, sexual adventure, and social event. Byron wrote to Thomas Moore:

> I think very highly of Hogg as a poet; but he, and half of these Scotch and Lake troubadors, are spoilt by living in little circles and petty societies. London and the world is the only place to take the conceit out of a man—in the milling phrase . . . Lord, Lord, if these home-keeping minstrels had crossed your Atlantic, or my Mediterranean, and tasted a little open boating in a white squall— or a gale in ' the Gut '—or the Bay of Biscay, with no gale at all— how it would enliven and introduce them to a few of the sensations! —to say nothing of an illicit amour or two upon shore, in the way of an essay upon the Passions, beginning with a simple adultery, and compounding it as they went along.

It is true that small provincial circles are most restrictive unless the members happen to be well chosen. And London until, say, 1914, was a wonderful place for polishing one's wits. Friends were not too busy making a living; or too fatigued by the noise of traffic, or too short-handed in the house to spend long hours together. When a man returned from a tour abroad, his friends would gather round and keep him posted with what had been happening in the world since they last saw him. My experience, when I come to London from Majorca for an annual fortnight or three weeks, is that people ask *me* what is happening!

However, Byron is over-stating the case for physical sensation: I doubt whether Shakespeare, when his early deer-stealing days had ended, ever so much as hired a wherry for a visit to the Isle of Dogs. And as for compound adultery: it never did Byron himself much good, and poets have written well enough without it.

Perhaps the nearest approach to an acceptable, all-purpose moral code for a poet is Swift's:

> *Stoop not to int'rest, flattery or deceit,*
> *Nor with hired thoughts be thy devotion paid;*
> *Learn to disdain their mercenary aid.*
> *Be this thy sure defence, thy brazen wall,*
> *Know no base action, at no guilt turn pale.*

Let me say a word or two about parody. A parody is not a poem, of course, yet the Muse at times commissions a parodist, such as Calverley or Lewis Carroll, to express her disapproval of poets who have behaved ridiculously. Parody is a form of destructive magic, like that employed by Russian forest-witches: the witch walks silently behind her victim, mimicking his gait, his carriage, and his gestures. After establishing a complete rapport with him, she pretends to stumble over a tree root. The victim inevitably does the same; but while the witch falls soft, he falls hard. No true poem can be parodied; because no true poem can be imitated. Calverley parodied Morris's *Two Red Roses Under the Moon* with his *Butter and Eggs and a Pound of Cheese;* and Carroll parodied Southey's *Old Father William;* in each case so successfully that the originals could never be recited again without a blush. But Jane Taylor's *Twinkle, Twinkle, Little Star* survives, undaunted by *Twinkle, Twinkle, Little Bat.*

Wordsworth often parodied himself so unmercifully that J. K. Stephen's lines are supererogatory, if just:

Two voices are there: one is of the deep;
It learns the storm cloud's thunderous melody,
Now roars, now murmurs with the changing sea,
Now bird-like pipes, now closes soft in sleep:
And one is of an old half-witted sheep
Which bleats articulate monotony,
And indicates that two and one are three,
That grass is green, lakes damp, and mountains steep:
And, Wordsworth, both are thine. . . .

And Tennyson, late and early, also parodied himself.

She stood upon the castle wall,
  Oriana:
She watch'd my crest among them all,
  Oriana:
She saw me fight, she heard me call,
When forth there stept a foeman tall,
  Oriana:
Atween me and the castle wall,
  Oriana.

Calliope once passed word to substitute the brutal phrase ' *Bottom Upwards!* ' for the romantic invocation ' *Oriana!* ' Try it for yourselves, especially from the point where Tennyson writes:

The battle deepened in its place,
But I was down upon my face,
  Oriana.

They should have stabb'd me where I lay,
  Oriana!
How could I rise and come away,
  Oriana?
How could I look upon the day?
They should have stabb'd me where I lay,
  Oriana—
They should have trod me into clay,
  Oriana.

THESE BE YOUR GODS, O ISRAEL!

I was never one to stroll down the street with a catapult and break windows just for the fun of hearing the tinkle of glass and seeing furious faces peering out as I scuttle away. But to break windows *from the inside* amounts, at times, to a civic duty. One smells gas, bursts open the kitchen door, turns off the oven-tap, wraps a towel around one's fist and breaks every pane in the kitchen window; for which a commendatory word or two may be expected from the magistrate—or from the coroner, according as the suicide is successful or not.

An anonymous leader-writer in *The Times Literary Supplement,* discussing the poetry of today, has described ours as an ' Age of Consolidation '. I find ' Consolidation ' too active a word, and should prefer ' Age of Acquiescence ' or ' Age of Acceptance '; which, of course, in the Welfare State, covers a wider range of subjects than poetry and literature in general. Most of my younger contemporaries have been acquiescing in an organized attempt, by critics, publicists, and educationalists, to curtail their liberty of judgement, and make them bow the knee before a row of idols, whose rites are quite incompatible with devotion to the Muse herself.

Idolatry is nothing new. The Goddess, or the God, being held too mysterious and exacting a figure for public worship, idols are set up as intermediaries—like the hero-images in Classical Greece—to focus the vague yearnings and aspirations of the unenlightened mass. As Isaiah remarks:

> He maketh a god even his own graven image and falleth down unto it and prayeth unto it and saith: ' Deliver me, for thou are my God! '

Yet the ancients at least waited until Homer and Virgil were decently dead before they paid them heroic honours. The living poet hero is a modernism; I think I am right in saying that Petrarch was the first poet to receive quasi-divine honours during his lifetime. And once an idol is set up it cannot easily be removed; but slowly moulders down the years, as Byron's and Wordsworth's have done. Tennyson's idol began to moulder soon after his death, because it had become identified with much that was unpopular in Victorianism. Thus Thomas Hardy wrote in his *An Ancient to Ancients* twenty-five years later:

> *The bower we shrined to Tennyson,*
> > *Gentlemen,*
> *Is roof-wrecked; damps there drip upon*
> *Sagged seats, the creeper-nails are rust,*
> *The spider is sole denizen;*
> *Even she who voiced those rhymes is dust,*
> > *Gentlemen!*

In 1910, when I first made poetry the most important thing in my life, no idols were forced on me. English literature did not form part of the curriculum at Charterhouse, and I could go foraging for myself in blessed freedom. Moreover, war broke out just when I should have gone to Oxford; I volunteered and took a commission in an unliterary line-regiment, where I spent the next four and a half years. I had never met a poet of my own generation until, by a stroke of luck, Siegfried Sassoon was posted to my battalion; and through him and Edward Marsh (who had befriended me while I was still at school) I came to know several of the real poets then extant—including Hardy, William Davies, and Wilfred Owen.

A wave of popular excitement had been raised, two or three years before the War, by Masefield's bold use of the word ' bloody ' in his *Everlasting Mercy;* but so dim were the other poetic lights of the period that he was the only modern poet whom Max Beerbohm found topical enough for inclusion in his *Poet's Corner*—except the insufferable Kipling (swapping 'ats with 'is gal Britannia on 'Ampstead 'Eath). Max wrote:

> *A swear word in a rustic slum*
> *A simple swear word is to some,*
> > *To Masefield. something more.*

A second wave of popular excitement was raised by the death of Rupert Brooke during the Dardanelles campaign. Brooke's patriotic sonnet ' If I should die . . .' was included in Edward Marsh's *Georgian Poetry,* and the subsequent three volumes set poetical taste for the duration of the War, and for some years after.

But there were no living idols even in the early 'twenties. Thomas Hardy was known mainly for his novels; Charles Doughty for his *Arabia Deserta;* William Davies for his *Autobiography of a Super Tramp;* A. E. Housman for his Latin scholarship. I was still young then, yet could regard them as my friends and colleagues; simply because the current text-books of English literature stopped at Tennyson and Swinburne—we were all equally post-Canonical. Thus, though I had been attracted at the age of sixteen by the soft music of Yeats's *Countess Cathleen* and *Wanderings of Oisin,* he was not yet a ' required ' poet; and I had felt no compunction about going behind him to literal translations of the Irish texts from which he quarried.

How things have changed since those days! Contemporary English literature has insinuated itself into the Public School and Secondary School curriculum. It is now recognized by the English Faculty here too. Even I have my niche in the popular text-book: I am briefly mentioned with the Georgian War Poets of 1914–18 (*see* p. 11), successors to the Imagists (*see* p. 1) and themselves superseded (*see* p. 11) by the Modernist Movement of the 'twenties; which merged (*see* p. 111) into the Left Wing Movement of the 'thirties; which was suffocated (*see* p. 141) by the 1939–45 War; which gave a pause for reflection, the new poets being few and inhibited. And for the setting up of five living idols—namely Yeats, Pound, Eliot, Auden, and Dylan Thomas (*see separate chapters devoted to each*).

Are you men and women of culture? Then you are expected not only to regard these five as the most ' significant ' modern writers but to have read all the ' significant ' literature that has grown up about them; because ' Age of Consolidation ' implies ' Age of Criticism '. The educational emphasis is now on appreciation of contemporary as well as ancient literature, and since to appreciate no longer means ' to evaluate ', as it did in earlier days, but has become a synonym for ' to admire ', there must be recognized objects of official appreciation —namely idols.

Ladies and gentlemen, relax! None of this lore is necessary for your

salvation, once you have satisfied the examiners. There are only
poems, very few of these in any generation, and there are periodic
verse-fashions. And as for the old-clothesman of literature, the critic
who starts by writing D.Phils. on such subjects as *W. H. Auden and
the Freudian Theory of Transference,* or *T. S. Eliot as Anticipated by
Duns Scotus;* and who then applies for a Foundation Research Fellowship, because he is compiling a scholarly edition (with cancelled first
drafts) of all Dylan Thomas's advertisement copy for Messrs. J.
Walter Thompson's *Night Custard* account; or perhaps a polyglot concordance to Pound's *Pisan Cantos*—as for the old clothesman, leave
him to his industry! Waste no money on books *about* poetry; not even
on mine. Build up a library of plain texts: the poet who pleads his
case before Dame Ocupacyon is expected to present a plain, un-
annotated text of his poems, and no supporting documents or testi-
monials whatsoever. I am here to remind you that poets are not idols,
nor are idols poets; and that the Muse alone deserves your love. The
idols are well swaddled against anything less destructive than a cobalt
bomb; and all my iconoclastic zeal, so far from turning the whole
temple blue, will not so much as dent a protective sandbag. Nevertheless, here it comes.

First, William Butler Yeats. The younger Yeats had wit, industry,
a flexible mind, a good ear, and the gift of falling romantically in love
—admirable qualities for a beginner. His less admirable qualities were
greed, impatience, and a lack of proportion, or humour, for which no
amount of wit can compensate. Yeats's father once confided to my
father: ' Willie has found a very profitable little by-path in poetry ';
and this was fair enough. The early poems fall short of the pathetic
only by their genuine feeling for Ireland and their irreproachable
anvil-craft. They are the work of a negligently-dressed, misty-eyed,
murmuring Dubliner, living in the Fenian past; ' a darling man ' to his
friends Douglas Hyde, Dr P. W. Joyce, A.E., J. M. Synge, Lionel
Johnson, Lady Gregory, and the rest, who supplied him with certain
up-to-date convictions. What he would most have liked to do was
what his American contemporary, Vachel Lindsay, had done—to
hawk his own ballads about the countryside; but he lacked Lindsay's
simple courage. And how good a poet Lindsay could be, when he
really said what he meant—as in *Bryan, Bryan, Bryan*—and was not
being corny or coy! A literary event which startled critics in the
'twenties was the emergence of a new, well-groomed, cynical Yeats,

with a manly voice, florid gestures, and an attractive wife, who had
cast his singing robes away and his wild harp flung behind him. Yeats
explained that he had been plagued by a swarm of imitators; this new
technique was the only way to be rid of them. It is now claimed that
the transmogrification was largely the work of Ezra Pound, who persuaded Yeats that the Celtic Twilight belonged to yesterday, and that
today's sun beamed on the buccaneer and smart-stepping salesman.
But Yeats needed little persuasion; he had written to Sturge Moore
that he preferred the violent expression of error (as in Bernard Shaw
or Schopenhauer) to the reasonable expression of truth which cor-
rupts by its lack of pugnacity.

When I returned to Oxford, after the War, Yeats was lodging above
the Shamrock Tearooms in the Broad; but curiosity never drew me
there. Now, Yeats was Irishman enough to realize that, however great
a man's industry, however careful his craftsmanship, all is sounding
brass and tinkling cymbal, unless divine ' grace ' is added. (Pleasant
to be able to quote St Paul and not get into trouble!) ' Grace ' is the
presence of the Muse Goddess; but she does not appear unless her
poet has something urgent to say and to win her consent a poet *must*
have something urgent to say. Yeats had a new technique, but nothing
to say, unless one counts the literary ballads written for the Irish War
of Liberation—in which he took no active part. Instead of the Muse,
he employed a ventriloquist's dummy called Crazy Jane. But still he
had nothing to say. What will a poor countryman do if he has no
sheep of his own to shear and badly needs a warm waistcoat? He will
go out with a bag into his neighbour's fields and collect strands of
wool from hedges and brambles. This Yeats did.

Raymond Mortimer recently called Yeats ' a bower bird collecting
bright coloured rags and pebbles from the Hebrew *Kabbalah,* the
Vedanta, the *Mabinogion,* the alchemists, Swedenborg, Blake, Nietzsche, and the Theosophists.'

That is correct. He was now using his wife as a medium, and took
the spirit babblings of a certain sixteenth-century Moor, a previous
incarnation of his own, as inspiratory material for his poems. This explained a dialogue reported to me by an undergraduate visitant to
No. 4. Broad Street, which had seemed a *non sequitur:*

UNDERGRADUATE: Have you written any poems recently, Sir?
YEATS: No, my wife has been feeling poorly and disinclined.

A few years later Yeats came to Majorca with an Indian disciple, and worked there on an English version of the *Upanishads*. That was the period of his Voronoff operation and its tragi-comic sequels, which were café gossip there for months. He confessed:

> *You think it horrible that lust and rage*
> *Should dance attention upon my old age;*
> *They were not such a plague when I was young;*
> *What else have I to spur me into song?*

While in Majorca, he wrote asking Laura Riding and myself, as co-authors of *A Survey of Modernist Poetry,* for advice: which younger English poets should he include in his new anthology? We suggested James Reeves, whose first book we had just published. Yeats rejected Reeves with this really devilish comment:

> Too reasonable, too truthful. We poets should be good liars, re-membering always that the Muses are women and prefer the embrace of gay, warty lads.

So we declined to contribute ourselves.

Raymond Mortimer goes on to say that Yeats could turn any rubbish borrowed from the planchette, or Rosicrucianism, or Mme Blavatsky, into hard and burnished gold, and that few poets have written verse so strong in the three virtues of terseness, tensity, and eloquence.

Yes; Yeats thought of himself as an alchemist, but (as I wrote somewhere) the alchemists never succeeded in making gold out of anything but gold; though they did manufacture muriatic acid, a solvent for gold. They disguised their secret formulae in a mythological cypher, which delighted Yeats and has since excited Jung, though neither of them was chemist enough to crack it. The early-medieval German monk Rugerus wrote:

> The Gentiles (Arabs) have an underground house walled with stones above and below, with two very small apertures, hardly wide enough to admit light. Here they place two old cocks of twelve to fifteen years old and feed them well. When they are fattened, the heat of their good condition makes them come together and lay eggs. The cocks are then removed and toads introduced to hatch them; these are given bread for food. Chickens then emerge like hens' chickens, but after seven days grow serpent's tails, and but for the

stone pavement would disappear into the earth. To guard against this, the owners take large, round, narrow-mouthed brass vessels, perforated all over, and put the chickens inside, closing the mouths with copper and burying them underground, where the creatures are fed for six months by the fine earth which enters by the holes. They then take the vessels out and heat them under a generous fire until the creatures are completely burned. The corpses are then left to cool, removed, carefully ground, mixed with the third part of the blood of a red man which has been dried and pulverized. . . .

And so on. The cocks here are sulphates of copper and iron; the eggs are lumps of gold ore. The chickens are fumes of sulphuric acid. The toad is nitrate of potash. The blood of a red man is muriate of ammonia. Fine earth is muriate of soda. . . . If Yeats had got hold of this passage, what fun he would have had with it! What tersity, what tensity, what eloquence—what hard, burnished rubbish!

Rugerus and his fellow-alchemists (I repeat) never made gold out of anything but gold: as poets can never make poems out of anything but poetry. However, the alchemists and their less mystical successors invented numerous glittering alloys, one of which is pinchbeck. The elder Pinchbeck (died 1732), who was an honest craftsman, produced some very pretty necklaces and brooches; but went to prison because his salesmen tried to pass them off as gold. The younger Pinchbeck, who was no craftsman but more careful of the law, mass-produced what is now called ' costume-jewellery '. ' Pinchbeck's curious metal ' contains five parts copper to one of zinc. I mention this because copper is a metal traditionally sacred to the Love-goddess, as gold is to her royal victims. But zinc, the intrusive metal which lends copper that hard, bright, delusive brilliance, has no poetic sanctity.

Here is Yeats in his early copper period:

> *Who dreamed that beauty passes like a dream?*
> *For these red lips, with all their mournful pride,*
> *Mournful that no new wonder may betide,*
> *Troy passed away in one high funeral gleam,*
> *And Usna's children died. . . .*

Who ever would have thought that the author would live to introduce the low word *bum* into a Classical fantasy? Or to combine blasphemy with obscenity in *The Stick of Incense,* a *double-entendre* about St Joseph? Well: here is the new-model Yeats, em-Pounded as far as he was capable, writing a poem called *Chosen:*

> *I struggled with the horror of daybreak,*
> *I chose it for my lot! If questioned on*
> *My utmost pleasure with a man*
> *By some new-married bride, I take*
> *That stillness for a theme*
> *Where his heart my heart did seem*
> *And both adrift on the miraculous stream*
> *Where—wrote a learned astrologer—*
> *The Zodiac is changed into a sphere. . . .*

He has taken bold poetic licences: *astronomer* rhymes with *sphere* —though, by the rule on which he was brought up, even if one rhymes (say) *verily* with *sigh, sigh* must come in the first rhyming line and *verily* in the second. He also here rhymes *on* with *man,* which can be done decently in Scotland alone; the convention being (I think) that half-rhymes are justified by poetic necessity only where a prevailing mood of gloom, doubt, mental stress or confusion would be denied by too perfect an answering chime. And in his younger days, Yeats would not have dared publish three lines as imprecise as these:

> *. . . If questioned on*
> *My utmost pleasure with a man*
> *By some new-married bride. . . .*

where the awkward syntax suggests, at first, that he was questioned about his utmost pleasure with some man while someone else's bride lay close by. Even after the reader has mentally corrected this confused image, he is still left with a question by the new-married bride which seems to pre-suppose sexual commerce between Yeats and a man, not her husband. The imprecision is developed by the astrologer's remark that ' The Zodiac is changed into a sphere,' to which Yeats supplies the following note:

> The ' learned astrologer ' was Macrobius, and the particular passage was found for me by Dr Sturm, that too little known poet and mystic. It is from Macrobius's comment upon ' Scipio's Dream ' (Lib. I, Cap. XII, Sec. 5): ' . . . when the sun is in Aquarius, we

> sacrifice to the Shades, for it is in the sign inimical to human life; and from thence, the meeting-place of Zodiac and Milky Way, the descending soul by its defluction is drawn out of the spherical, the sole divine form, into the cone.'

But suppose we happen to have read Macrobius, who is not everyone's meat, what then? Macrobius does not say that the *Zodiac* becomes turned into a sphere, or anything of the sort. He says that the *soul* when it reaches a certain point in the Zodiac, conceived as a girdle, is drawn from the spherical form into the conical. But what *that* means, even Dr Sturm has not elucidated.

Yeats's reference to *Usna's children,* in the early poem I quoted, can be defended: the tale of *The Three Sons of Usna* was familiar to his Gaelic Revivalist readers. But, as I was saying last week, to publish a poem strewn with references to which not one reader in ten million has the key, is regarded as impudence by Dame Ocupacyon. The case becomes worse when the poet misquotes; as so often happens with Ezra Pound.

Pound, an Idaho man, left America with a patchy education and settled in London while Edward VII still sat firmly on the throne. London was then the acknowledged literary centre of the English-speaking world. Pound's early poems were influenced by William Morris, Browning, and Yeats, particularly Yeats. Pound wrote in Yeatsian style:

> *For I was a gaunt, grave councillor*
> *Being in all things wise, and very old,*
> *But I have put aside this folly and the cold*
> *That old age weareth for a cloak. . . .*

But Pound had no inkling of English tradition, and when he tried to write a Villonaud in eighteenth-century English style, could get no closer to it than the shockingly illiterate:

> *Drink we a skoal to the gallows tree,*
> *François and Margot and thee and me,*
> *Drink we to Marienne Ydole*
> *That hell brenn not her o'er cruelly . . .*
> *Those that we love shall God love less*
> *And smite always at their faibleness?*

He ordered his songs to cock a snook at Mr Strachey, Editor of *The Spectator;* and published among them a Latin poem in which the future indicative of *gaudeo* was given as *gaudero;* and wrote *Maelids* for *Meliads* in a poem allegedly based on Ibycus. The Thames was not set on fire.

Before his arrival on these shores he had been teaching English Literature in a small mid-Western college, where he was not appreciated, and left soon after his arrival. It is my impression that Pound never forgave his country this rebuff, and that he thereafter ranked himself as a great teacher whose talents were too stupendous for the classroom and at whose knees all illuminated rebels would gather. He made his peace with Walt Whitman whom he had hitherto despised, and wrote in Whitmanesque vein:

> *Go, my songs, seek you praise from the young and the intolerant,*
> *Move among the lovers of perfection alone.*
> *Seek ever to stand in the hard Sophoclean light.*

With T. E. Hulme and others he issued the *Imagiste* manifesto, which offered a hard, precise image as the *summum bonum* of poetry; but Imagism never caught on here. It seemed both precious and metrically undisciplined, and (worse) could not be harnessed to the war effort of a nation in arms. Slowly the frustrated Pound went mad-dog, and bit the other dogs of his day; he even, as I have said, fastened his teeth in Yeats's hand, the hand that had fed him.

I did not meet Pound until 1922, in T. E. Lawrence's rooms at All Souls'. He happened along for a discussion of Provençal poems, on which Lawrence was an authority. Lawrence introduced us: ' Pound, Graves; Graves, Pound; you'll dislike each other.' From his poems, I had expected a brawny, loud-voiced, swashbuckling American; but he was plump, hunched, soft-spoken and ill-at-ease, with the limpest of handshakes. Afterwards I asked Lawrence: ' What's wrong with that man? ' Lawrence answered cryptically: ' Pound has spent his life trying to live down a family scandal: he's Longfellow's grand-nephew.'

Gilbert Highet parodied Pound in 1942:

> *. . . And there sat the well-oiled fire-engine*
> *all ready to strain its gutmost*

> *eek ow ouf honk honk*
> *unable to think, but ready to quote and paraphrase*
> * in six languages*
> *including Provençal . . .*
> *ei didl didl*
> * li chat e li fidl*
> *   it took a man like Ezra to kill Provençal poetry*
> *   for us . . .*

' The well-oiled fire-engine ' is T. S. Eliot's tribute to Pound's verse technique. And again:

> *the Emperor is at Ko*
> *but No*
> *silken strings shiver no longer, clashing of smilax, dark*
> *nuts on the dry bough, nuts on wet earth, nuts*
> *it's lonesome too being the only one who understands Caius*
> *   Properzius,*
> *   'Alkaios,*
> *   Li Pu,*
> * all great guys,*
> *an' I know 'em, see? . . .*

However, Pound's bravado paid in the long run. He knew little Latin, yet he translated Propertius; and less Greek, but he translated Alcæus; and little Anglo-Saxon, yet he translated *The Seafarer*. I once asked Arthur Waley how much Chinese Pound knew; Waley shook his head despondently. And I don't claim to be an authority on Provençal, but Majorcan, which my children talk most of the time, and which I understand, is closely related to it. When my thirteen-year-old boy was asked to compare a Provençal text with Pound's translation, he laughed and laughed and laughed.

Pound's admirers explain that his translations should not be read as such; that his free treatment of the original has supplied him with many interesting new ideas. Well, I don't know. . . . It is true that Michelangelo advised young painters to seek inspiration (when at a loss) from the damp patches and cracks on their bedroom walls. But the corresponding source of poetic inspiration would, I suppose, be the litter left behind by foreign students in a Bloomsbury hostel; it

seems unfair on Alcæus and Li Po and Propertius to treat them so
cavalierly. Pound's passionate feelings became centred later in politics
and popular economic theory: he even succeeded for a while in persuading Yeats of the brutal virtues of Fascism. He also convinced
himself that the Jews had invented usury, and that the jew (with a
small j) was the evil genius who degraded our superior Christian culture, from which only a revolution of intellectual aristocrats could
dislodge him. It is an extraordinary paradox that Pound's sprawling,
ignorant, indecent, unmelodious, seldom metrical *Cantos,* embellished
with esoteric Chinese ideographs—for all I know, they may have been
traced from the nearest tea-chest—and with illiterate Greek, Latin,
Spanish, and Provençal snippets (the Italian and French read all right
to me, but I may be mistaken) are now compulsory reading in many
ancient centres of learning. If ever one comes across a relatively
simple Blake-like passage in the *Cantos,* sandwiched between direct
quotations from history text-books, and snarling polyglot parentheses,
this is how it sounds. Forgive me; but we are all adults here:

> *S . . . t on the throne of England, s . . . t on the Austrian*
>   *sofa,*
> *In their soul was usura and in their minds darkness*
> *and blankness, greased fat were four Georges*
> *Pus was in Spain, Wellington was a jew's pimp* [small j]
> *and lacked mind to know what he effected.*
> *' Leave the Duke, go for gold! '*
> *In their souls was usura and in their hearts cowardice,*
> *In their minds was stink and corruption.*
> *Two sores ran together, Talleyrand stank with shanker,*
> *and hell pissed up Metternich.*
> *Filth stank as in our day . . .*

Even Whitman's barbaric yawp was hardly as barbaric as that. But
remove the layers and layers of cloacinal ranting, snook-cocking,
pseudo-professorial jargon and double-talk from Pound's verse, and
what remains? Longfellow's plump, soft, ill-at-ease grand-nephew remains![1]

---

[1] Mr Gordon Wharton has recently written about Pound in *The Times Literary
Supplement* that: ' whatever total judgement one makes on his works, one has

T. E. Lawrence wrote in 1912 to his brother Will, who had come under Pound's influence:

> Pound has a very common American affectation of immense learning in strange things. If you can read history and *Bertrand* together you would not dream of following him. . . . I think *The Goodly Fere* is by far his best thing. . . .

Bertrand de Born was a Provençal hero whom Pound used as one of his own *personae,* or masks; but who deserved a better fate. Lawrence means that *The Goodly Fere,* a rousing old-world Salvationist ballad about Jesus Christ, the muscular fisherman, is honest Longfellow: by *Blind Bartimaeus* out of *The Wreck of the Hesperus.* T. S. Eliot omitted it from his critical edition of Pound's poems with the lame, if aristocratic, excuse that it was ' too well known '.

T. S. Eliot, another American, had been a graceful writer of songs and conventional poems at Harvard (until he read philosophy and ceased for a while). He came to Europe a year or two before the First

---

to admit that his whole poetic career has been dominated by an ambition to achieve major form.' As an example of major writing he quotes Pound's lyric:

> *O Lynx, guard this orchard,*
>   *Keep from Demeter's furrow*
> *This fruit has a fire within it,*
>   *Pomona, Pomona,*
> *No glass is clearer than are the globes of flame*
> *What sea is clearer than the pomegranate body holding the flame?*
>   *Pomona, Pomona,*
>   *Lynx, keep watch on this orchard*
>   *That is named Melagrana*
> *or the Pomegranate field*
>   *The sea is not clearer in azure*
>   *Nor the Heliads bringing light*
> *Here are lynxes*   *Here are lynxes,*
> *Is there a sound in the forest*
>   *of pard or of bassarid*
> *or crotale*   *or of leaves moving?*

This makes little sense to me, though I am as good as the next man in seeing through a brick wall. I can get as far as where a lynx is improbably asked to keep from Demeter's furrow a clear flaming pomegranate-like fruit in an orchard sacred to Pomona. But there the trail goes cold, despite Heliads, pards and bassarids ' such as a college easily supplies ' (Dr Johnson on *Lycidas*). What is the Goddess Pomona doing among pards, lynxes and bassarids, none of which occurred in her limited Latin territory? And what or who is *crotale?* Only *crotalon* appears in *Liddell and Scott* and means a rattle, either real or metaphorical.

World War and found it a more congenial continent than his own.
Yet even so he was bored to screaming by tea-parties, and art-
students' chatter, and lodging-house society, and cocktail-bars, and
London fog, and hymns in London churches; already he began to feel
bald and old and useless. This reaction accounts for *Prufrock* (published in 1917). I first met Eliot in 1916: a startlingly good-looking,
Italianate young man, with a shy, hunted look, and a reluctance
(which I found charming) to accept the most obvious phenomenon
of the day—a world war now entering its bloodiest stage, and showing every sign of going on until it had killed off every man in London
but the aged and neutrals. I was due to return to the Somme any day,
and delighted to forget the war too in Eliot's gently neutral company.

When the Armistice delivered us all, he had no war-neurosis to
slough off, and stepped forward as a prophet of the uninhibited, anti-
Romantic early 'twenties. In *The Hippopotamus* he guyed the Church
irreverently:

> *Flesh and blood is weak and frail,*
> *Susceptible to nervous shock,*
> *While the True Church can never fail,*
> *For it is based upon a rock. . . .*
>
> *The hippo's feeble steps may err*
> *In compassing material ends,*
> *While the True Church need never stir*
> *To gather in its dividends.*

He was as polyglot as Pound: Greek, Latin, French, German, Italian,
Sanscrit tags alternate in his poems, but he took decent care to check
their accuracy, and had a far better ear for verse.

Pound accepted Eliot as a disciple, or Poundling, and was rewarded
for his blue-pencilling of *The Waste Land* by the dedication: *Il miglior
fabbro*. This celebrated poem was, I believe, the first to apply the
current art-fashion of *collage* to English verse—*collage* being the
technique of pasting, say, autumn leaves, bus-tickets, metal shavings,
cigar bands, fur, playing cards, and artificial flowers on a sheet of
paper, in order to create a ' significant ' composition. What the composition is ' significant ' of, is never explained. Here Eliot pasted frag-
ments of the Elizabethan ornate against skilfully chosen examples of

the modern nasty (though never using words which would have barred him from the drawing-room); and in his notes asked the reader to find, despite the continual change of subject and metre, a connecting thread of sense. Dame Ocupacyon will not be pleased when she reads:

> Not only the title, but the plan and a good deal of the incidental symbolism of the poem were suggested by Miss Jessie L. Weston's book on the Grail legend: *From Ritual to Romance* (Cambridge). Indeed, so deeply am I indebted, Miss Weston's book will elucidate the difficulties of the poem much better than my notes can do; and I recommend it (apart from the great interest of the book itself) to any who think such elucidation of the poem worth the trouble. To another work of anthropology I am indebted in general, one which has influenced our generation profoundly; I mean *The Golden Bough;* I have used especially the two volumes *Atthis Adonis Osiris*. Anyone who is acquainted with these works will immediately recognize in the poem certain references to vegetation ceremonies.

Eliot had meanwhile been encouraged by Pound to voice the anti-Jewish obsession:

> *My house is a decayed house*
> *And the jew* [small j] *squats on the window sill, the owner,*
> *Spawned in some estaminet of Antwerp*
> *Blistered in Brussels, patched and peeled in London. . . .*

(Eliot himself, though afterwards patched and peeled in London, was not spawned, but decently begotten by a God-fearing Christian father.) And again, in the Venice poem, we find:

> *The rats are underneath the piles*
> *The jew* [small j] *is underneath the lot.*
> *Money in furs. The boatman smiles. . . .*

(Eliot's family kept clear of the fur trade: machinery was more respectable.)

Well, the libertarian movement of the 'twenties got bogged, as the text-books explain, in the political 'thirties; and before these were over, Eliot who, unlike Pound, had no grudge against the world, but only a shyness of it, made his peace with the Hippopotamus and was well on his way to Rydal Mount. Instead of *The Ecclesiastical Sonnets* he wrote *Murder in the Cathedral,* and *The Rock*—the Rock against which he had stubbed a toe—in aid of ecclesiastical charities:

> *With Seneca, with Cicero,*
> * With cockney fun he makes amends;*
> *The cheerful clerics grin, not slow,*
> * To gather in fresh dividends.*

He became a churchwarden, edited Kipling, and recanted his former aspersions on Milton. Kathleen Nott has wickedly said: ' He reminds me of a dignified landlady who, without a word, retrieves the tribal ornaments from the cupboard where the guest has hidden them, and puts them back on the mantelpiece.'

Eliot, being an ex-banker and less naïve in his economics, resisted Pound's anti-usury fixation—for once he was penny-wise, not Pound-foolish—and matured into a rugged, if retiring, businessman. Yet he had once been, however briefly, a poet—I refer to the haunting blank verse passages in *The Waste Land*—and if he found the demands of the Goddess too severe, who can blame him? I shall always be grateful to Eliot for having been the only publisher in London with the courage to print my long *White Goddess*. And his rejection of *The Nazarene Gospel Restored* was charming: he explained that he ' would have published it if it had been more drily written.' And I admire Eliot's courageous loyalty to old friends in trouble: he was the prime mover in a protest against the unceremonious treatment accorded to U.S. Traitor Pound when the G.I.'s caught up with him in Italy at the end of the War. Eliot asked me to sign, but I make it a rule not to interfere with the domestic affairs of another nation.

The Four Quartets, which had appeared in the middle of the War, correspond with Wordsworth's *River Duddon* volume, in so far as they were written to reassure Elliot's public that he still had a pen in his hand:

> *O dark dark dark. // They all go into the dark . . .*
> *The captains, merchant bankers, // eminent men of letters . . .*
> *Distinguished civil servants, // chairmen of many*
> *   committees . . .*
> *And dark the Sun and Moon, // and the Almanach de Gotha*
> *And the Stock Exchange Gazette, // the Directory of Directors,*

So here I am, in the middle // way, having had twenty years—
Twenty years largely wasted, // the years of l'entre deux
    guerres—
Trying to learn to use words, // and every attempt . . .
Is a new beginning, // a raid on the inarticulate
With shabby equipment // always deteriorating . . .

I suppose he mentions the two Wars because the unusual passions
they aroused provoked him to write on wholly personal subjects. But
why is he complaining? Who forced him, during the Battle of the
Somme, to attend London tea-parties presided over by boring host-
esses? Or, in after years, to become a chairman of many committees,
and figure in *The Directory of Directors,* instead of serving the Muse?
Does he require our commiseration because his shabby equipment is
always deteriorating and because he wasted twenty years in publishing the books of others instead of writing his own? In the passages I
quote he is true to a boyhood's admiration for Longfellow's *Evange-
line;* but has decided that Longfellow's smooth hexameter coach-
wheels run just a bit too tediously, he shortens and sufflaminates them
to suit the present bumpy age. For my part, I wish that he had
stopped at *The Hollow Men,* his honest and (indeed) heart-breaking
declaration of poetic bankruptcy, to the approved Receiver of poetic
bankruptcy, the Hippopotamus Church.

> *We are the hollow men*
> *We are the stuffed men*
> *Leaning together*
> *Headpiece filled with straw. Alas!*
> *Our dried voices, when*
> *We whisper together*
> *Are quiet and meaningless*
> *As wind in dry grass*
> *Or rats' feet over broken glass*
> *In our dry cellar*
>
> *Shape without form, shade without colour,*
> *Paralysed force, gesture without motion;*
>> For Thine is the Kingdom . . .
>> Life is very long . . .
>> For Thine is the Kingdom . . .

Eliot's introduction to Pound's *Poems* reveals that both based their
a-metrical practices on the example of Laforgue. But he does not explain the need. That Laforgue tried to wriggle out of the strait-jacket
of the French Classical alexandrine seems irrelevant to the case; English has worn no strait-jacket since the Age of Obsequiousness, and
if strait-jackets exist only to be wriggled out of, why did both Pound
and Eliot set such immense store on Pope, admiration for whom Eliot
(in this introduction) makes the test of a truly poetic mind? Am I
being obtuse? At any rate, what I like most about Eliot is that though
one of his two hearts, the poetic one, has died and been given a
separate funeral, in Jewish style (capital J) he continues to visit the
grave wistfully, and lay flowers on it.

I have never met W. H. Auden—and, so far as I recall, have never
written to him more than once. During 1928–9 I was printing books
by hand, and he subscribed to them. I had to suggest that the half-
guinea he paid for Laura Riding's *Love as Love, Death as Death*, gave
him no right to borrow half lines and whole lines from them for in-
sertion in his own verse.

> LAURA RIDING: *The standing stillness,*
> *The from foot-to-foot . . .*
> *Is no real fever . . .*

> W. H. AUDEN: *This gracious greeting,*
> *' Good day. Good luck ',*
> *Is no real meeting . . .*

> LAURA RIDING: *' Yes! ' to you is in the same breath*
> *' No! no! ' to Death.*
> *But such love turns . . . etc.*

> *After we have fictitiousness*
> *Of our excess,*
> *All will be as before*
> *We shall say, love is no more*
> *Than waking, smiling,*
> *Forcing out ' Good morning,'*
> *And, were it more, it were*
> *Fictiousness or nothing.*

W. H. AUDEN: *From yes to no,*
For no is not love; no is no,
And saying yes
Turns love into success . . .
And were this all, love were
But cheek to cheek
And dear to dear.

He is as synthetic as Milton, who borrowed his inspiration in *Paradise Lost* from Browne, the two Fletchers, Davies, Silvester and a host of others. Like Tennyson (whom he has admiringly edited), Auden went to Spain in warlike ardour by a comrade's side; like Tennyson he saw no fighting. But, unlike Tennyson, he played plenty of ping-pong in a hotel at Sitges. Just before World War II he emigrated to the United States, subsequently becoming a U.S. citizen, and there developed his real talent, which is for light verse. His Phi Beta Kappa poem (Harvard, 1946) is a *tour de force:*

Ares at last has quit the field,
The bloodstains on the bushes yield
To seeping showers,
And in their convalescent state
The fractured towns associate
With summer flowers.

Encamped upon the college plain
Raw veterans already train
As freshman forces;
Instructors with sarcastic tongue
Shepherd the battle-weary young
Through basic courses.

Among bewildering appliances
For mastering the arts and sciences
They stroll and run,
And nerves that never flinched at slaughter
Are shot to pieces by the shorter
Poems of Donne. . . .

The cockney rhyme of *slaughter* and *shorter* expresses his contempt of the young fools who allowed themselves to get caught in the War.

There are, by the way, no fighting men among the idols—no successors to Ben Jonson who once 'killed his man in the sight of both
armies'; which is paradoxical in an age that has sentenced every second man to ordeal by battle. Auden's is now the prescribed period
style of the 'fifties, compounded of all the personal styles available;
but he no longer borrows whole lines, as for his first volumes, or even
half-lines. It is a word here, a rhythm there, a rhetorical trope, a
simile, an ingenious rhyme, a classical reference, a metrical arrangement. Auden's zinc-bright influence is even stronger than Yeats's,
Pound's, or Eliot's. He has been saluted as the Picasso of contemporary English poetry; and, indeed, if Auden's verse makes me feel uncomfortable so, I confess, does a Picasso design, however firmly
drawn, when I recognize the source, or sources, of his inspiration—a
fourteenth-century Spanish plate, a wooden mask from the Congo, a
Hittite seal, a Baffinland Eskimo ivory, an Etruscan tomb painting,
a Carthaginian clay figure, an Aztec calendar illustration. 'Ah, yes,'
says his admirers, 'these ignorant savages anticipated him.'

So we come to the last of the modern idols: Dylan Thomas. At
what interval after the death of a young poet is it decent to tell the
truth about him? Despite the splendid orations spoken at his grave,
more eulogistic than any poet has earned since Byron's death at
Missolonghi, was Thomas either a master-poet or a 'great Christian
gentleman'? He himself never pretended to be anything more than a
young dog—witty, naughty, charming, irresponsible, and impenitent.
But he did give his radio-audience what they wanted.

Thomas had all the rich musical eloquence of a South Welshman.
Did anyone ever hear a Welsh choir, either in a concert hall, or a
chapel, or when fortuitously assembled in a motor-bus or railway carriage, sing out of tune? It is a Welsh national characteristic to sing in
tune and be eloquent: just as the Egyptian *fellah* lays a tennis-court
dead flat without the aid of a spirit-level, or the old Majorcan shepherd never misses his mark with a sling-stone. But the Welshman
seldom really cares what the tune is, whether *Marchog Jesu,* or *Saspan
Fach,* or *Roll out the Barrel,* so long as he can sing it as a part-song.

Dylan Thomas was drunk with melody, and what the words were
he cared not. He was eloquent, and what cause he was pleading, he
cared not. He had a rich voice, could put on the *hwyl* like any Rev.
John Jones, B.A., Bangor, albeit in English as spoken in Langham

Place; and, when I listened to him broadcasting, I had to keep a tight hold of myself to avoid being seduced. As when once, in 1916, I listened to a war speech given by Lloyd George to the Honourable Society of Cymrodorion.

I never met Thomas; but when he was sixteen, he sent me from Swansea a batch of his early poems. I wrote back that they were irreproachable, but that he would eventually learn to dislike them. I forget what more I said; but I remember thinking that whereas musical prodigies like Mozart, or mathematical prodigies like William Rowan Hamilton, are not uncommon (and, when they grow up, continue happily as they began), poetic prodigies are monstrous and ill-omened. Young poets stumble and make a thousand clumsy errors, and though one may hope or guess that they will be something in the end, there is only promise, not performance. A sense of poetic protocol develops very slowly indeed. (The sole exceptions are such inspired young women poets as Juana de Asbaje, or Christina Rossetti; but a girl is often a woman when her elder brother is still a child.) Even experts would have been deceived by the virtuosity of Dylan Thomas's conventional, and wholly artificial, early poems.

In order to conceal this defect in sincerity, he learned to introduce a distractive element. He kept musical control of the reader without troubling about the sense. I do not mean that he aimed deliberately off-target, as the later Yeats did. Thomas seems to have decided that there was no need to aim at all, so long as the explosion sounded loud enough. The fumes of cordite would drift across the target and a confederate in the butts would signal bull after bull. Nevertheless, as in double-talk, a central thread of something like sense makes the incrustations of nonsense more acceptable. Listeners, as opposed to readers, are easily convinced, in such cases, that they are obtuse and slow to follow the workings of the interlocutor's mind, especially when the musical content is so rich. But professionally-minded English poets ban double-talk, except in satire, and insist that every poem must make prose sense as well as poetic sense on one or more levels. The common report that most of Thomas's poems came out of the beer barrel cannot be accepted. It is true that he drank a great deal of beer, and that beer is a splendid drink before one takes one's place in a male voice choir; but the poems show every sign of an alert and sober intelligence. The following typical stanza is nonsense, but

Dylan's golden voice could persuade his listeners that he was divulging ineffable secrets:

> *If my head hurt a hair's foot*
> *Pack back the downed bone. If the unpricked ball of my breath*
> *Bump on a spout let the bubbles jump out.*
> *Sooner drop with the worm of the ropes round my throat*
> *Than bully ill love in the clouted scene.*[2]

Stephen Spender, who often prognosticates next year's poetic skirt-length or waist-line long before the autumn collections, wrote of Thomas in 1946:

> He is a poet who commands the admiration of all [*sic*] contemporary poets. He has influenced a number of writers who see in him an alternative to the intellectual [*sic*] writing of Auden. Of the

---

[2] When I delivered this lecture, I offered a £1 note to anyone who could make sense of these lines. The ingenious Mr M. J. C. Hodgart of Pembroke, a member of the Cambridge English Faculty, has since come forward to claim the award. He suggests that the child about to be born is here addressing his mother. The child cries out that if he is to cause her any pain by his birth, let him not be born at all. 'If I were to hurt so much as a hair of your head in process of birth push my downy, but bony, head back into the womb.' . . . Birth (Mr Hodgart adds) is represented here as a violent movement like a bouncing ball; and the child's breath before birth is compared to an unpricked bubble. Therefore: 'If even this soft bubble of breath should hurt you by bouncing on your spouting blood, prick it and let my life run out in bubbles.' And: 'I would sooner be born hanged with my navel-string coiled around my throat than bully you when I appear on a scene made wretched by baby-clouts, or clouts on the head.'
There are flaws in this argument. The hair's foot, misleadingly identical in sound to *hare's* foot, is not a hair's *root*. Also, the physical situation is blurred by the apparent contact of the baby's downy head with the mother's hairy one, and by the description of the navel-string as 'the worm of the ropes'—why 'ropes' in the plural? And by the metaphor of an unpunctured ball bouncing on the top of a spout—as in pleasure fountains; how the bubble of breath could bounce on the flow of lochial blood is not easy to see (blood is not mentioned in the poem). And why should the unpricked bubble become 'bubbles'? And is the infant experienced or ignorant? If ignorant, how can it anticipate baby-clouts, and balls bouncing on fountains? If experienced, how can it make so absurd a suggestion as that the mother should push its head back again to relieve her labour pains? And if it is so considerate and saintly as Mr Hodgart suggests, why should it ever turn bully?
I have a conscience about paying my debts, but though Mr Hodgart may have identified the thin thread of sense on which the enormous and disgusting hyperboles of the child's address are strung, this is not enough: the five lines taken as a whole remain nonsensical.

poets under forty-five, he is perhaps the only one capable of exercising a literary influence as great as that of Auden.

Yeats, Pound, Eliot, Auden, and Thomas are credited with having delivered English poetry from the shackles of the past. And the people said: ' These be thy gods, O Israel, which brought thee up out of the land of Egypt! '

Need I also dwell on the lesser idols now slowly mouldering: on sick, muddle-headed, sex-mad D. H. Lawrence who wrote sketches for poems, but nothing more; on poor, tortured Gerard Manley Hopkins?

Despite the great spate of commercial jazz, there has always been a small, clear stream of living jazz music; despite the great outpouring of abstract or semi-abstract art (the more abstract, the more imitative and academic) there has likewise been a thin trickle of admirable painting and sculpture. The same is true of poetry. To take only the United States: Robert Frost, E. E. Cummings, John Crowe Ransom, Laura Riding, have all written living poems in their time. I refrain from invidiously singling out their English counterparts still alive, who are no fewer in number. But I do find it remarkable that the extraordinary five years of Siegfried Sassoon's poetic efflorescence (1917–21) should be utterly forgotten now. For the rest it will be enough to say that William Davies, though at times his simplicity degenerated into artfulness, put his near-contemporary Yeats to shame; and that Norman Cameron, who died last year within a month or two of Thomas, and worked in the same office for a while, was indisputably the truer poet; and that so was Alun Lewis, killed during the Second World War.

This is Alun Lewis writing from the Welch Regiment in Burma to his Muse in Wales:

> . . . My longing is more and more for one thing only, integrity, and I discount the other qualities in people ruthlessly if they lack that fundamental sincerity and wholeness.

> . . . And although I'm more engrossed with the *single* poetic theme of Life and Death, for there doesn't seem to be any question more directly relevant than this one, of what survives of all the beloved, I find myself quite unable to express at once the passion of Love, the coldness of Death (Death is cold), or the fire that beats

against resignation, ' acceptance '. Acceptance seems so spiritless, protest so vain. In between the two I live.

With this quotation, I make my bow, and thank you for your continued patience. If, in the course of these lectures, I have said anything out of order, pray forgive me doubly; I am no longer a stranger here.

VARIOUS ESSAYS ON POETRY

MOTHER GOOSE'S LOST GOSLINGS

Mother Goose is famous for her nursery rhymes, but not many of them were composed as such. Sometimes what appears to be nonsense is no more than long out-of-date topical satire; sometimes the nonsense element has been added later, either because the original words were garbled or forgotten, or because their meaning had to be suppressed for political or moral reasons. Two or three hundred years of oral tradition in the nursery had played havoc with the texts before Haliwell collected and printed them in 1846.

Deliberately nonsensical rhymes for children first appeared in the eighteenth century, as a reaction against the over-decorous verse of the over-sane Augustan Age, and even these were a fairly restrained sort of nonsense, based on puns and manifest self-contradiction. It was not until the time of Edward Lear and Lewis Carroll that nonsense of brilliant inconsequence studded with newly invented words came to be composed. Typical of the eighteenth century is:

> There was a man of London Town
> And he was wondrous wise:
> He jumped into a quickset hedge
> And scratched out both his eyes.
> But when he saw his eyes were out,
> With all his might and main
> He jumped into another bush
> And scratched them in again.

The metre supplies the date. Goldsmith used it in his satire on Madame Mary Blaize. In her youth,

> *Her love was sought, I do aver,*
> *   By twenty beaux or more;*
> *The King himself has followed her—*
> *   When she has walked before.*

Also typically eighteenth-century in their restraint are:

> *The man of the wilderness asked of me:*
> *' How many strawberries grow in the sea? '*
> *I answered him as I thought good:*
> *' As many red herrings as grow in the wood.'*

and:

> *On Paul's Cathedral grows a tree*
> *As full of apples as can be.*
> *The little boys of London Town,*
> *They come with hooks to pull them down;*
> *Then they run from hedge to hedge*
> *Until they come to London Bridge.*

But these must be distinguished from such mildly satiric rhymes as *The Grand Old Duke of York* and *Little Jack Horner.*

> *The Grand Old Duke of York,*
> *   He had ten thousand men.*
> *He marched them up to the top of the hill*
> *   And he marched them down again.*
>
> *And when they were up, they were up,*
> *   And when they were down, they were down,*
> *And when they were only half-way up*
> *   They were neither up nor down.*

H.R.H. Frederick Augustus, Duke of York—and incidentally Bishop of Osnaburg since infancy—commanded the British Army in Flanders successfully enough from 1793 to 1795, and though he failed in the Helder expedition of 1799, that was not altogether his fault. In 1809 he was obliged by the Whig Opposition to resign his appointment as Commander-in-Chief of the Forces because his mistress, the notorious Mary Anne Clarke, had taken bribes to secure promotion for Army Officers. The rhyme is an undeserved Whig libel on his military capacity. It may have been composed to offset the thanks voted him by both Houses of Parliament at the conclusion of the Napoleonic Wars.

A companion piece has survived only in two very nonsensical versions. It runs:

> *King William was King James's son*
> *And many a gallant race did run,*
> *And on his breast he carried a star*
> *And that's the way to the pickle-jar!*

or—I owe this one to Miss Alice R. Benson, who recorded it in Virginia:

> *King William was King James's son*
> *By the royal race he run:*
> *Upon his breast he wore a star*
> *That points the way to the Governor's door.*
>
> *Go choose your east, go choose your west,*
> *Go choose the one that you love best;*
> *And if she will not take your part,*
> *Go choose another with all your heart.*
>
> *Down on this carpet you must kneel,*
> *As sure as the grass grows in the field.*

The star and the name William suggest the Sailor King William IV, sometimes called ' King Tarry-Breeks ', who was King George III's son and famed for his amours and drinking. The last line of the first version has originally, I think, been borrowed from Hogg's: ' That's the way for Billy and me.' The lines which explain ' many a gallant race ' seem to have been variously censored by parents or nurses; but the Virginian version develops the love interest in the second stanza. The original may have run:

> *Prince William was King George's son*
> *And many a gallant race did run.*
> *For on his breast he carried a star—*
> *That was the way of Billy the Tar.*
>
> *For all the ladies upon the shore*
> *It shone the way to the Governor's door,*

And down on the carpet they must kneel
As sure as the grass grows in the field.

Go sail to east, go sail to west,
Go choose the lass that you love best,
And if she will not play the part,
Go choose another with all your heart.

Little Jack Horner has been quoted as another Whig satire, with
' Jack ' substituted for ' Frank ':

> *Little Jack Horner*
> *Sat in a corner*
> *　Eating his Christmas pie.*
> *He put in his thumb*
> *And pulled out a plum*
> *　And said: ' What a good boy am I! '*

Francis Horner, Scottish economist and member of Parliament during the Napoleonic Wars, was one of the few thoroughly honest
statesmen of his day; he even refused a Treasury secretaryship in
1811 because he could not afford to live on the salary. In 1810 he
had been secretary to the Parliamentary Committee which investi-
gated inflation and persuaded the House to check the issue of paper-
currency unsupported by bullion. Horner exercised a moral as well
as an intellectual influence on his fellow-members, which galled the
Whig Opposition. A ' plum ' in the slang of the time was £100,000;
it appeared even in such sober reports as: ' The revenue is about
£90 plum, to be increased by funding.' But here critical caution is
needed. Though the Whigs may have mischievously applied the
rhyme to Horner, as an accusation that he had secretly enriched himself by bribes from the City, while protesting his incorruptibility, it
was already at least a century old. Henry Carey quotes it in his
Namby Pamby satire on Ambrose Phillips in 1725. The Wiltshire
Horners were a rich family who had profited from Henry VIII's
dissolution of the monasteries, and seem to have been notorious for
their self-righteousness.[1]

---

[1] I have to thank Peter and Iona Opie, authors of the *Oxford Dictionary of
Nursery Rhymes*, for putting me right on this point.

The nearest to deliberate nonsense written in the seventeenth century had been the Bedlamite verse put in the mouth of ' Poor Tom ' or his sweetheart ' Merry Mad Maudlen '; but this was no more than wild fancy, not in the least Jabberwocky, nor even self-contradictory in the eighteenth-century style.

Mad Maudlen's song:

> *My staff hath murdered Gyants,*
> *My Bag a long Knife carries*
> *To cut Mince-pyes from Children's thighs*
> *With which I feast the Fairies,*

is of the same order of extravagance as the contemporary dancing song:

> *If all the world were paper*
> *If all the seas were ink,*
> *If all the trees were bread and cheese,*
> *What would we do for drink?*
>
> *If all the vessels ran-a*
> *And none but had a crack,*
> *If Spanish apes ate all the grapes*
> *What would we do for sack?*

' If all the world were paper, if all the seas were ink ' (originally a Rabbinic formula) points to the Inns of Court as the place of composition; the law-students were weary of quill work and wanted to drink and dance.

Another fanciful rhyme, of about the same date, is:

> *Four and twenty tailors*
> *Went to catch a snail,*
> *Even the bravest of them*
> *Durst not touch her tail—*
>
> *She stuck out her horns*
> *Like a little Kyloe cow.*
> *Run, tailors, run*
> *Or she'll get you all ere now.*

This is a simple popular satire on the supposed cowardice of tailors; Kyloe lies in Northumberland. As for:

> *There were three cooks of Colnbrook.*
> *And they fell out with our cook:*
> *It was but for a pudding he took*
> *From those three cooks of Colnbrook—*

I should date this to the Civil Wars. Colnbrook in Buckinghamshire was far too small a place to have supported so many cooks except for a week or two in November 1642; then the Royalist Army encamped there while Charles I negotiated with Parliament. The tune is a bugle-call, which suggests that the cooks were regimental ones stealing from one another in the old Army tradition. It is perhaps the earliest of a long series, mostly mid-Victorian, which now includes the officers' mess-call:

> *Officers' wives have puddings and pies,*
> *But soldiers' wives have skilly;*

the no-parade call:

> *Hooray, hooray, hooray,*
> *There's no parade today!*
> *The Colonel's got a belly ache*
> *And the Adjutant's gone away.*

and the post-call, which ends:

> *A   postcard   from   your   mother-in-law*
> *And a letter from Lousy Lou.*

The jingle about Little Miss Muffet and the spider can safely be dated to the second half of the seventeenth century. One Dr Muffet wrote the treatise *A Theatre of Insects* which, in 1658, was bound up with the Rev. E. Topsell's *History of Four-footed Beasts and Serpents*. In it Muffet eulogized the Spider as follows:

> The skin of it is so soft, smooth, polished and neat that she precedes the softest skin'd Mayds and the daintiest and most beautiful Strumpets. She hath fingers that the most gallant Virgins desire to have theirs like them, long, slender, round, of exact feel, that there is no man, nor any creature, that can compare with her.

Dr Muffet (as W. S. Bristowe, the arachnologist, has pointed out)
had a daughter named Patience who probably did not share her
father's entomological enthusiasms; but the occasion of the rhyme
may have been the comical incident recorded in Doctor Muffet's
diary, when a swarm of wasps spoilt his family picnic in Epping
Forest.

Another satiric rhyme:

> *I do not like thee, Dr Fell.*
> *The reason why I cannot tell,*
> *But this I know, I know full well,*
> *I do not like thee, Dr Fell.*

is known to have been written in 1678 by Thomas Brown of Christ
Church, Oxford. Brown merely translated Martial's epigram:

> *Non amo te, Sabidi, nec possum dicere quare . . .*

changing Sabidius's name to that of Dr Fell, then Bishop of Oxford
and the energetic Dean of Brown's own College. Dr Fell is best remembered now as the designer of the Fell type, one of the best
English founts, and for having, albeit reluctantly, expelled the philosopher Locke from Oxford.

The rhyme *Goosey-goosey-gander,* made nonsensical only by its
corruptions, was coined, I suspect, at the same mint. That its first
mention in print is 1816 signifies nothing; 'chamber' had been
obsolete in the sense of 'room' for a hundred years. Though recalling five lines of *The Image of Hypocrisy,* an anti-clerical poem in
Skeltonic verse written about 1535:

> *Doctor Bullatus*
> *Will brabble and prate thus:*
> *How Doctor Pomander*
> *As wise as a gander*
> *Wots not where to wander,*

Goosey-goosey-gander should be read as a mocking chorus sung
in 1689 by anti-Papal undergraduates to bait the Rev. Henry Gandy,
an Oxford University Proctor who had remained loyal to the deposed
King James II. 'Goosey', apparently suggested by 'Gandy', had
meant 'stupid' since the time of Chaucer. After holding out for a
year, Gandy was deprived of his Oriel fellowship for refusing to

take the oath of allegiance to William III. (In 1716 he became one of the Rev. Jeremy Collier's private creation of non-juror Jacobite bishops.) The 'old man who would not say his prayers' must be Gandy himself, and the prayers, those that he refused to offer for King William and Queen Mary; but since he was no more than forty at the time of his deprivation 'old man' is perhaps a nursery simplification of 'proctor', which makes a pleasant alliteration with 'prayers'. For 'my Lady' we should read 'thy Lady'. It is not clear, however, whether he is here accused of intrigue—if he had a powerful patroness; or of immorality—Oxford fellows were not allowed to marry and usually kept mistresses in disreputable St Ebbe's; or of secret Romanizing—if 'thy Lady' refers to the Virgin Mary. Probably the charge is immorality, since in those days a gander meant a lecherous fellow and the 'gander-month' was the month of a woman's lying-in when the husband considered himself justified in illicit love-making. It is the sort of charge that undergraduates would delight in bringing against their proctor whose main business it was to keep them out of taverns and brothels. On the other hand, 'thy Lady's chamber' may be St Mary's Hall, then an undergraduate lodging house adjoining Oriel, now the 'Stimmery Quadrangle' of the College and adorned with Cecil Rhodes' statue. The original perhaps ran:

> *Gandy, Goosey-Gander,*
> *Whither dost thou wander?*
> *Upstairs, or downstairs,*
> *Or in thy Lady's chamber?*
>
> *If e'er we catch a proctor*
> *That will not say his prayers,*
> *We'll take him by his long legs*
> *And fling him downstairs.*

The Lion and the Unicorn can be dated by its metre to half a century earlier, and goes to the popular ballad-tune of *Cuckolds all a-row*.

> *The Lion and the Unicorn*
> *Were fighting for the Crown;*
> *The Lion beat the Unicorn*
> *All round the town—*

> *Some gave them white bread,*
> *Some gave them brown,*
> *Some gave them good plum cake*
> *And drummed them out of town.*

Commentators have hitherto been content to point out that the Lion and the Unicorn, the supporters of the Royal Arms of England and Scotland, are turned rampant towards each other as if contending for the Crown. But the Lion heraldically represents England; and the Unicorn, Scotland; and these beasts did fight fiercely for the Crown after the execution of Charles I in 1649. What happened was that the Scots then proclaimed Charles II as King not only of Scotland but of England, though England was now a Commonwealth. When Cromwell's hands were free of other business he marched against Charles and beat him at Dunbar on September 3, 1650. But the victory did not prove decisive: in the New Year Charles was crowned at Scone, and in April moved south at the head of another Scottish army. On September 3, 1651, Cromwell met him again at Worcester and it was at this town that the Lion beat the Unicorn so unmercifully. Charles fled in disguise to the Continent, and his Restoration nine years later doubtless accounts for the nonsensical way in which the ballad now ends. I amend it as follows, remembering the pride of the New Model Army in their buff-coloured uniforms and their scorn of the gay Highland plaids.

> *The Lion and the Unicorn*
> *Were fighting for the Crown;*
> *The Lion met the Unicorn*
> *Nigh Worcester Town—*
> *One Clad in Hyland Plaid,*
> *One Clad in Brown—*
> *Roll Prince Charlie in the Mire*
> *And Drub him out of Town!*

The metre of:

> *Hark, hark, the dogs do bark*
> *The beggars are coming to Town;*
> *Some in rags and some in jags*
> *And some in a velvet gown,*

also points to seventeenth-century England. Here again there is no nonsense, only satire. At the Restoration, survivors of ruined Cavalier families swarmed to Court to petition rewards for their loyalty and compensation for their losses; some of them almost in rags. With them, however, came many petitioners who had kept on good terms with Cromwell and were as well off as before the Civil Wars, which accounts for the ' velvet gown '. It is from this rhyme that the last four lines of the familiar version of *The Lion and the Unicorn* seem to have been borrowed, to replace the merciless Roundhead ones; but further softened by the substitution of ' good plum cake ' for ' a good horse-whip '.

There is no mystery about how these political and topical rhymes came to be accepted among Mother Goose's goslings. Nursemaids and parents will sing the first thing that comes into their heads, to keep children amused or send them to sleep. I remember my old nurse, about the year 1898, crooning to the tune of *Quibbs was a Quaker:*

> *Our dear little Bobby,*
> *Our wide-awake Bobby,*
> *Our dear little Bobby,*
> *Has turned out the Whigs.*

She must have been in her 'teens when Sir Robert Peel, who had founded the Conservative Party in 1831, was returned to power ten years later amid great popular enthusiasm. The particular Whigs, celebrated in the song, whom he turned out were the Whig Ladies of the Bedchamber; he considered them to have an injurious effect on young Queen Victoria's politics. But I knew nothing of this at the time. And when my married daughter in New Zealand croons to her children as she baths them:

> *Whiter than the snow,*
> *Whiter than the snow!*
> *Wash me in the water*
> *Where you washed your dirty daughter*
> *And I shall be whiter than the snow.*

they are certainly unaware that this is a parody of a Salvation Army hymn which I picked up in the trenches in World War I and used to sing to their mother on similar occasions. The fourth line is really:

> *Where the Lamb was led to slaughter.*

Yankee Doodle entered the English nursery at the conclusion of the American War of Independence. It had long been used to sing Revolutionary children to sleep, being almost the only song that the American Army knew. But the English had a scurrilous parody, composed by the unfortunate Major André whom Washington hanged as a spy, and it was this that they brought back to Europe with them.

Several ' Mother Goose ' rhymes of Northern origin have been altered for the benefit of Southern children who would not have understood them otherwise. For example, the painstakingly nonsensical:

> *There was a man and he had naught,*
> *Yet robbers came to rob him.*
> *He climbed up to a chimney pot*
> *And then they thought they had him . . .*

can easily be returned to the late eighteenth-century Yorkshire original:

> *There was a man and he had nowt,*
> *He climbed up by a gutter-spout*
> *He climbed up by a gutter-spout*
> *And there they thowt to nob him. . . .*

Then there is the famous rhyme:

> *How many miles to Babylon?*
> *Threescore miles and ten!*
> *Can I get there by candlelight?*
> *Yes, and back again.*
> *If your feet be nimble and light*
> *You can get there by candlelight.*

This is revealed as eighteenth-century Scottish—and incidentally robbed of all its magic—when one recognizes *Babylon* as *Baby Land,*

and restores the whimsical comment on the threescore and ten years which separate childhood from second childhood.

> *Hoo mony miles tae Babby Lond?*
> *Three scair miles an' ten.*
> *Sall I win yon by condle-licht?*
> *Ay, and hame agen.*
> *Gin your feet be nimble and licht*
> *Ye sall be hame before the nicht.*

Once the original date and provenience have been fixed for a lost poem that has fallen into the rag-bag of nonsense, and the text has been amended accordingly, the strangest things may shine out. For example:

> *Two grey kits and the grey kits' mother*
> *All went over the bridge together.*
> *The bridge broke down and they all fell in—*
> *' The rats go with you! ' says Tom Boleyn.*

The rhymes ' mother ' and ' together ' point to a Scottish or Northern English origin, though the poem has survived only in the United States. Tom Boleyn, or Tomalyn, is easily recognized as Thom o' Lin or Tomalyn, a mysterious popular hero who has given his name to a country dance, first recorded in 1549; and is shown in the ballad of *Young Tam Lin,* first recorded in 1558, to have been connected with the British witch cult. The grey kits and their mother were witches—two witches and their queen, or a witch and her familiars. Grey or ' brinded ' was the favourite colour of witch cats, as Shakespeare mentions in *Macbeth* and *King Lear.* ' The rats ' seems to be a worn-down form of ' Auld Scratch ', or ' Auld Scrat ', the Devil. Witches were made powerless by being immersed in running water. So the rhyme is a sixteenth- or seventeenth-century charm against witches:

> *Twa grey kits and the grey kits' midder*
> *A' went ower the brigg togidder.*
> *The brigg brak doon and they tummelled in.*
> *' Auld Scrat gae wi' ye! ' says Tam o' Lin.*

Then again:

> *Grey goose and gander,*
> *Waft your wings together*
> *And carry the good king's daughter*
> *Over the one-strand river.*

In a recent London newspaper correspondence about its sense, the
only solution offered was that *strand* did not mean *thread,* but *shore,*
and that the ' one-strand river ' was the ocean. This was correct up
to a point, but did not explain either the geese or the king's daughter,
which were dismissed as charming fancies.

The metre cannot be later than the middle sixteenth century and,
to judge by the rhymes ' together ' and ' river ', the poem comes
from Scotland or the Scottish Border. The recovery of the original
text is perhaps best shown in three stages of emendation.

FIRST STAGE: *Grey goose and gander,*
> *Waft your wings togidder,*
> *And carry the gude King's dochter*
> *Owre the ane-strand river.*

No: in the ballad-poetry of Scotland and the Border *gander* would
never have rhymed with *dochter;* also *gander* was usually spelt *ganer.*
Daughter has evidently been suggested by the ' King of Spain's daughter ' in another of Mother Goose's rhymes, or by the ' King's daughter
of Norraway ' in the *Ballad of Sir Patrick Spens.* The rhyme needed
is *banner,* or *baner* as it was then spelt.

SECOND STAGE: *Grey goose and ganer,*
> *Waft your wings togidder*
> *And carry the gude King's baner*
> *Owre the ane-strand river.*

No: *waft* means ' blow gently ' and is likely to be a Southern English modification of the vigorous Northern *wap,* which is what wild
geese in flight do with their wings. And the heavy alliteration of the
other lines is missing in the third, which suggests that *carry* has been
substituted for *bear ye.* But why should wild geese in their summer
flight across the cold northern ocean to their breeding grounds in the
Arctic Circle, or near it, be asked to carry a King's banner?

Surely, because a banner goes ahead of the king's army, and be-

cause the wild geese in British folklore are the *Cwm Annwm,* or
Hounds of Hell, a ghostly pack used by the Wild Hunter—Arawn,
Bran (hence the names ' *Brant*-goose ' and, by metathesis, ' *Barn*acle-
goose '), Herne, Gwyn, Gabriel, or what you will—when he con-
ducts the souls of kings and heroes (and, in later popular tradition,
the souls of unbaptized children or suicides or excommunicated
heretics) to the pre-Christian Otherworld at the back of the North
Wind. In Scotland he was known as Arthur, or ' Arthur of the
Bower ', and to die was to ' rest in Arthur's bosom '. The cry of the
barnacle-goose is almost indistinguishable from the music of a pack
of hounds on a hot scent. To quote the *Whitby Glossary* (1876):

> *Gabriel Hounds:* the flocks of wild-geese high in the air migrat-
> ing southward in the twilight evenings of autumn, their cry being
> more audible than the assemblage is visible. As the foreboders of
> evil, people close their ears and cover their eyes until the phalanx
> has passed over.

The Hounds of Hell are also variously known as ' Yeth Hounds ',
' Wish Hounds ', ' Yell Hounds ', ' Gabriel Ratchets ', ' Gobble-
ratches ' and so on. Hounds and Wild Hunter are carved in stone
outside the church door of Stoke Gabriel in Devon. The ' ane-strand
river ' is, in fact, the ocean of Death, across which no traveller can
hope to return.

   Then at what time in the sixteenth century did a Royal Scottish
banner need to be conveyed by wild geese across the one-strand
river? The history books supply only one answer. On September 9,
1513, near Flodden Edge, in battle with the Earl of Surrey, James
IV was killed fighting at the head of almost the entire chivalry of
Scotland. So dreadful was the carnage dealt by the English ' brown
bills ' that the royal corpse was not found for some days after; and
when finally it was recognized by a glove and plaid, it could not be
given Christian burial because the Pope had excommunicated James
for his unprovoked attack on his ' brother ', King Henry VIII of
England. There remained only a single refuge for the unhoused
soul: the ancient pagan paradise of his royal ancestors.[2] Indeed, he

---

[2] On November 29, 1513, the Pope, at King Henry's request, gave permission
for James's body to be buried with regal honours in St Paul's Cathedral. But,
as we read in Stow's *Survey of London:*

> . . . after the battle the body of the said king being found, was enclosed
> in lead, and conveyed from thence to London, and so to the monastery

had no choice; for as a Scottish rhyme says:

> *The King o' Scots wi' a' his power*
> *Canna stop Arthur o' the Bower.*

But why ' grey goose '? Because the grey goose is also known as the ' lag ' from its habit of lagging behind when the barnacle-goose has migrated to its breeding grounds in Spitsbergen, and other varieties have flown to Iceland, Greenland, and Lapland. In early September the ' lag ' would be the only wild goose likely to be encountered by a poet in the neighbourhood of Flodden.

FINAL STAGE: *Grey goose and ganer,*
> *Wap your wings togidder*
> *And bear ye the gude King's baner*
> *Owre the ane-strand river.*

Gif ye wad ask me quhy this sang was made and quhilk was his maker, I answer: Ye man understond that whenas our brave King Jamie iiii was slaine fechting dughtely at the heid of his grand battaile of Skottishe lairds and knichtis, on the morowe ane auld menstorall fortuned to come be fflodden hylls and Brankstone Muir quhair lay the lykis of the foresaid King and his deid lairds and knichtis, all manglit in peses and abandonat starke nakid amang the wods and scrogs. Quhairat he made meikle dule that the sowl of King Jamie, and the sowlis of them that holp him, being excomminicat by the Pope of Rome, micht na be receivit intil the Paradise of our swete Saviour Jesu Crist. Bot espying ane parcel of grey geese quhilk swom upon a water nere to hand (as fouls slow to flee after ther kin to the heich court and bower and septemtrionall tilt-yard of him quhilk men call Arthur) this same auld menstorall waefully strook the stringis of his harp and, being inspirit of the Muse Calliope, made him the sang quhairof I tell yow.

---

of Shene in Surrey, where it remained for a time, in what order I am not certain; but since the dissolution of that house, in the reign of Edward VI . . . I have been shown the same body so lapped in lead, close to the head and body, thrown into a waste room amongst the old timber, lead, and other rubble. Since the which time workmen there, for their foolish pleasure, hewed off his head; and Launcelot Young glazier to her majesty, feeling a sweet savour to come from thence, and seeing the same dried from all moisture, and yet the form remaining, with the hair of the head and beard red, brought it to London to his house in Wood street, where for a time he kept it for the sweetness, but in the end caused the sexton of that church [St Michael's, Wood Street] to bury it amongst other bones taken out of their charnel. . . .

THE OLD BLACK COW

Pawb yn llosgwrn ei henfon, 'every man to the tail of his cow' as the Welsh say, and the cow whose tail Professor Gwyn Williams[1] follows is the old black bardic Llywiadwr which gives whey instead of milk: not shining white Olwen, 'she of the white track', known in Ireland as the Glas Gabnach. This Olwen was a moon-cow and once yielded creamy milk in such rivers that it formed the Milky Way.

I was introduced to Welsh poetry nearly fifty years ago, when my father became an enthusiastic pan-Celt; and, this noun being new to Merioneth where we lived, he had a famous argument with Mr Postoffice-Griffiths as to whether it would count as one word in a telegram, or cost a half-penny more as two words. Mr Postoffice-Griffiths finally conceded the point: 'Very well, sir, one half-penny it shall be: on the analogy of a pancake I shouldn't wonder.' To our house came numerous Welsh bards, including Ceiriog ('the Welsh Wordsworth') whose non-bardic name I forget, and who was a stationmaster on the Cambrian Railway; also gentle Canon Owen Edwards, whose bardic name I forget; and the formidable, booming Arch-Druid Dyfed himself. It amused Canon Edwards to teach me the ninety-odd rules for writing the bardic *englyn,* which is to the Welsh what the *tanka* is to the Japanese; and in 1906 my father took me to the Carnarvon Eisteddfod where I watched his friends (dressed up in antique druidic robes, with Sunday-go-to-meeting boots and trouser-legs showing underneath, and bowler hats on their heads against the soft summer rain) assemble for the mock-antique opening ceremony.

But by then I was reading the *Mabinogion,* in Lady Charlotte

---

[1] *An Introduction to Welsh Poetry from the Beginnings of the Sixteenth Century,* by Gwyn Williams. Faber, 25s.

Guest's translation; and an inspired fishmonger from Criccieth had brought its wonders to life. He took me up into the hills and pointed out, on the enormous panorama of Merioneth and Carnarvon stretched before us, by what road a King of Dyfed once pursued the wizard Gwydion in an attempt to recover his pigs; and where the refugees fled from the drowned *cantrevs* of Gwynedd in the days of Prince Seithenyn; and, turning about, showed me the distant knoll of Mur-y-Castell, the scene of Llew Llaw's murder by the treacherous Flower-goddess Blodeuwedd. So Welsh poetry for me now meant the *Mabinogion,* not the Eisteddfod contest for the Chair; though, as I knew from Canon Edwards, *eisteddfod* contests were of very ancient origin, and *englynion* in a primitive form dated back to the Battle of Catraeth—fought as long ago as 565 B.C., and celebrated by Aneirin in his *Gododdin,* a Cymric poem not unlike the *Chanson de Roland.*

It is not generally known that the Cymry were once as much foreigners in Wales as the hated Saxons who followed them. Soon after the Romans decamped, an army of adventurers from Kirkcudbright and Wigtown invaded North Wales under King Cunedda and, linking up with their Brythonic kinsmen in mid-Wales, imposed a barbarous aristocracy on the Goidelic and pre-Celtic peoples who then occupied the country. The Goidels were Aryans, like the Cymry, but being in numerical inferiority to the pre-Celtic tribes, had been converted to their matrilincal culture and accepted institutions which the battle-scarred Cymry rejected with scorn. Presently the Cymric kings, still behaving as foreigners, became Christianized, and the master-poets of the old religion—tellers of the earliest *Mabinogion* tales—were driven from their seats of learning, replaced by ecclesiastical bards of inferior education and powers, and forced to become wandering minstrels, or *kerddorion.*

Professor Williams is referring to the effects of this literary revolution when he writes:

> In Wales, to say that a man is a poet immediately induces an attitude of respect for him . . .

and goes on to explain:

> Most of the poetry of the present century has been written by Nonconformist ministers and University professors.

This respectability he traces to Hywel the Good, a tenth-century King of North Wales who claimed descent from Cynedda, and whose laws regulated Welsh society before the coming of the Normans:

> Poets ranked high in the civil service of the Welsh kings. According to the laws of Hywel Dda, a poet became a *penkerdd,* or chief poet, when he won a chair, that is a seat in the immediate entourage of the king or prince. In the hall he then sat next but one to the *edling,* or heir to the throne, the priest sitting between them.

But on reaching down a dusty copy of *Cyvreithiau Hywel Dda*— ' how *do* you manage for books in Majorca, Mr Graves? '—from my legal shelf, I find that Professor Williams has not been quite accurate. Hywel Dda himself seems to have had little respect for poetry, since in the earliest version of the *Cyvreithiau* (Peniardd MS. 28) the *penkerdd* is not mentioned as having any place at court, and a version called the Demetian Code denies his right to one. Moreover, in the later Venedotian Code, the seat allotted him carries less honour than those of such minor functionaries as chaplain, steward, chief falconer, chief groom and page of the chamber; his worth is six score and six kine—not above that of the porter and the queen's candle-bearer.

In Ireland, where Christianity was not forcibly imposed on the Courts, and the master-poet, who was required to attend a twelve-year university course in the arts and sciences, exercised corresponding power, the Welsh bard would have been derided as an unqualified practitioner—and, indeed, that is the meaning of ' bard ' in Irish. He had served only a short apprenticeship and, as the Anomalous Laws suggest (Book iv, 2, p. 397) have appointed directly by the king—for his morals rather than his poetic qualities. He held his chair on the understanding that he praised God Almighty and his lord at set times, in set metres, in set diction, and that he avoided all ' untruth '—meaning any exercise of the imagination that would puzzle the Chief of the Household's mead-sodden brain or bring a frown to the mutton-gorged chaplain's brow. Poetry was defined for him as: ' grammatically accurate expressions, clothed in exalted diction, beautified with becoming and approved epithets, signifying praise of good, dispraise of evil.' He might also, as a dispensation, write poems proper to the *teulwr,* or poet of the second category (namely gnomic stanzas, upright and stereotyped amatory verse, and rhymed lives of the saints), but nothing else. He never ceased to be under the strict moral control of the Chaplain and Chief of the Household, and could be fined or imprisoned for satire, parody or mimicry; for speaking disrespectfully of religion; for dicing in taverns; for quarrelsomeness; or for suggesting that any woman in Wales would ever, under any circumstances, behave with impropriety. His use of mythology was restricted to the ' Triads of Wales ', a dry *memoria technica,* already meaningless, of the ancient pre-Cymric tales which had been banned by the Church as ' untruths '. Thus a *penkerdd* might praise his prince as having ' the might of Aergwl, the disposition of Alexander, the strength of Alun, the energy of Beli, the sword-stroke of Peredur, and the courtesy of Medrod '— without in the least knowing who these personages were. The Irish master-poet, on the other hand, was required to know three hundred and fifty ancient tales, each of them a night's entertainment, and could recite any one of them correctly at a moment's notice.

Professor Williams, while dwelling proudly on the official bards of Wales, has no word of praise for the *kerddorion,* the descendants of the dispossessed pre-Cymric master-poets, from whom royal favour continued to be withheld—and who managed to preserve a few of the old tales, despite all efforts to suppress them; yet one *kerddor,* Geoffrey of Monmouth's ' Bledhericus ', or Bleiddriw, introduced the tales to the Norman-French *trovères,* thus setting a fashion of Arthurian romance throughout Western Europe. And it was these same outcasts—rather than, a Professor Williams would like to think, the *teuluwr*—whose obstinate adherence to their ancient poetic principles brought about the fourteenth-century renascence in Welsh poetry. When Professor Williams briefly mentions the *Preiddeu Annwfn,* ' The Spoils of Tartarus ', because of a reference to King Arthur's harrowing of Hell, he allows his readers to suppose that it is official verse, rather than a poem of ' untruth '—a biting satire by a *kerddor,* who called himself Gwion Bach of Llanfihangel, on the ignorance, cowardice and boastfulness of the official bards.

This would pass as old-fashioned conservative obscurantism, were it not for the praise which Professor Williams inconsistently showers on the fourteenth-century Dafudd ap Gwilym who, being a real poet, behaved exactly as a *penkerdd* should not. Like his gifted friends

Gruffudd ap Ada and Madog Benfras, Dafudd used non-Classical metres, versified tales of untruth, diced, whored, blasphemed:

> *For God's sake, no more bread and water,*
> *Throw aside Lenten watercress,*
> *For Mary's sake, cease your thin prayers,*
> *The Romish monks' religion:*
> *Be not a nun in Springtime,*
> *The grove is better than a nunnery . . .*
> *Come to the spreading birch*
> *The cuckoo's woodland church,*
> *Where none will mock at us*
> *For seeking Heaven in a green grove;*
> *Keep Ovid's book in mind*
> *And pray, not too much faith!*

and when he should have roused the Welsh to perish magnificently in a rebellion against the English oppressors, was exchanging *englynion* with charming but disreputable Gwerfil Mechain—who had written:

> *I am the hostess of the irreproachable Ferry Tavern,*
> *A white-gowned moon welcoming*
> *Any man who comes to me with silver—*

about his and her sexual anatomy. Dafudd often refers to himself as a wandering minstrel; but since he came of a noble family, and towards the end of his life humorously reverted to the twenty-four Classical metres—the Job's potsherd with which Welsh bards still scrape themselves—used by his more respectable contemporaries, his moral shortcomings are here ascribed to the breakdown of Welsh social life after the conquest of Wales by the English. ' When a nation is defeated,' Professor Williams observes charitably, ' there are sensitive spirits for whom politics and religion cease to be serious concerns.'

Besides, Dafudd is long dead, poetry in dangerously free metres has come and gone, respectability is respectable again:

> The competition for the Chair at this year's Eisteddfod requires a poem of not more than three hundred lines in full *cynghanedd* [a form of balanced cross-alliteration] employing any number of Davydd ap Edmwnd's measures [Davydd ap Edmwnd was the bard

who, in 1451, ' tightened up *cynghanedd* to a pitch of craziness '],
including at least one *awdl* measure; and the winner may well be a
shepherd, a postman, a preacher, or a journalist.

As Gwion Bach, who had taken the trouble to give himself a proper
poetic education in Ireland, remarked on a similar occasion about
eight hundred years ago:

Ni obrynaf lawyr llen llywiadur—

meaning: ' I have a poor opinion of official Welsh literature.'

THE ESSENTIAL E. E. CUMMINGS

A REVIEW OF SIX NONLECTURES[1]

I get a warm feeling when I remember that, in the late 'twenties, I was probably the first Englishman to say a good word for E. E. Cummings as the author of *Is* 5 and other poems; and that I persuaded Jonathan Cape to publish his *Enormous Room,* the most hilarious account of prison-camp life that two world wars have produced. Since then Cummings has written little—his only other long work, *EIMI,* a cross-grained comic diary of a visit to Soviet Russia is twenty years old now—and gone forward little; but neither has he gone backwards nor sold any pass. I bought his *Collected Poems* a year or two ago to see what had been happening since *Is* 5 and *XLI Poems* and the play *HIM:* and the poems stood up, all stalwart and American, saying: ' Sure, read us if you like! '; which I did with a deal of pleasure. But—if *but* be the right copulative—I realized for the first time his close kinship with Nicholas Vachel Lindsay, who though neither so classically educated, so tough-shelled, so precise in language and punctuation; nor capable of such wicked and often pornographic satire; nor (being born into an elder generation of Puritan Progressives) so openly and happily devoted to carnality—nevertheless was as ingenuous, noble-hearted, gentle, courageous, and liberty-loving as Cummings. And Lindsay proved equally apt, when least expected, to write an unforgettable line or two, or even six or seven in a row; and also equally capable of deep, brilliant, unblushing, folksy-homesy sentimentality.

Both in fact are/were ideally representative of what an American poet might once hope to be: a thing which apparently, as Lindsay

[1] Geoffrey Cumberlege, Oxford University Press, 24s.

admitted by his suicide, and as Cummings here indicates by his rage against ' the spiritually impotent pseudo-community grovelling before the materialization of their own death wish ', no American poet can plausibly hope to be again.

Lindsay in his youth tramped around the States peddling *The Village Magazine,* written and illustrated by himself—I remember one pretty stanza:

> *' Which is superior to which? '*
> *Asked the snob when she came to the City.*
> *' I want to know people to kick,*
> *I want to know people to pity.'*

and preaching the Gospel of Beauty. Anti-snob Cummings has been preaching the Gospel of *Is*ness, as he calls poetic or artistic integrity, since at least 1922; and recently Harvard University, a beleaguered stronghold of U.S. academic freedom, invited him to lecture on it. This is the poetic *is*ness he then defined:

> Fine and dandy: but, so far as I am concerned, poetry and every other art was and is and forever will be strictly and distinctly a question of individuality. If poetry were anything—like dropping an atom bomb—which anyone did, anyone could become a poet merely by doing the necessary anything; whatever that anything might or might not entail. But (as it happens) poetry is being, not doing. If you wish to follow, even at a distance, the poet's calling (and here, as always, I speak from my own totally biased and entirely personal point of view) you've got to come out of the measurable doing universe into the immeasurable house of being. I am quite aware that wherever our so-called civilization has slithered, there's every reward and no punishment for unbeing. But if poetry is your goal, you've got to forget all about punishments and all about rewards and all about self-styled obligations and duties and responsibilities etcetera ad infinitum and remember one thing only: that it's you—nobody else—who determine your destiny and decide your fate. Nobody else can be alive for you; nor can you be alive for anybody else. Toms can be Dicks and Dicks can be Harrys, but none of them can ever be you. There's the artist's responsibility; and the most awful responsibility on earth. If you can take it, take it—and be. If you can't, cheer up and go about other people's business; and do (or undo) till you drop.

In the first two nonlectures, as he prefers to call them, he described his old-hickory-cut New Hampshire father: crack shot, fly-fisherman, scholar, woodsman, clergyman, sailor, actor, photographer, painter, carpenter, plumber, ornithologist, taxidermist, Harvard lecturer, and hero. And his Roxbury mother: poetry-lover, Quaker, charity worker, heroine. And himself as a child, secure in a home which was all that an ideal American poet's home should be; and where he read Scott, Dickens, Jules Verne, Harrison Ainsworth, Malory, Froissart, the *Holy Bible, Robinson Crusoe, The Swiss Family Robinson, Gulliver's Travels, Lorna Doone, Treasure Island,* and *The Arabian Nights*— odd! no Twain, Alger, Fenimore Cooper, or Melville!—and now thanks a beneficent Providence that he passed through his childhood without

> ever once glimpsing that typical item of an era of at least pen-ultimate confusion—the uncomic non-book. No paltry supermen, no shadowy space-cadets, no trifling hyperjunglequeens and pantless pantherwomen insulted my virginal imagination.

One of the penalties of this New English education was that he learned at an early age ' the one and only thing which mattered about a poem was what it said: it's so-called meaning '. He records:

> A good poem was a poem which did good, and a bad poem was a poem which didn't: Julia Ward Howe's Battle Hymn of The Republic being a good poem because it helped free the slaves. Armed with this ethical immutability, I composed canticles of comfort on behalf of the griefstricken relatives of persons recently deceased; I implored healthy Christians to assist poor-whites afflicted with The Curse Of The Worm (short for hookworm); and I exhorted right-minded patriots to abstain from dangerous fireworks on the 4th of July.

And being a good son and citizen he has never altogether divested himself of this obsession about goodness, even after celebrating a sort of Doge-wedding with the vicious Seine at Montparnasse; nor indeed of the red H which his mother knitted into his first jersey and which, printed on his heart, sent him to read Classics at Harvard forty years ago and has now called him back there again to deliver his nonlectures. Towards the close of each of these he read out his favourite poems, and what were they? *The Ode on the Intimations of Immortality,* in full, for his mother's sake; a passage from *Prometheus Unbound,* for Liberty's sake; a border ballad in memory of Harvard's

Professor Francis James Child, who had baptized him; two pieces from Dante; three from Shakespeare; Burns's *Red Red Rose;* Keats's *Grecian Urn;* Swinburne's *When the Hounds of Spring;* and (in frank tribute to Old Carnality) Donne's *To His Mistress Going to Bed.*

By thus loyally keeping his first loves in poetry always before his eyes, and not realizing how unworthy some of these are (judged by his own standards of *is*ness) to be set beside some of the others, he does his heart more credit than his five sound senses. Nor is he abashed to write, endite and publicly recite so intrinsically corny a sonnet as the one beginning:

> *i thank You God for most this amazing*
> *day: for the leaping greenly spirits of trees*
> *and a blue dream of sky; and for everything*
> *which is natural which is infinite which is yes*
>
> *(i who have died am alive again today,*
> *and this is the sun's birthday; this is the birth*
> *day of life and of love and wings: and of the gay*
> *great happening illimitably earth)*

In 1945 he ran, as he reminds his nonlectured, to the rescue of ' this self-styled world's greatest and most generous literary figure, who had arrived at our nation's capital, attired in half a G.I.'s uniform, and ready to be hanged as a traitor by the only country which has ever made even a pretence of fighting for freedom of speech '—with the plea that this nontraitor had been ' true to the illimitable country of his own personal art '. Thereupon he rages against ' the supermechanized submorons . . . dedicated to a proposition that massacre is a social virtue because murder is an individual vice.' Here I personally cannot follow him; the self-styled world's greatest literary figure had compromised his *is*ness by raving anti-poetic generalities over the Fascist radio, and recommending that all Jews in Italy, as in Germany, should be sent to the gas-chamber. And the G.I.'s who made a buckshow of him when they caught him were, I assume, acting *is*ly, on individual impulse; castigating not the artist but the truth-perverting tool of *is*nesslessness.

Cummings is at his best here when, as a ' burlesk addict of long standing ', he mimics the voice of the America that he hates yet continues to live among:

> John viii, 7.
>   So now let us talk about something else. This is a free country because compulsory education. This is a free country because nobody has to eat. This is a free country because not any other country was is or ever will be free. So now you know and knowledge is power.
>   An interesting fact when you come right down to it is that simple people like complex things. But what amounts to an extraordinary coincidence is mediocre people liking first-rate things. The explanation can't be because complex things are simple. It must be because mediocre people are first-rate.
>   So now let us pull the wool over each other's toes and go to Hell. John viii, 7.

I regret that he did not include in the readings from his own work such jocund verses as *She being brand-new,* describing Old Carnality in terms of the internal combustion engine; and the well-worn but ever-living mock-heroic stanzas beginning:

> *come, gaze with me upon this dome*
> *of many coloured glass, and see*
> *his mother's pride, his father's joy,*
> *unto whom duty whispers low*
>
> *' thou must! ' and who replies ' I can! '*
> *—yon clean upstanding well dressed boy*
> *that with his peers full oft hath quaffed*
> *the wine of life and found it sweet—*
>
> *a tear within his stern blue eye,*
> *upon his firm white lips a smile,*
> *one thought alone: to do or die*
> *for God for country and for Yale*

. . . Yale, not Harvard! And therefore with the shocking pay-off at the close.

JUANA DE ASBAJE

afterwards JUANA INÉS DE LA CRUZ

(with two of her poems)

Every few centuries a woman of poetic genius appears, who may be distinguished by three clear secondary signs: learning, beauty, and loneliness. Though the burden of poetry is difficult enough for a man to bear, he can always humble himself before an incarnate Muse and seek instruction from her. At the worst this Muse, whom he loves in a more than human sense, may reject and deceive him; and even then he can vent his disillusion in a memorable poem—as Catullus did when he parted from Clodia—and survive to fix his devotion on another. The case of a woman poet is a thousand times worse: since she is herself the Muse, a Goddess without an external power to guide or comfort her, and if she strays even a finger's breadth from the path of divine instinct, must take violent self-vengeance. For a while a sense of humour, good health, and discretion may keep her on an even keel, but the task of living to, for, and with herself alone, will sooner or later prove an impossible one. Sappho of Lesbos, Liadan of Corkaguiney, and Juana de Asbaje belonged to this desperate sisterhood: incarnations of the Muse-goddess, cut off from any simple gossiping relation with their fellow-women, who either adored them blindly or hated them blindly, and from any spiritual communion with men on equal terms. Though a woman so fated cannot help feeling physical desire for a man, she is forbidden by her identity with the Goddess from worshipping or giving herself wholly to him, even if he desires to worship and give himself wholly to her. It is possible that Clodia was another of these unfortunates, so that the harder Catullus tried to please her, the more despairingly she fought him off: playing the society harlot rather than consent to burn with him in a mutual flame.

About Clodia little is known, and about Catullus no more than his poems reveal. Even the story of Sappho survives only in fragmentary form. We learn that she was early married on Lesbos to one Cercolas, a man of no distinction, and bore him a daughter; that her learning and inventive faculties were memorable; that she tutored girls of literary promise; that she rejected the advances of Alcaeus, the leading poet of his day; that she fled to Sicily from some unnamed trouble and, after an unhappy affair with one Phaon, a common sailor, ' took the Leucadian leap ': which implies some spectacular act of self-destruction. The inter-relation of these bare facts remains obscure; yet it seems that a possessed woman poet will rather subject herself to a dull husband or ignorant lover, who mistrusts her genius and may even ill-treat her physically, than encourage the love of a Catullus or Alcaeus, which demands more than it is hers to give.

The story of Liadan is also fragmentary. She was a brilliant young Irish *ollamh* (or master-poet) of the seventh century A.D., privileged to make semi-royal progresses from one great mansion to another, preceded by a peal of golden bells, and followed by a train of lesser bards and pupils. On one of these she went to Connaught, where the *ollamh* Curithir welcomed her to an ale feast. After the long exchange of riddling poetic lore in Old Goidelic, customary on such occasions, he burst out suddenly: ' Why should we not marry, Liadan? A son born to us would be famous.' She was startled into answering: ' Wait until my progress is done; then visit me at Corkaguiney and I will come with you.' He did so, only to find that Liadan, regretting her lapse, had meanwhile taken a religious vow of chastity. In despair and anger, Curithir took a similar vow, and when they went away to-gether, as agreed, it was to the monastery of Clonfert, where Liadan insisted on placing herself under the spiritual direction of St Cummin, a hard and severe abbot. Curithir followed suit. Cummin found them two separate cells, offering Curithir the choice of either seeing Liadan without addressing her, or addressing her without seeing her. He chose the second alternative; and Liadan consented to this arrangement. They were then each in turn allowed to wander around the other's wattled cell; until Liadan persuaded Cummin to grant Curithir greater freedom, of which she must have known that he would try to take ad-vantage. As a result, he was banished from Clonfert, and sailed away to the Holy Land; but Liadan let herself die of remorse, because she had foolishly involved him in her ruin.

Unlike Sappho and Liadan, Juana de Asbaje was born into a society where she must have seemed as portentous as a talking dove, or a dog which does long division. Neither in Lesbos nor ancient Ireland had limits been set to a woman's learning. Sappho was no freak, but merely the truest of several famous women poets. Liadan, to win her peal of golden bells, had passed the *ollamh's* twelve-year course in literature, law, history, languages, music, magic, mathematics, and astronomy—one of incredible stiffness—and that a woman should so distinguish herself was not considered abnormal. In seventeenth-century Mexico, however, the Church had gained such a stranglehold on learning and literature that women, doctrinally debarred from the priesthood, and despised as the intellectual and moral inferiors of their fathers and brothers, could nurse no aspirations beyond a good husband, many children, and a Christian death. Only at the Viceregal Court might a lady read poems or romances, and thus equip herself for the games of chivalry in which etiquette required her to assist the courtiers; but even so, a confessor always stood by to check all signs of vanity or immodesty.

Juana, born on November 12, 1651, was the daughter of Don Pedro Manuel de Asbaje, an immigrant Vizcayan, and Doña Isabel Ramirez, whose father, the head of a family long established in Mexico, owned a substantial estate near Chimalhuacán, and seems to have been a man of some cultivation. Juana's mother, however, could neither read nor write and, when she died some thirty years later, it transpired that Juana and her two sisters had all been born out of wedlock: presumably because the father had left behind a wife in Spain. Though he seems to have legitimized the three of them before they grew up, it has been suggested that the shame of having been born a bastard encouraged Juana to excel as a poet, while it soured her against marriage; but this is mere speculation.

One morning, when she was three years old, her sister said: 'Mother cannot have you about the house today. Come with me to school and sit quietly in a corner.' Juana went . . .

> . . . and seeing that they gave my sister lessons, I so burned with a desire to know how to read that, deceiving the teacher, as I thought, I told her that my mother had ordered her to give me les-

sons. She did not believe this, as it was incredible, but to humour
me, she acquiesced. I continued to attend and she to teach me, not
in mockery now, because experience had undeceived her; and I
learned to read in such short time that when my mother (from
whom the teacher had hidden the matter in order to give her the
pleasure and receive the reward all at once) found out, I was already
proficient. I, too, had concealed it, thinking that they would whip
me for acting without orders. She who taught me still lives, God
preserve her, and can testify to the truth. . . . I recall that in those
days I had the appetite for sweets and delicacies that is common at
such an age, but that I abstained from eating cheese because I had
heard it said that taking this made one dull-witted; for my desire to
learn was stronger than the wish to eat, which ordinarily is so powerful in children.

At the age of six or seven, she pleaded to be enrolled at Mexico
City University and, since the statutes barred women from taking the
course, to have her hair cut and be dressed as a boy. When her mother
laughingly refused, Juana took possession of her grandfather's library,
which no punishment could deter her from reading; and when she
found that the most desirable books were in Latin, mastered the elements in fewer than twenty lessons and, before she was eight, could
read and enjoy Plato, Aristophanes, and Erasmus. Juana now made
life so difficult for her mother that she was sent to her uncle's house
in Mexico City, where she taught herself literature, science, mathematics, philosophy, theology, and languages. At the age of thirteen
she was presented at Court by the uncle; there her exceptional talents,
vivacity, and beauty—wide-set chestnut-coloured eyes, broad brow,
quick smile, straight nose, determined chin, delicate fingers—qualified
her to be the darling and first lady-in-waiting of the Vicereine. For
three years Juana took part in all the gallant diversions of the Viceregal Court, the cultural centre of the New World, and became its
principal ornament, next to the regal pair themselves: studying every
book that came to hand, and writing a profusion of court verse in
Castilian, Latin, and Aztec—besides theatrical sketches, satires, verses
of commendation and occasional trifles, some of them ' highly sea-
soned '; and finding time for poetry of a truer and more personal kind.
A great many well-born young men asked her hand in marriage, but
she behaved with admirable discretion and refused their offers, though
the Viceroy and Vicereine would doubtless have provided a dowry.

When she reached the age of sixteen, the Viceroy heard her decried as having only a smattering of knowledge, and therefore summoned forty learned men—University professors, theologians, poets, mathematicians, and historians—to examine her in their various subjects. He afterwards recorded with satisfaction:

> Like a royal galleon beating off the attacks of a few enemy sloops, so did Juana fight clear of the questions, arguments and objections that so many specialists, each in his own department, propounded. . . .

Father Calleja, of the Society of Jesus, her first biographer, asked Juana what impression this triumph, capable of puffing up even the humblest soul to self-importance, had made upon her. She replied: ' It left me with no greater satisfaction than if I had performed a small task of hemstitching more neatly than my embroidery-teacher.' About this time she first expressed a total aversion to marriage. Her motives have ever since been hotly debated. Father Calleja suggests that she recognized the glitter of Court life as empty delusion; never fell in love with a man; and soon realized that only service to God could give her lasting happiness. This is still the view of the Church, despite her plainly autobiographical love-poems, written at the age of sixteen: *Este amoroso tormento que en mi corazón se ve,* and: *Si otros ojos hé visto, matenme, Fabio, tus airados ojos;* and the poems of disillusion which followed, especially the famous:

> *Hombres necios que acusáis*
> *a la mujer sin razón;*

and the two scorching farewell sonnets to Silvio, whom she hates herself for having loved so well.

Juana presently decided to become a nun, although, as she wrote later: ' I knew that the estate implied obligations (I am referring to the incidentals, not the fundamentals) most repugnant to my temperament.' In this course she was encouraged by her confessor, Father Antonio Nuñez de Miranda, to whom ' she broached all her doubts, fears, and misgivings '. Her first attempt failed: after three months as a novice among the Barefoot Carmelites, her health broke down, and she withdrew on doctor's orders. Fourteen months later, however, she was well enough to enter a Jeronymite convent and in

February 1669, having completed a short novitiate, took the veil as
Sor Juana Inés de la Cruz, the name by which she is now generally
known.

Father Antonio did not insist that she should abandon her studies
and, since the Jeronymites were the most liberal of the Orders in
seventeenth-century Mexico, her cell soon became an academy, lined
with books and filled with the instruments of music and mathematics.
Juana learned to play several instruments, wrote a treatise on musical
harmony, made a name as a miniaturist, became proficient in moral
and dogmatic theology, medicine, canon law, astronomy, and advanced mathematics. Her library swelled to four thousand books, the
largest in the New World, and it is recorded:

> . . . the *locutorio* of the Jeronimas was frequented by many of the
> highest in Mexico, thanks to the renown of Sor Juana. She had loved
> solitude but [her presence] brought her many distinguished visitors.
> Not a Viceroy of that epoch but desired to know her and, from the
> highest to the lowest, they all consulted Juana on weighty affairs. A
> natural affability and graciousness made her lend herself with good
> will to these fatiguing visits.

Juana continued to write verses, though none for publication:
mostly birthday and name-day greetings addressed to her friends at
Court, dedications, epitaphs, commemorations, rhymed letters of
thanks for books or musical instruments—all smooth, eloquent, and
highly rhetorical. To these she added sacred sonnets, dirges, rounde-
lays, carols, panegyrics of saints, lively allegories, and religious plays.
She was also a famous cook and for ever sending her friends gifts
of confectionery: almond rings, nuns' sighs (to use the politer
phrase), cakes, and puff pastry of every kind. Accompanying these
went humorous verses, such as this:

> *To Her Excellency again, with a shoe embroidered in*
> *Mexican style, and a parcel of chocolate:*
>
> > *A cast glove is challenge:*
> > *Contrariwise,*
> > *A cast shoe, my Lady,*
> > *Surrender signifies.*

Frequent balls, concerts, and ballad-recitals were given in the
Convent and patronized by the Viceregal pair who never failed to

attend vespers there as an excuse for amusing and instructive conversation with the 'Mexican Phœnix'. It was an easy life, since no limit was put on the number of Indian serfs owned by the sisters; one convent of a hundred nuns had five hundred such serving-women working for them. Juana was unlucky, at first, to be under a jealous and narrow-minded prioress, at whom she once shouted in exasperation: 'Hold your tongue, you ignorant fool!' The prioress complained to the then Archbishop of Mexico who, as an admirer of Juana, endorsed the prioress's complaint with: 'If the Mother Superior can prove that this charge is false, justice will be done.'

Juana performed all the religious tasks laid on her, though not greedy of ecclesiastical advancement and, when on one occasion unanimously elected prioress, declined the honour. The gay times at the Convent seem to have ended with the Viceroy's term of office; but her 'passion to know' remained as strong as ever, and this, she wrote, subjected her to more criticism and resentment than the massive learning she had already acquired. On one occasion a 'very holy and candid prelate' ordered her to cease from her studies. She obeyed in so far as she read no more books . . .

> . . . but since it was not within my power to cease absolutely, I observed all things that God created, the universal machine serving me in place of books.

During the three months of the prelate's continuance in office, she studied the mechanics of the spinning top, and the chemical reactions of convent cookery, making important scientific discoveries. Later, when she fell seriously ill, the doctors also forbade her to read, but . . .

> . . . seeing that, when deprived of books, her cogitations were so vehement that they consumed more spirit in a quarter of an hour than did four days' reading,

they were forced to withdraw their prohibition.

Juana's confessor, still the same Father Antonio, now tried to dissuade her from seeing and writing to so many friends and learned laymen, on the ground that this was irreconcilable with her profession; and when she would not listen to him, resigned his charge. Next, she was ordered by an unnamed superior to refute an admittedly unorthodox sermon preached by a famous theologian, the Portuguese Jesuit Father Antonio Vieira; which Juana did in a letter of such masterly argument, that when it was published (without her knowledge or permission) the most learned doctors of Spain and Portugal were highly diverted to find that this Mexican nun had completely demolished Vieira's thesis; and sent her profuse congratulations. But one old friend, the Bishop of Puebla, qualified his praises with the suggestion that the letter proved how sadly she had wasted her talents in writing shallow verses and studying irrelevant and profane subjects; instead, she should have devoted herself to the unmasking of doctrinal error, now so rife in Christendom. Juana, deeply offended, replied that she made no claim to academic distinction, had written the letter only because ordered to do so and, when she saw it in print, had burst into tears, ' which never come easily to me '. Then, rather than become a theologian, to the exclusion of all her other studies, she grimly sold her entire library for the benefit of the poor, together with all her musical and mathematical instruments; and submitted to the severest conventual discipline, which Father Antonio, returning in joy, unsuccessfully begged her to moderate. This spectacular event created such a stir that the new Archbishop of Mexico similarly sold all his books, jewels, valuables, and even his bed.

In 1695, some of the sisters fell ill of the plague, and Juana, though weakened by nearly two years of rigorous penance, set herself to nurse them; but presently caught the infection and succumbed. The Jeronymity records contain this sentence, scratched with Juana's fingernail dipped in her own blood—because she had renounced the use of pen and ink:

> Immediately above will be noted the day, month and year of my death. For the love of God and of His Purest Mother, I pray that my beloved sisters, both those now living and those who have gone before, will recommend me to Him—though I have been the worst woman in the world.
>
>   Signed: I, Juana Inés de la Cruz.

Juana de Asbaje wrote true poetry before she was seventeen; but what of her heiress and successor, Sor Juana Inés de la Cruz? We can applaud the dazzling fantasy of Sor Juana's religious verse, its perfect sense of rhythm and sure balance of phrases, its essential clarity, which shames the interlaced extravagances of contemporary Gongor-

ists, and the universality of knowledge displayed by the incidental
references. Yet the appeal is almost wholly to the intellect. Juana
never became mystically involved with Christ. She accepted Him as a
theological axiom, rather than as the divine bridegroom whom St
Teresa knew, and of whom the medieval Irish nun wrote:

> *Jesukin, my Jesukin*
> *My small cell doth dwell within!*
> *With prelates have I nought to do:*
> *All's untrue but Jesukin.*

She was no longer the Muse of every Mexican gallant, though flat-
terers continued to call her ' The Tenth Muse '; and as an intelligence
she now functioned in a field which the ecclesiastics, to whom she had
promised obedience, were always seeking to reduce; being forced to
play a religious part in which she could not wholly believe, because
it was repugnant to her temperament, yet at last playing it so successfully as at once to shame them and defeat her own ends. When she had
sold her books and cut herself off from the world, the only solace left
was the fellowship of her ignorant sisters, and even this seems hardly
to have been an unmixed blessing:

> It happened that among other favours, I owe to God an easy and
> affable nature and the nuns loved me for it (without taking notice,
> like the good people they were, of my faults) and greatly enjoyed
> my company; knowing this and moved by the great love I had for
> them—since they loved me, I loved them more—there were times
> when they intruded somewhat, coming to me to console themselves
> and to give me the recreation of their company.

It was in no spirit of mock-humility that she described herself as
the worst of women; writing the confession in her own blood. She
meant that when she first took the Leucadian Leap by becoming a
nun, it had not been into the sea of pure religion. Still keeping her
intellectual pride, her thirst for scientific knowledge and her pleasure
in profane authors, lay visitors and the minor pleasures of the flesh,
she could remember what it had been to love and to write poetry; and
her ancient powers still occasionally reasserted themselves, for instance in some of the songs, based on the *Canticles,* which enliven
her religious play *The Divine Narcissus.* Juana called herself the
worst of women, it seems, because she had lacked sufficient resolution

either to stick it out as a Muse, or make a complete renegation in the style of Liadan.

Now, though both Liadan and Juana were young and famous women poets who took vows of celibacy and submitted to ecclesiastical discipline, it was Juana's Irishness, rather, that first led me to compare them. Juana not only combined Christian ethics with pagan emotion, and profound learning with easy lyricism, like the *ollamhs,* but had inherited their technique by way of the early medieval Latin hymns and the anti-monastic ballads of the Goliards. She too loved the short rhymed quatrain, and the internal rhymes of her *Carol to St Peter:*

> *Y con plumas y voces veloces*
> *Y con voces y plumas las sumas*
> *Cantad . . .*

were in the purest Bardic tradition, like St Bernard of Cluny's *Rhythm,* which begins:

> *Hora novissima, tempora pessima*
> *Sunt; vigilemus*
> *Ecce minaciter imminet arbiter*
> *Ille supremus . . .*

Moreover, she excelled in satire of the scorching Irish sort that would raise blotches on the victim's face: her *Lines to Sour-Faced Gila* might have been written by the arch-*ollamh* Seanchan Torpest himself, notorious for having rhymed rats to death.[1] Perhaps Juana's Vizcayan blood was at work; an ancient tie of kinship and religion bound the Western Irish with the Northern Spanish—both peoples had worshipped the same pre-Christian Muse-goddess and the doomed hero Lugos, or Lugh, her gifted son.

---

[1] *See* pp. 52–54.

POEMS BY JUANA DE ASBAJE,
WITH TRANSLATIONS

ARGUYE DE INCONSECUENTES EL GUSTO Y LA CENSURA
DE LOS HOMBRES QUE EN LAS MUJERES ACUSAN
LO QUE CAUSAN

Hombres necios que acusáis
a la mujer sin razón,
sin ver que sois la ocasión
de lo mismo que culpáis,

si con ansia sin igual
solicitáis su desdén
¿por qué queréis que obren bien
si las incitáis al mal?

Combatis su resistencia
y luego, con gravedad,
decís que fué liviandad
lo que hizo la diligencia.

Parecer quiere el denuedo
de vuestro parecer loco,
al niño que pone el coco,
y luego le tiene miedo.

Queréis, con presunción necia,
hallar a la que buscáis,
para pretendida, Thais,
y en la posesión, Lucrecia.

¿Qué humor puede ser más raro
que el que, falto de consejo,
él mismo empaña el espejo
y siente que no esté claro?

Con el favor y el desdén
tenéis condición igual:
quejándoos si os tratan mal,
burlándoos si os quieren bien.

Opinión ninguna gana,
pues la que más se recata,
si no os admite, es ingrata,
y os admite, es liviana.

Siempre tan necios andáis
que con desigual nivel
a una culpáis por cruel
y otra por fácil culpáis.

¿Pues cómo ha de estar templada
la que vuestra amor pretende,
si la que es ingrata ofende
y la que es fácil enfada?

Mas entre el enfado y pena
que vuestro gusto refiere
bien haya la que no os quiere
y dejaos en hora buena.

Dan vuestras amantes penas
a sus libertades alas,
y después de hacerlas malas
las queréis hallar muy buenas.

¿Cuál mayor culpa ha tenido,
en una pasión errada,
la que cae de rogada,
o el que ruega de caído?

¿O cuál es más de culpar,
aunque cualquiera mal haga,
la que peca por la paga
o el que paga por pecar?

Pues ¿para qué os espantáis
de la culpa que tenéis?

Queredlas cuál las hacéis
o hacedlas cual las buscáis,

dejad de solicitar
y después, con más razón,
acusaréis la afición
de la que os fuere a rogar.

Bien con muchas armas fundo
que lidia vuestra arrogancia,
pues, en promesa e instancia
juntáis diablo, carne y mundo.

AGAINST THE INCONSEQUENCE OF MEN'S DESIRES
AND THEIR CENSURE OF WOMEN
FOR FAULTS WHICH THEY THEMSELVES HAVE CAUSED

Ah stupid men, unreasonable
  In blaming woman's nature,
Oblivious that your acts incite
  The very faults you censure.

If, of unparalleled desire,
  At her disdain you batter
With provocations of the flesh,
  What should her virtue matter?

Yet once you wear resistance down
  You reprimand her, showing
That what you diligently devised
  Was all her wanton doing.

With love you feign to be distraught
  (How gallant is your lying!
Like children, masked with calabash,
  Their own selves terrifying),

And idiotically would seek
  In the same woman's carriage

A Thais for the sport of love,
  And a Lucrece for marriage.

What sight more comic than the man,
  All decent counsel loathing,
Who breathes upon a mirror's face
  Then mourns: ' I can see nothing.'

Whether rejected or indulged,
  You all have the same patter:
Complaining in the former case,
  But mocking in the latter.

No woman your esteem can earn,
  Though cautious and mistrustful;
You call her cruel, if denied,
  And if accepted, lustful.

Inconsequent and variable
  Your reason must be reckoned:
You charge the first girl with disdain;
  With lickerishness, the second.

How can the lady of your choice
  Temper her disposition,
When to be stubborn vexes you,
  But you detest submission?

So, what with all the rage and pain
  Caused by your greedy nature,
She would be wise who never loved
  And hastened her departure.

Let loved ones cage their liberties
  Like any captive bird; you
Will violate them none the less,
  Apostrophizing virtue.

Which has the greater sin when burned
  By the same lawless fever:
She who is amorously deceived,
  Or he, the sly deceiver?

Or which deserves the sterner blame,
   Though each will be a sinner:
She who becomes a whore for pay,
   Or he who pays to win her?

Are you astounded at your faults,
   Which could not well be direr?
Then love what you have made her be,
   Or make as you desire her.

I warn you: trouble her no more,
   But earn the right to visit
Your righteous wrath on any jade
   Who might your lust solicit.

This arrogance of men in truth
   Comes armoured with all evil—
Sworn promise, plea of urgency—
   O world, O flesh, O devil!

VILLANCICOS QUE SE CANTARON EN LA CATEDRAL DE MÉXICO,
EN LOS MATINES DEL PRÍNCIPE DE LA IGLESIA,
SEÑOR SAN PEDRO,
EL AÑO DE 1677

Estribillo

Serafines alados, celestes jilgueros,
templad vuestras plumas, cortad vuestros ecos,
y con plumas y voces aladas,
y con voces y plumas templadas,
cantad, escribid de Pedro los hechos;
y con plumas, y voces
   veloces,
y con voces y plumes
   las sumas
cantad, escribid de los hechos de Pedro.

Coplas

Reducir infalible
quietud, del viento inquieto las mudanzas,
es menos imposible,
que de Pedro cantar las alabanzas,
que apenas reducir podrán a sumas,
de las alas querúbicas las plumas.

Más que al Cielo de estrellas
número hay de excelencias, que le asista;
¿pues qué diré de aquellas,
que imperceptibles son a nuestra vista?
¿si a decir las sabidas no acertamos,
cómo podré cantar las que ignoramos?

Poner Pedro la planta
adonde Cristo la cabeza puso,
misterio es, que adelanta
el respeto que el Cielo nos impuso:
pues de besar el pie Cristo se precia
a Pedro por cabeza de la Iglesia.

Que él es Pedro, responde
Cristo cuando el Dios vivo le ha llamado;
porque tal gloria esconde
este nombre de Pedro venerado,
que no hallando a su fe, que satisfaga,
sólo en llamarle Pedro Dios le paga.

No le dijo, que él era
cabeza de la iglesia militante,
ni que era la primera
puerta para pasar a la triunfante,
ni que a la redondez; que alumbra el día;
su pescador anillo ceñiría.

Ni que entre justos tantos
tendrá el primer lugar entre los hombres;
gocen allá otros Santos
de gloriosos altísimos renombres,

cual la palma inmortal, cual verde cedro,
que a mi Pedro le basta con ser Pedro.

Pues si tal enseñanza
nos muestra vuestro título y nobleza,
y que vuestra alabanza
encierra en vuestro nombre más grandeza,
no quiero yo alabaros de otro modo:
Pedro sois, y en ser Pedro la sois todo.

CAROL SUNG IN THE CATHEDRAL OF MEXICO CITY AT THE
MATINS OF OUR LORD SAINT PETER,
PRINCE OF THE CHURCH,
A.D. 1677

Winged seraphin, celestial linnets,
Trim your feathers, still your echoes,
And with feathers and winged voices
Sing, write the deeds of Peter:
O, with feathers and voices
    Swift-flying,
O, with voices and feathers,
    Singing and writing,
Sum the deeds of Peter!

What? Reduce to infallible quiet
The shifts of the unquiet wind?
Even that were less impossible
Than to sing Peter's praises
Which the very feathers of the cherubs' wings
Could scarce reduce to a sum.

More than the stars of Heaven in number
Are the merits that attend him.
How then to celebrate such finenesses
As must elude our vision?
If we cannot certify things known to us,
How chant of things we know not?

That Peter his sole rested
Where Christ rested His head,
Is a mystery enhancing
Awe which Heaven has upon us laid:
Since by Christ's kissing of that foot
Peter was hallowed as the Church's head.

' Thou art Peter,' Christ replied
When greeted by him as the Living God—
For the reverend name of Peter
Enshrines such glory
That, finding other fee too poor,
God recompensed his faith with this alone;

And did not manifest him as the head
Of the Church Militant,
And the first gate wherethrough
The Church should pass triumphant,
Nor told him that the Fisherman's ring would loop
The round horizon beamed upon by day;

Nor that of all men ever born
He would hold first place among the just.
O then, let other Saints in Heaven enjoy
Honours most glorious and most high,
Be it deathless palm, or cedar evergreen;
My Peter it suffices to be Peter.

Envoie

Wherefore, since Christ's Own declaration
Blazoned your title and nobility,
And since your praise must rest upon
The supreme grandeur which your name encloses,
I would not praise you otherwise than thus:
' Peter thou art and, being so, art all!'

THE POET AND HIS PUBLIC:

A HOME SERVICE BROADCAST

Here I sit, alone in a sound-proof room, at a table bare but for my papers, a pencil, and a glass of water. I am supposed to be addressing my public, as members of other professions in this series have addressed theirs. An awkward situation. The chances are that not more than one person in every hundred has read my poems even by mistake —except perhaps a few rhymes which I wrote nearly forty years ago and which have got fossilized in school anthologies. The chances are equally against any immediate increase in the number of my readers because of this broadcast.

The B.B.C., you will notice, have not supplied me with an audience to make encouraging noises and laugh in the right places, as they do for highly-paid comedians. I dare say they might have raked together a sympathetic audience, if I had insisted. (I was an old friend of the Corporation's while it was still only a Company, and announced itself as 2 LO; when you veteran listeners were using home-made crystal sets with cat's whiskers; and every time a bus went down the Strand you heard the rumble.) But a poet needs no audience: he can do very well without the giggle or horse-laugh so necessary for the comedian. The comedian tries to make his public as large as possible, and loses no opportunity of meeting it in person; he takes it out to dinner (so to speak) and pets it, and gives it photographs signed in enormous round handwriting—' To my own darling Public, from your adorer Charlie.' And he joins in every merry romp that will bind him and it more lovingly together. The poet behaves quite differently towards his public— unless he is not really a poet but a disguised comedian, or preacher, or space-buyer.

Frankly, honest Public, I am not professionally concerned with you, and expect nothing from you. Please give me no bouquets, and I will give you no signed photographs. That does not mean that I am altogether untouched by your kindness and sympathy, or that I dislike the money which two or three thousand of you invest in new volumes of my poems. All I mean is that these poems are not addressed directly to you in the sense that the comedian's jokes are; though I don't in the least mind your reading them. Of course, I also write historical novels, which is how I make a living. My motive or excuse is usually to clear up some historical problem which has puzzled me, but I never forget that these novels have to support me and my large family. So I think of the average, intelligent, educated general reader, and try to hold his attention by writing as clearly and simply and unboringly as the subject allows. Money's tight these days, and I should think very ill of myself unless I made the novels as lively as possible—just as the greengrocer or butcher prides himself on selling the freshest, tastiest produce of the market, and at a reasonable price. Here duty and self-interest go hand in hand; because once one tries to pass off bad stuff as good, the customer will shop elsewhere and advise his friends to do the same.

Towards my poetry-reading public, however, I feel no such tenderness. By this I do not mean that I have stricter standards in prose than in poetry. On the contrary, poems are infinitely more difficult to write than prose, and my standards are correspondingly higher. If I re-write a line of prose five times, I re-write a line of verse fifteen times. The fact is, that I could never say: 'Funds are low, I must write a dozen poems.' But I might well say: 'Funds are low, it's time I wrote another novel.' Novels are in the public domain, poems are not. I can make this last point clear by talking about important letters. Most of the important letters you write fall into two different categories. The first is the business letter—'Sir: I beg to advise you in reply to your communication of the 5th ultimo . . .'—written with an eye on office files. This sort of letter is in the public domain. But not the other sort, the personal letter beginning: 'Darling Mavis, when we kissed good-bye last night . . .' Or: 'Dear Captain Dingbat, you go to blazes!'—in each case written to convey a clear and passionate message, and without a thought for any libel suit, or breach of promise action, in which it may one day be produced as evidence against you. So with poems. We must distinguish those written with a careful eye to the public files from those written in private emotion. Of course, this comparison is not quite exact. Though some poems (for example, most of Shakespeare's *Sonnets*) are in the love-letter category, and others (for example, a couple of the same *Sonnets*) are in the ' You go to blazes! ' category; yet in most cases the poet seems to be talking to himself, not either to his beloved or to his enemy.

Well, then, for whom does he write poems if not for a particular Mavis or Captain Dingbat? Don't think me fanciful when I say that he writes them for the Muse. ' The Muse ' has become a popular joke. ' Ha, ha, my boy! ' exclaims Dr Whackem, the schoolmaster, when he finds a rude rhyme chalked on the blackboard. ' So you have been *wooing the Muse,* have you? Take that, and that, and that! ' But the Muse was once a powerful goddess. Poets worshipped her with as much awe as smiths felt for their god Vulcan; or soldiers for their god Mars. I grant that, by the time of Homer, the ancient cult of the Muse had been supplanted by the cult of the upstart Apollo, who claimed to be the god of poets. Nevertheless, both Homer's *Iliad* and Homer's *Odyssey* begin with a formal invocation to the Muse. When I say that a poet writes his poems for the Muse, I mean simply that he treats poetry with a single-minded devotion which may be called religious, and that he allows no other activity in which he takes part, whether concerned with his livelihood or with his social duties, to interfere with it. This has been my own rule since I was fourteen or fifteen, and has become second nature to me.

Poems should not be written, like novels, to entertain or instruct the public; or the less poems they. The pathology of poetic composition is no secret. A poet finds himself caught in some baffling emotional problem, which is of such urgency that it sends him into a sort of trance. And in this trance his mind works, with astonishing boldness and precision, on several imaginative levels at once. The poem is either a practical answer to his problem, or else it is a clear statement of it; and a problem clearly stated is half-way to solution. Some poets are more plagued than others with emotional problems, and more conscientious in working out the poems which arise from them—that is to say more attentive in their service to the Muse.

Poems have been compared to pearls. Pearls are the natural reaction of the oyster to some irritating piece of grit which has worked its way in between its valves; the grit gets smoothed over with layers of mother-of-pearl until it ceases to be a nuisance to the oyster. Poems have also been compared to honey. And the worker-bee is driven by some inner restlessness to gather and store honey all summer long, until its wings are quite worn out, from pure devotion to the queen. Both bee and oyster, indeed, take so much trouble over their work that one finds the geography books saying: ' The oysters of Tinnevelly yield the most beautiful pearls on the Indian market,' or: ' The bees of Hymettus produce the sweetest honey in the world.' From this it is only a step to the ridiculous assumption that the oyster is mainly concerned in satisfying the Bombay pearl merchants' love of beauty; and the bees in delighting gourmets at the world's most expensive restaurants. The same assumption, almost equally ridiculous, is made about poets.

Though we know that Shakespeare circulated a few of his less personal sonnets among his friends, he is unlikely to have had any intention of publishing the remainder. It seems that a bookseller-publisher, one Thorp, bought the manuscript from the mysterious Mr W.H., to whom they were addressed, and pirated the whole series. Nevertheless, a poem is seldom so personal that a small group of the poet's contemporaries cannot understand it; and if it has been written with the appropriate care—by which I mean that the problem troubling him is stated as truly and economically and detachedly as possible—they are likely to admire the result. The poem might even supply the answer to a pressing problem of their own, because the poet is a human being, and so are they. And since he works out his own problems in the language which they happen to share, there is a somewhat closer sympathy between his public and himself, even though he does not write directly for it, than between the oyster and the oyster's public, or the bee and the bee's public.

A poet's public consists of those who happen to be close enough to him, in education and environment and imaginative vision, to be able to catch both the overtones and the undertones of his poetic statements. And unless he despises his fellow-men, he will not deny them the pleasure of reading what he has written while inspired by the Muse, once it has served his purpose of self-information.

Young poets tend to be either ambitious, or anxious to keep up with fashion. Both these failings—failings only where poetry is concerned, because they are advantages in the business world and in most of the professions—encourage him to have designs on the public. The attempt to keep up with fashion will lead him to borrow the style of whatever poet is most highly approved at the time. . . . Now, I have known three generations of John Smiths. The type breeds true. John Smith II and III went to the same school, university and learned profession as John Smith I. Yet John Smith I wrote pseudo-Swinburne; John Smith II wrote pseudo-Brooke; and John Smith III is now writing pseudo-Eliot. But unless John Smith can write John Smith, however unfashionable the result, why does he bother to write at all? Surely one Swinburne, one Brooke, or one Eliot are enough in any age?

Ambition has even worse results. The young poet will try to be original; he will begin to experiment: a great mistake. It is true that if an unusually difficult problem forces a poet into a poetic trance, he may find himself not only making personal variations on accepted verse forms but perhaps (as Shakespeare and Hardy did) coining new words. Yet innovation in this sense is not experiment. Experimental research is all very well for a scientist. He carries out a series of routine experiments in the properties (say) of some obscure metallic compound, and publishes the results in a scientific journal. But poetry cannot be called a science; science works on a calm intellectual level, with proper safeguards against imaginative freedom.

And what is all this nonsense about poetry not paying? Why should it pay? Especially when it is experimental in the scientific sense? Poets today complain far too much about the economic situation, and even expect the State to support them. What social function have they? They are neither scientists, nor entertainers, nor philosophers, nor preachers. Are they then 'unacknowledged legislators' as Shelley suggested? But how can unacknowledged legislators be publicly supported by the legislature itself? If a poet is obsessed by the Muse and privileged to satisfy her demands when he records his obsessions in poetry, this in itself should be sufficient reward. I doubt whether he should even bargain with the public, like Wee MacGregor (wasn't it?) with his school-friend: 'Gie me a bite of your apple, and I'll

show you my sair thumb! ' It always surprises me to find that my personal poems have a public at all; probably most of my readers buy
them because of my novels—which I think is a very poor reason.

So much for the poet in his unjustified search for a public. Now
about the public in its justified search for a poet. Public, you sent me
a one-man delegation the other day in the person of a worthy, well-
educated, intelligent, puzzled paterfamilias, who happened to be
closely connected with the publishing trade. This is how he began:
' I must be getting old and stupid, Robert, but I can't really follow
more than an occasional line of this modern poetry. I feel quite
ashamed of myself in the presence of my boy Michael and his friends.'

I asked him to explain. ' Well,' he said, ' when I was young and
keen on modern painting I had a fight with my father because he
couldn't appreciate Toulouse-Lautrec or the Douanier Rousseau. And
now an important Toulouse-Lautrec fetches as much as a Botticelli;
and if you own a Douanier Rousseau, you have to install a burglar
alarm. . . . Michael and his friends take the same line about Mr
X and Mr Y; and so does everyone else at Cambridge. Mr X's *Collected Poems* have recently sold ten thousand copies, and Mr Y is
regarded as the highest apple on the tree. *All* the critics can't be
wrong.'

' Why can't all the critics be wrong? ' I asked. ' If you mean the
un-poets who set the Paris fashions. Who decides on this year's skirt-
length? Not the women themselves, but one or two clever man-milliners in the Rue de la Paix. Similar man-milliners control the fashions in poetry. There will always be a skirt-length. . . . And as
William Blake said: " In a Commercial Nation impostors are abroad
in every profession." How do you know that twenty years hence
Messrs X and Y won't be as old-look as Humbert Wolfe and John
Freeman, who were public idols twenty or thirty years ago? '

He said: ' Toulouse-Lautrec and Rousseau aren't old-look.'

I pacified him by agreeing that it would take a lot to kill either; or,
for that matter, Botticelli. Then he asked the question that you are all
itching to ask me: ' How can you tell good poetry from bad? '

I answered: ' How does one tell good fish from bad? Surely by the
smell? Use your nose.'

He said: ' Yes, perhaps with practice one can tell the clumsy from
the accomplished. But what about the real and the artificial? '

'Real fish will smell real, and artificial fish will have no smell at all.'

He thought this rather too slick an answer, so I explained: ' If you prefer the painting metaphor, very well. The test of a painting is not what it looks like in an exhibition frame on varnishing day; but whether it can hang on the wall of your dining-room a year or two after you bought it without going dead on you. The test of a poem is whether you can re-read it with excitement three years after the critics tell you it's a masterpiece. Well, the skirt-length of fashion has wandered up and down the leg from heel to knee since I first read my elder contemporaries Thomas Hardy and William Davies and Robert Frost; and my younger contemporaries Laura Riding, Norman Cameron and James Reeves. They have all at times written below their best, and none of them are in fashion now, but their best does not go dead on the wall.'

To conclude. The only demands that a poet can make from his public are that they treat him with consideration, and expect nothing from him; and do not make a public figure of him—but rather, if they please, a secret friend. And may I take this opportunity for appealing to young poets: not to send me their poems for my opinion? If they are true poems, they will know this themselves and not need me to say so; and if they are not, why bother to send them?

BEST MAN, BORE, BAMBOOZLE, ETC.

Not long ago, because I had described myself as an ex-member of the Anglican Communion, a Northern daily newspaper branded me as a ' renegade protestant '. When they tried to justify the libel by quoting the *Concise Oxford English Dictionary,* I replied that the *Concise O.E.D.* sacrifices accuracy to brevity, and referred them to the 13-volume *O.E.D.* itself to prove that before qualifying as a renegade one must embrace a rival faith—such as Mohammedanism or Judaism—which I had demonstrably not done. Only there, I insisted, can one hope to find the whole meaning and atmosphere of English words unequivocally set out with illustrative quotations.

The newspaper proprietors printed the apology I demanded, not venturing to argue further. Yet the *O.E.D.* has no official standing of the sort enjoyed in France by the great Dictionary which the *Académie Française* sponsors and keeps up to date. It abstains from such critical judgements as ' This is correct English; that is incorrect ', and is no more than a large dated collection of verbal usages, some of them plainly ignorant or perverse. The validity or need of many forms may be disputed—for instance, the forms of *refectorian, refectorary* and *refectorer* are all dubious variants of *refectioner,* meaning the official in charge of the *refectory;* yet their literary occurrence must be accepted as historical because noted in the *O.E.D.*—and they can therefore be quoted as precedents by writers who wish to use them again instead of either *refectioner* or *refectuary,* which is how the word should properly be formed from the medieval Latin *refectuarius.* The English language is, in fact, regulated by judge-made law, rather than by a Code or by Acts of Parliament.

No other dictionary of English, of course, comes within measurable distance of this, and every poet should have continuous access to it.

I would sooner part with my overcoat than with my much-travelled
set. When it is supported by the 6-volume *Dialect Dictionary,* a Slang
Dictionary and a Dictionary of Americanisms, most questions about
the date, derivation and meaning of any word can be satisfactorily
settled. But not, I admit, all questions. I have consulted my *O.E.D.*
on an average three times a day for the last twenty-five years, and
have often enough been left dissatisfied or doubtful. Only yesterday,
for instance, I looked up the heraldic term *lion leopardée* and read
that, in French heraldry, it means a *lion passant* (walking and turning
full face) as in our Royal coat of arms. Yet in an authoritative Majorcan sixteenth-century *armorial,* the so-called *lion leopardée* which
appears on the Bonapart coat is *rampant gardant*—like the crowned
lion which, with the unicorn, supports the Royal Crown. Since therefore Majorcan heraldry was French and the Bonaparts came from
Languedoc, did the author of the *armorial* perhaps blazon the arms
incorrectly? Or is the *O.E.D.* wrong in suggesting that a *lion leopardée*
cannot ramp?

Best man is a convenient example of an entry which fails to pass
muster. The editors have defined the word as ' groomsman, or friend
of the bridegroom ', rather than as ' paranymph, or bridegroom's ad-
jutant '. *Paranymph* (correctly defined in a later volume) is the more
accurate term because, as the quotations under *groomsman* show, a
bridegroom may have any number of groomsmen, but only one paranymph; and because a ' best man ' is not necessarily the bridegroom's
friend—cases have been known in which a titled relative of the bride's
family, whom the bridegroom has never met, is foisted on him at the
altar steps to give the wedding greater cachet. Worse, the meaning
of *best* is not defined here—are the criteria of his excellence, moral,
physical or social?—and ' of Scottish origin ' though supported by the
two earliest quotations given (1814 and 1823) is shown to be incorrect by Robert Plot's *Natural History of Oxfordshire* (1705).
Plot writes in Chapter 8, illuminating the whole question:

> We may reckon many ancient customs still retain'd here, abolish'd
> and quite lost in other *Counties,* such as that of *Running* at the
> Quinten . . . once a trial of *Manhood* between two *Parties;* since
> that, a Contest among *Friends,* who should wear the *gay Garland,*
> but now only in request at *Marriage* and set up in the way for

Young Men to ride at, as they carry home the Bride, he that breaks the Board being counted the *Best Man*.

Again, Plot's use of the word *Board* as a synonym for *quinten,* or *quintain,* is not listed; nor is *gay Garland,* as specifically meaning a flowery wreath awarded to men for prowess in rural sports; though *the garland* is noted as worn by the elected May Queen, or ' by girls as a prize for some kind of competition '.

The adverb *so so,* defined as ' in an indifferent, mediocre, or passable degree ' is given the same derivation as the adjective *so so,* which is similarly defined as ' indifferent, mediocre, of middling quality '. Now, the adverb *so so* (like *sae sae* in Scotland, *zoo zoo* in Dutch, and *so so* in German) has lost the accompanying gesture which its French and Spanish equivalents retain. *Comme çi, comme ça,* and *asi asi* are spoken with a see-sawing motion of the hand to suggest ' sometimes better, sometimes worse '. But the Spanish adjective *soso,* spoken with a gesture of dismissal, and seemingly derived from the Latin *sopire,* ' to deprive of feeling, or sense ', is unconnected with *asi asi.* It means ' downright dull, vapid, tasteless '. And since the English adjective *soso,* first used by Nicolas Udall (1542), is spelt as one word and applied by him to weak wine, it seems to be the borrowed Spanish adjective rather than an adaption of the earlier English adverb *so so.*

The editors define the verb *bore* as ' to weary by tedious conversation, or simply by the failure to be interesting ', and the noun *bore* as ' the malady of ennui '; but cannot agree on an etymology for either. While avoiding the usual explanation that the Biblical use of *bore,* ' to insist upon a hearing ', accounts for both the noun and the verb, they presume a French origin and unconfidently mention *bourre,* ' padding ' or ' triviality ', and *bourrer,* ' to satiate ' as perhaps the words implicated. But they say nothing of the Spanish words *aburrir,* ' to bore ', and *burrada,* ' a boring occasion ', which come much closer in sense to *bore,* and are derived from *burro,* ' ass '. *Aburrir* is ' to make an ass of ' by rustic and relentless shouting. Moreover, this sense of *bore* recalls the earlier one found in the *Life of Thomas Cromwell* (1602): ' One that hath gulled you, that hath bored you, sir,' and Fletcher's *Spanish Curate* (1622): ' I am laughed at, baffled

and bored, it seems . . .' where ' made an ass of ' comes closer to the
intended sense than anything that the *O.E.D.* can adduce.

Another word for which no derivation has been suggested is *jamboree,* though the quotations supplied point to a solution. The entry
runs:

> *Jamboree:* U.S. slang. A noisy revel; a carousal or spree.
> 1872. Scribner's Mag. iv. 363 (Farmer) There have not been so
> many dollars spent on any jamboree; 1878. W. H. Daniels, *That
> Boy,* xv. 236. He enjoyed a drinking bout or jamboree as well as
> if he couldn't write the finest poetry in the language; 1895.
> W. O'Brien. *On the Eve,* 25/2. The Orange bad boys who . . .
> would be making the air of Belfast hideous about this time of the
> year with their annual jamboree over the July anniversaries.

Here the second and third references securely connect the word with
Ireland. *Jamboree* is now generally associated with the Boy Scout
Movement, because Sir Robert Baden-Powell, the founder, applied it
in 1902 to his camp-rallies at which noisy songs were sung and buns
and ginger-pop consumed; and it is more likely that Sir Robert borrowed *jamboree* from the campfire talk of his regiment, the 13th
Hussars, who were largely recruited from Ireland, then from U.S.
slang, which by 1902 had made little headway in the British Army.
Can the word be Irish Gaelic? Admittedly, Gaelic has no *j.* Its place
is taken by *sh;* thus *John* becomes *Shawn,* and *James* becomes
Shamus. But all Irish dictionaries agree that *Shan* means ' great ', and
Bairghín (pronounced *barreen*) means ' a circular shape, especially
that of a large cake baked for wakes or other jollities '. *Shan Bairghín*
would connote ' a great circle of feasters ', and, when Anglicized, the
n of *Shan* would easily become *m* before *b;* as the cant word *benbouse* used by Fletcher in his *Beggar's Bush* (1622)—' a can of benbouse '—had formed the word *bamboozle* by 1700. Thus *Shan
Bairghín,* written *jambarreen,* is shortened to *jamboree,* on an analogy
of *spree, whoopee,* and other jollificatory words; except in Australia
where, either on the analogy of *hullabaloo,* and to provide a rhyme
for kangaroo, it becomes *jamboroo.*

Here we have stumbled on another weakness in the *O.E.D.* The
note to *bamboozle* is:

> Probably of cant origin. The statement that it is a Gipsy word wants
> proof.

No mention is made of *benbouse,* which is the vagabonds' version of the French *bon boisson,* 'good drink' and the second syllable of which survives in the familiar English *booze.* To *bamboozle* is, apparently, to make a man drunk with a view to defrauding him.

It will be noticed that four of the entries here criticized come under B—the A.B. volume was prepared between 1882 and 1888, before the editors and their research teams had settled down into their stride. The inadequacy of the treatment has not been altogether repaired in the *Supplement* published, after the dictionary was finally completed, in 1928. Yet my frequent wonder is not that the *O.E.D.* contains occasional sins of omission or commission, but that there are not a hundred times as many, considering the frightful size of the task that the editors set themselves.

And now, as I write these last words, proofs of a new book of mine arrive and I notice that the printer has queried the adjective *protocatarctical*—' the protocatarctical cause of the Trojan War was the apple inscribed " To the Fairest " which Eris rolled at the feet of the three Goddesses at the marriage feast of Peleus and Thetis.' Turning to the *O.E.D.* to check the spelling, I find that the word, which I first met in some seventeenth-century pamphlet or other—but which? —is not given. I consult the Greek Lexicon and confirm the existence of an adjective *catarcticos,* from which *protocatarctical* would be correctly formed to mean, as I meant it to mean, ' of the very first beginnings '. There is no synonym of the same resonance and I do not propose to search for one. The question is: whether my authority will be considered reputable enough for the inclusion of this handy word in future editions, or whether *protocatarctical* will be allowed to die again after a brief airing.

I remember that when I stayed with Thomas Hardy in 1920 he complained to me: ' Yesterday I was not quite sure of a rustic word which I wanted to use in a poem, and once again found myself at a loss: because the only authority quoted for it in the *Oxford English Dictionary* was my own " Under the Greenwood Tree, 1872 ".'

THEFT

There are many forms of theft: some tolerable and even praiseworthy, some dubious, some reprehensible, some quite intolerable. The ethical aspect has been confused by the simplified definition that the Law is forced to make of theft: namely, the unauthorized removal from others of such property as has market value. The penalty imposed varies, roughly, with the market value of the stolen goods. In England, once, the theft of property having the value of five shillings or over was a capital crime. (Merciful juries sometimes reckoned a stolen guinea as worth only four shillings and elevenpence.) The Law has now been softened, but market value still remains the ruling consideration. There are others: whether the thief is a first offender, or a minor, and whether the theft was accompanied by violence. But two even more fundamental considerations play surprisingly little part in the assessment of crime: the degree of distress caused to the victim, and the question of title, which the very fact that thieves exist proves to be an ambiguous concept. The thief who snatches a woman's handbag from a counter—purse, keys, glasses, private letters, shopping list and all—is likely to cause far more acute distress than the thief who abstracts a lesser work of art from a public gallery. Yet the difference in gaol-sentence, if both are caught, may be between weeks and years; though the first thief has violently challenged the woman's confidence in the fact of possession, whereas the second is merely playing a game of chance with an object that seems attached to nobody in particular.

Mental annoyance, like the ' sentimental ' value of stolen objects, cannot be easily assessed. The Law will dispute that a gold-headed cane, an exact replica of which could be made for a few pounds, is worth a hundred times that amount to its owner because it once belonged to his grandfather. As for the theft of non-marketable *intangibilia,* the Law is admittedly equipped to deal only with economic values, not with emotional ones. Though a wife or husband may be awarded monetary compensation for stolen affections, this will represent the economic loss incidental to loss of love, rather than loss of love itself.

Three main kinds of thief are to be distinguished: the thief who prides himself on confounding property distinctions, stealing for the sensation of power it gives him; the thief who is ashamed of his thefts; and the thief who neither knows nor admits that he is a criminal, stealing from mere vagueness of property-sense.

Dillinger and his gun-moll, American Public Enemies of the 1930's, took pride in their thieving. They robbed from the rich and did not adopt the Robin Hood practice of sharing their spoils with the poor; the act of daring was a sufficient end and justification for them. Such major theft, on account of which the practitioner accepts outlawry and often becomes a hero of ballad literature, should be distinguished from minor stealing by swindle, which is simple effrontery within the social scheme. Swindlers make no positive attacks on property, but avail themselves of weaknesses in the laws framed for protecting property. If these laws were foolproof, the swindler would presumably be an honest man: his daring is in the comic, rather than the heroic, vein. The notorious Horatio Bottomley belonged to this class and, among his intimates, was jocularly proud of it. ('Suckers have to learn their lesson!') An office-boy once came up before him, charged with stealing a one-and-sixpenny postal order from an entry to a *John Bull* competition. Bottomley remarked in an indulgent aside: 'Well, I suppose he has to begin *somewhere.'*

The second kind of thief is instanced by the well-dressed shoplifter, who figures regularly in the news and often faints for shame when charged—the impulsive thief who cannot account for the act even to herself, except as a temporary loss of her social sense. A vision of luxury seduced her for the moment; yet in a normal frame of mind she has always respected her economic limitations.

The thief who neither knows nor admits that he is a thief seldom comes into court. And this is the most dangerous sort, because the market value of his stolen property cannot be economically assessed: he is the thief of his neighbour's privacy, patience, time, energies, and of his very identity. How are such thefts licenced? By the general axiom that man, being a gregarious creature, enjoys, or should enjoy, casual visits from his neighbour whenever he is not ill, engaged in making love, or working concentratedly at his trade or profession. He is held to have stored up a certain amount of social pleasantness, and this he must share with his fellow-creatures when they are impelled to call on him by a vague feeling of self-insufficiency—with which they also credit him. Like themselves, he must need ' company '. Thus they are following the conventions of social interchange: being neither decently interested in his personal problems, nor willing to accept any burden of responsibility towards him. This neighbour-dogma is added to the theory that all aberrations from normal behaviour are ' news ' and therefore public property (social pleasantness heightened to social excitement); the person who first secures the news, far from being a thief, is entitled to a reward from the news-hungry public. Indeed, nine out of every ten people are willing to share themselves with the public to a most generous extent—the hatchet-slayer summons the reporters and asks anxiously: ' This is front-page stuff, isn't it? '

Neighbour-dogma is strongly held by country people, for whom any refusal by a newcomer to go further than ' good-morning ' and ' good-evening ', when amicably greeted in the shop or post office, constitutes a social danger; and his privacy will be assailed in a hostile, though surreptitious, way. Yet once he has admitted the first caller (the local parson) inside the house, his time and energies will be at the mercy of all neighbours belonging to the same social class, who feel entitled to share his humanity. And in the city, where nobody is expected to know even the occupants of the flat above, or the flat below, there is always the State—brusquely presenting itself, on one bureaucratic pretext or another, with inspections, demands, subpœnas, and forms to be completed. Such thefts of time and energy are excused on the plea that everyone is a member of the State and enjoys a claim on the attentions of all fellow-members; the assumption of social community being based on that of national community. If a private citizen feels victimized by thievish officialdom, the remedy is held to lie in his own hands as a national or municipal voter. Furthermore, continuous thefts are committed in the name of Business, Politics, Charity —invasions of privacy, draining of energy, wasting of time, legitimized by an extension of the neighbour-dogma. That this organized theft is hardly ever challenged, suggests that few people still consider themselves private individuals.

The question of what may rightly be called one's inalienable own, safe from encroachment, grows most confused in the case of private amenities. According to the democratic view, each of us may control his immediate surroundings to a reasonable extent, only the too ' particular ' people being regarded as freaks and troublemakers. Between one person and another a no-man's-land of property is assumed to exist, over which neither has any special control. And if we dislike the new buildings going up along a favourite old street of ours, the sole grounds on which we are allowed to protest are those of impersonal artistic taste: though entitled to our private opinion, we can claim no right to be consulted. The favourite old street is ' ours ' only in a manner of speaking. Its architectural effect must be regarded as public property subject to our control through the municipal system alone; our personal reactions as individual citizens do not, and cannot, interest this remote and stubborn authority.

Few even of our purely local amenities are protected by Law. A successful action might perhaps be brought, on economic grounds, against the planting of a glue-factory next door to a tea-garden, or of a kennels next door to a hospital for psychopaths; and the Law does take cognizance of ' ancient lights '. But no remedy can be found against the spoiling of the view from one's rural sitting-room by the erection of a gas-works or a neo-Gothic castle. Nor can a neighbour be prevented from raising a tall structure in his garden which will command a view of our own and thus destroy its privacy; unless his actions when posted there are noisy, offensive, or menacing. Again, though we may sue a neighbour for stealing flowers from our garden (and recover their market value), we are powerless against him if he steals the affections of our cat by giving it richer food than we choose to give it at home. Actions have been successfully brought against fashion-pirates who make surreptitious sketches of new models at a private preview; but can a woman prosecute a neighbour who plagiarizes her individual way of dressing and thus steals from her the sense of looking fastidiously like herself? I may sue a publisher for an infringement of copyright, but not a man who tells my favourite story or joke as his own, and thus steals from me the peculiar flavour of wit that is part of my social identity. An inventor may sue a manufacturing company for an infringement of patent, but what remedy have I against an acquaintance who copies the interior decoration of my house and thus steals the dignity of its uniqueness?

Private taste is, in fact, at the mercy of public depredation. If we enjoy a particular view, we cannot prevent its being spoilt, precisely because our liking rests on taste, not on mere material considerations. If we fancy a particular combination of colours and express it in the decoration of our sitting-room, we are powerless to prevent a visitor from imitating what can be described as ' only a matter of taste ': the sensibilities associated with taste being too subtle for recognition in the register of public property. We do not really own the view on which we have bestowed thoughtful choice when we designed the house, and which has played an important part in our local orientation; nor do we own that thoughtfully devised sitting-room colour-scheme. We possess no more than a taste for a certain kind of view, or a taste for a certain colour-scheme. Our consolation must be that this taste cannot be taken from us by even the cleverest of thieves.

Two proverbs licensing plagiarism are ' *de minimis non curat lex* ' —which implies that people must not make a fuss about petty theft so long as the police protect the house from burglary; and ' imitation is the sincerest form of flattery '—which implies that the object of adopting certain peculiarities in dress or household furnishings is to call attention to oneself, or to influence others, rather than to be oneself as simply and honestly as possible. If imitation were said to be the sincerest form of respect, this proverb might easily be refuted. But the sneer conveyed by ' flattery ' imposes a shamed silence. ' Perhaps,' one thinks, ' I have, after all, been over-demonstrative, even a little theatrical.'

It is commonly supposed that a crowd cannot be reduced to a single integer by a process of division. I find this untrue: the integer of the crowd is the thief. Crowds will gather outside a church at the close of a wedding, or outside a hospital when an ambulance drives up, with thievish anxiety to steal the private feelings of the principals. Crowds are nourished by the theory that everyone has a share in certain common possessions. But these common possessions are so vague in substance that the collective sense of ownership remains unsatisfied; and the crowd swoops down on any available private experience or entity and claims it thievishly for its own. News is one manifestation of this methodical thieving; fashion, the pseudo-honourable convention by which something private is publicized, is another. But what of the original inventor? The fashions which the crowd adopts are never original inventions, always vulgarizations of such inventions by some super-thief. The super-thief has a keen eye for what is 'different' and knows how to convert the different into the stylish, or the topical, shrewdly by-passing the laborious processes by which the different was achieved. He would not reproduce the original even if he could; his sole interest lies in reproducing its 'atmosphere'. Most public characters, from dictators downwards, must be counted among these super-thieves, and stand in need of the three qualities demanded from the Elizabethan pick-pocket—an eagle's eye, a lion's heart, a lady's hand.

But: 'Isn't everyone a thief?' We must concede the existence, if not of an immediate, collective property, at least of a common stock, or 'cultural inheritance', on which even the most inventive mind must draw. The inventor of the phosphorus-match, for example, merely combined two earlier discoveries—the tinderbox and the ignitability of phosphorus by friction. A woman with an individual sense of clothes rarely weaves her own dress-materials, or designs the buttons, or the jewels, or the gloves. The most original poet starts with a given language and certain inherited metrical conventions. That there is nothing new under the sun is a sweeping consolation to the uninventive and would, if true, be a justification for theft. But it is not true. Though a common historical background certainly exists, yet what we individually do, or are, today implies specific additions to and manipulations of this background. The crowd has a collective claim on the past, but not on the present. No living person can be collectivized, except by means of what he voluntarily contributes to the common stock: which is not himself, but only a statement about himself in relation to society. Such a statement may help others to understand their own problems; but a man's way of being is as uniquely private as his handwriting, his features, or his gait. There are, admittedly, millions of people whose subservience to a conventional pattern has made them resemble one another very closely; yet however slight the differences between them, every one is to some extent an original, not a thief, until he merges with the crowd.

What theft, then, is legitimate? The culling of property never individually owned, or temporarily without an individual owner—the raw material of living—is not stealing. Buttons and accessories, for example, are on sale in a great variety of materials, colours, and patterns. A woman carefully picks a certain set of buttons and a certain trimming to suit a dress that she has in mind, the cloth for which was also carefully chosen from a shop counter. No theft there. Theft occurs only when someone deliberately appropriates the effect of a neighbour's dress, disregarding its personal associations. Accidental thefts may occur by a coincidental similarity in circumstances; but more often they are due to the lazy indecisiveness of a mind on which impressions of things seen or heard exert an hypnotic power.

Nature provides convenient symbols of the legitimate and the illegitimate thief; the illegitimate being the cuckoo, who saves herself the trouble of nest-building and the care of her young; the legitimate being the hermit-crab, who uses discarded sea-shells to cover his unprotected softer parts. The jackdaw is a doubtful case. He steals in a haphazard and irresponsible way, cheerfully decorating his nest with whatever bright object can be carried off safely—a bit of broken glass, or a diamond earring left near an open window. The cuckoo must, we assume, be vividly conscious that she is stealing, whereas the jackdaw is seduced by vanity; we could hardly accuse him of deliberate intent to steal. Literary thieves are usually viewed, with indulgence, as jackdaws: literature being presumed to be a necessarily jackdawish profession.

Stealing, nevertheless, brings its own punishment. No one with sensibility enough to realize that he is a thief will be permanently content in the ownership of stolen goods; though an outlaw may try to be romantic about it.

> *Furto cuncta magis bella,*
> *Furto dulcior puella,*
> *Furto omnia decora,*
> *Furto poma dulciora.*

But can any integral part of one's life really get stolen? If a literary style, or a way of dressing, may be so exactly reproduced that there is nothing to choose between copy and original, can we be sure that the original was, after all, unique—and not a mere collection of commonplaces? Objects of sentimental value, too, may be tokens of either clear or uncertain memories. If of clear memories, then the object may be regarded as a superfluity; if of uncertain memories, then it is still less integral a possession.

Love remains the greatest single power that recruits thieves. Love in its popular sense, I mean—the desire to take complete possession. Such love leads many an otherwise honest man to imitate the ways of his beloved so closely that he hopes to appear her second self: her favourite flowers, songs, poems, colours, and places will be his favourites, and his objects in life male parodies of her female ones. This swindling technique of love must be distinguished from the robbery with violence glorified in melodramatic novels, but rarely resorted to in practice. If the swindler succeeds in winning a woman's affections, there has probably been swindling on both sides: an association of two thieves results, each happy in the possession of the other's purse. Jealous loves denotes rage that some property of the beloved has evaded theft; for instance, former friendships, or occupations, or her affection for a favourite dog or cat. Old successfully married couples often acquire a common gait, a common smile, and even a common handwriting. They have almost ceased to exist as individuals; and all that they have stolen from each other and held in common pool becomes synthetic mediocrity.

In art and literature, thefts are sometimes due to possessive love; if not sexual love, then disciple-love. The victim may feel embarrassed and annoyed, as a woman feels when a sudden stranger lays his heart at her feet. But since social custom demands that she shall pretend compassion in such a case, rather than express her boredom or annoyance, so with disciple-love which takes the form of a close imitation of style or matter. The victim seldom says, as he should: ' Run away, thief, and manage with what you have! ' This may be because he himself began as a thief, and looks upon such stealing wistfully, as a wholesome characteristic of youth. Nor is disciple-love the only cause for plagiarism. It is more often prompted by an envious desire for reputation: the thief naïvely reckoning that if he can outdo the master in his own field he himself will then be the famous one. Sometimes it may be prompted by light-hearted experimentation: ' How does it feel to write or paint like So-and-So, and then like So-and-So? '

The prevalence of thieving forces an almost morbid conscientious-

ness on naturally honest persons, or on thieves converted to honesty
by dissatisfaction with their spoils. That a friend owns a green tea-set
argues against my buying a green tea-set myself; even of a different
shade and design, and even if green is the colour that I should have
liked. If I discover that the two operative words in a line of my own
also occur in a line written by someone else, I instantly cancel them,
even if the sense I have conveyed is completely different, and even if
the words in question are the most natural ones for me to use. The
Chinese have a proverb commending such scrupulousness: ' When
passing through a neighbour's orange-grove, do not pause to lace
your hat; when passing through his melon-patch, do not stoop to lace
your shoe.'

But whose conscience is ever quite clear? And how could it ever
be? My mind, at least, is not card-indexed. I may even have stolen a
commonplace or two in composing this pure-hearted homily.

KYNGE ARTHUR IS NAT DEDE

Something can be done with Agamemnon and Menelaus as historical characters. I find no insuperable objections to the belief that they led a mixed armada of Greek-speaking warriors against Troy towards the close of the second millennium B.C. Certainly, Homer's account of these events is not always satisfactory, if only because he flourished after the Dorian Confederacy had laid Mycenae and Sparta in ruins. Something also can be done with Roland and Oliver as historical characters, despite the obvious inflation of the Roncevalles story; their liege lord Charlemagne is a dateable king, and I am ready to believe that a rearguard action was fought by raiders against the Moors who threatened his Pyrenean frontier. The German Dietrich saga may read crazily, but its central character the Emperor Theoderic did exist, and certain faint historical outlines can be recognized in the saga, which at least seems all of a piece. But what can be done with King Arthur, a key-figure in English poetic tradition?

Though Arthur is described as King of the Britons, leader of a group of knights fighting in fifteenth-century armour and sworn to the eleventh-century Provençal code of chivalry, he can be identified with no post-Conquest English sovereign. Among his enemies are the kings of Ireland, Denmark, Orkney, and Brittany; and an emperor of Rome, named Lucius, whose territories correspond with the Roman Empire at its maximum second-century extension. Yet Arthur's chief strongholds are Camelot (Winchester) and Caerlleon-upon-Usk, Roman camps abandoned when the legions were withdrawn from Britain; and he checks the advance of certain pagan Saxons whom wicked King Vortigern has invited to Britain. In his youth, after collecting the ritual token of royalty, a sword, in the precise manner of King Theseus of Athens, he is acclaimed the lost heir of Uther Pendragon, Ruler of Britain; and presently takes part in the Battle of Badon Hill, which is agreed to have been fought about A.D. 520. He inherits Uther's prerogative (as *Dux Britanniarum*) of flying a Red Dragon standard in battle. This standard which has since become the *Dra Goch* of Wales, oddly connects King Arthur with the Far East. The Chinese Dragon Standard, with its pocket-like body of vermilion silk and its gaping jaws, was borrowed by the Byzantines from their Hunnish archer allies, to serve a dual purpose: as a rallying point, and as a wind-indicator like the pocket-flags one sees on airfields. A glance at the standard on a gusty day told the archers how much to allow for deflection. The device must have reached Britain before the Romans left.

Arthur then fights the mythical Giant of St Michael's Mount, the Great Cat of Losane and the terrific Twrch Trwyth (in Latin, the *Porcus Troit*) and sails in his magic ship *Prydwen* to harry a pagan Hell from which, in pure Bronze Age style, he carries off an enchanted cauldron. He is buried in the Isle of Avalon (or Glastonbury), where the monks later disinter his gigantic bones from an oak-coffin burial which dates him about 1500 B.C. However, the inscription on the coffin, in monkish Latin, states that: ' Arthur King of the Britons and his wife Guinevere lie here.' Giraldus Cambrensis saw this coffin and so did Edward I. Yet an ancient Welsh Triad insists that Arthur's grave will never be found; and this corresponds with a legend current in various parts of South Wales that he lies asleep in a cave with a golden crown on his head, whence he will emerge only to rescue his ' honey isle ' from foreign oppression. Similarly, the Scottish King Arthur occupies a hidden cave in the Eildon Hills, whence he will emerge only when someone finds and blows the trumpet he lost in his last battle thereabouts. And as a child I was taken to the top of a hill near Snowdon and told that this was where the usurping Modred dealt King Arthur his mortal wound, and that when seven church steeples could be seen from there, and when a pair of twins, a boy and a girl, went looking for lost lambs on a Sunday afternoon they would find King Arthur's dinted crown rolled away under a bush of bracken.

In the Middle Ages Arthur was the object of deep and sincere belief. Caxton writes in his preface to Sir Thomas Malory's *Morte d'Arthur:*

> In hym that shold say or thynke that there was never suche a kyng callyd Arthur myght wel be aretted grete folye and blyndenesse, for there be many evydences of the contrarye. Fyrst, ye may see his sepulture in the monasterye of Glastynburye; and also in *Polycronycon,* in the fifth book the syxte chappytre, and in the seventh book, the twenty-thyrd chappytre, where his body was buryed and after founded and translated into the said monasterye. Ye shal se also in the ystory of Bochas, in his book *De Casu Principium,* parte of his noble actes, and also of his falle. Also Galfrydus, in his Brytysshe book, recounteth his lyf. And in dyvers places of Englond many remembraunces ben yet of hym and shall remayne perpetuelly, and also of his knyghtes: fyrst, in the abbey of Westmestre, at Saint Edwardes shryne, remayneth the prynte of his seal in reed waxe, closed in beryll, in which is wryton PATRICIUS ARTHURUS BRITANNIE GALLIE GERMANIE DACIE IMPERATOR; item, in the castel of Dover ye may se Gauwayns skulle and Cradoks mantel; at Wynchester, the Rounde Table; in other places Launcelottes swerde and many other thynges.

The best, in fact, that we can do with King Arthur is to accept him as a national obsession, and his paradoxes as peculiarly insular. He was anointed King by an archbishop and wore a cross on his shield; yet his sponsor was Merlin the Enchanter, begotten on a nun by the Devil himself, and according to the Taliesin poems in *The Red Book of Hergest:* ' erudite druids prophesied for Arthur.' And though he permitted a few knights of the Round Table—those with beautiful Germanic souls and a pleasure in living virginally on bread and water —to ride off in quest of the Holy Grail, he himself never joined them. Living heartily in feasting, hunting, bold bawdry and open manslaughter, he attended church parade like an Edwardian cavalry colonel, largely to set his captains and other ranks a good example. Then why this assemblage of authenticated religious relics, as though Arthur had been Christ; and Launcelot, Peter; and Gawain, John the Evangelist?

The truth is this: Arthur had long been converted into a counter-Christ, with twelve knights of the Round Table to suggest the Twelve Apostles, and with a Second Coming. For though the seigneurial class consented to fight for the Cross as an emblem of Western civilization, the ascetic morality preached by Jesus did not appeal to them in the least. Jesus's grave warning that 'he who lives by the sword shall perish by the sword' was read as a joyful reassurance to the true knight that if he always observed the code of chivalry he would die gloriously in battle, and be translated to a Celtic Paradise in the twinkling of an eye. Moreover, the Western conception of personal honour could not be reconciled with humility, turning the other cheek, and leaving God to avenge injuries. The concept of knight-errantry would have made poor sense in Israel. I recall no distressed damsels in the entire Bible, the heroes all being national deliverers, not individual adventurers. When an ancient Israelite fought in God's name, he fought ruthlessly: thrusting women through the belly with his javelin, dashing the little ones against the stones, and smiting the infirm or aged with the edge of the sword—churlish behaviour for which an Arthurian knight would have had his spurs lopped off by the common hangman. And the Israelite was realistic about yielding to superior force and allowing himself to be led away captive; not so the true knight. Sir Accolon would have killed Arthur with:

> many grete strokes, and for the moste party every stroke Accolon gaff wounded him full sore. And always King Arthur loste so much blood that hit was marvayle he stode upon his feete, but he was so full of knighthode that he endured the payne. And his swerde braste at the cross and felle on the grasse among the blood, and when he saw that, he was in grete feare to dye.

However, he would not yield:

> for I promised by the feythe of my body to do this batayle to the uttermost whyle my lyff lastith, and therefore I had liver to dye with honour than to lyve with shame.

So Arthur fought on with shield and sword pummel until the Damsel of the Lake disarmed Sir Accolon by magic; whereupon Arthur won the advantage, but generously spared Sir Accolon's life.

Launcelot's love for Guinevere is altogether un-Christian. He loved her truly and was found 'togyders abed with her in her chamber'. Later he rescued Guinevere from the fire to which she had been condemned by Arthur 'and kept her as a good knight should'. After Arthur's death, he repented as a matter of form, 'endured grete penaunce syx yere, and then dyed'.

> And so after mydnyght, ayenst day, the Bysshop that was hermyte, as he laye in his bedde aslepe, he fyl upon a grete laughter.

And therwyth all the felyshyp awoke and came to the Bysshop and asked hym what he eyled.

'A, Jesu mercy!' sayd the Bysshop, 'why dyd ye awake me? I was never in all my lyf so mery and so wel at ease.'

'Wherfore?' sayd syr Bors.

'Truly,' sayd the Bysshop, 'here was syr Launcelot with me, with mo angellis that ever I sawe men in one day. And I sawe the angellys heve up syr Layncelot unto heven, and the yates of heven opened ayenst hym.'

Arthur, of course, had no right to complain of having been cuckolded by Launcelot; he had himself begotten Modred on King Mark's queen in her husband's absence, similarly claiming that he could not resist the pangs of true love—though, according to some writers, the queen was his own sister.

Whenever the merchant and artisan classes turn Lollards or Levellers and repudiate the chivalrous tradition, King Arthur is publicized as a national hero. Milton would doubtless have written his projected Arthurian Epic in this sense at the time of the Great Rebellion, but for the unknightly thoughts which an unhappy marriage bred in his mind, forcing him to desert the Cavalier cause. He turned Hebrew prophet instead. Eventually Tennyson versified the legends in his *Idylls of the King,* as a means of strengthening the throne against Chartism and the chapels; but compromised sadly by introducing a heavy atmosphere of guilt and scandal into Malory's straightforward story of Launcelot and Guinevere. The 'manner of love in King Arthur's days' was therefore generally repudiated until William Morris wrote *The Defence of Guinevere;* since when the bonds of Christian marriage have become less and less burdensome to knight and lady. Thus the Briton's counter-Bible is the *Morte D'Arthur,* here for the first time available at a popular price in the best text,[1] that of the Winchester College MS.

Sir Thomas Malory, the author, was an eccentric Warwickshire knight who served at the siege of Calais in 1436, sat in Parliament nine years later, and then began a career of knight-errantry for which he suffered eight terms of imprisonment before his death at Newgate in 1471. The charges against him were cattle-raiding, rifling the Abbey of Blessed Mary of Combe, and twice forcing the wife of one

---

[1] *The Works of Sir Thomas Malory,* edited by Eugene Vinaver. Geoffrey Cumberlege, Oxford University Press, 1954, 21s.

Hugh Smyth—but Guinevere probably told Arthur that she had been twice forced by Launcelot. Malory makes no historical sense of King Arthur, but unifies the scattered legends in so masterly a fashion that their very contradictions and miracles give them almost gospel authority; justifying his faith that: ' Kynge Arthur is nat dede but shall come agayne.'

Shakespeare, another Warwickshire man, understood all this perfectly. He places the departed soul of his favourite knight-errant— a renowned leader and swordsman who loved feasting, drinking, adultery and the panoply of war—' neither in Heaven nor in Hell . . . but in Arthur's bosom, if ever man went to Arthur's bosom.'

DR SYNTAX AND MR POUND

(prompted by *The Poet as Translator;*
The Times Literary Supplement,
Sept. 18, 1953)[1]

DR SYNTAX: Now for our Propertius translation, boys. This morning
we begin with the lines:

> *Multi, Roma, tuas laudes annalibus addent*
> *Qui finem imperii Bactra futura canent.*
> *Sed, quod pace legas, opus hoc de monte Sororum*
> *Detulit intactâ pagina nostra viâ.*

(*Dr Snytax consults his teachers' crib, which reads: '* Multi, Roma,
many men, O Rome, *addent,* shall add, *tuas laudes annalibus,*
praises of thee to the annals, *qui canent,* prophesying, *Bactra
futura,* that Bactria shall form, *imperii finem,* thine imperial frontier [i.e. that the Parthian empire shall be absorbed], *sed,* but,
pagina nostra, my page, *detulit,* has brought down, *hoc opus,* this
work, *de monte Sororum,* from the mountain of the Sisters [i.e. the
Muses of Parnassus], *viâ intactâ,* by an untrodden path, *quod legas
pace,* for thee to read in time of peace [i.e. I alone have not joined
the cavalcade of popular war poets].' *He sighs and looks about
him.*)

THE BOYS: Only to the bottom of the page, Dr Syntax, Sir.

DR SYNTAX: Ha! Very well. Let me see! Whom shall I put on to con-
strue first? Surely our celebrated transatlantic scholar Ezra Pound
who only yesterday, perhaps inspired by George Borrow's felicitous

---

[1] Quotations from the *T.L.S.* eulogy of Pound are here printed in CAPITAL
LETTERS.

pseudo-translations from the Armenian and Polish, distinguished himself by rendering

Unde pater sitiens Ennius ante bibit

as if *sitiens* meant ' sitting ', not ' a-thirst '. Quiet, boys, no merriment! Come on, Pound; my Fabian *libra* of twelve *asses* in one, ha, ha! I can see you are yearning to outdo yourself.

POUND (*virtuously*): Please, Dr Syntax, Sir! I have translated the whole passage into free verse. I call it *Homage to Sextus Propertius,* Sir.

DR SYNTAX: Eh, what? How very industrious and thoughtful of you! Proceed! We are all attention.

POUND (*declaims*):
Annalists will continue to record Roman reputations.
Celebrities from the Trans-Caucasus will belaud Roman celebrities
And expound the distentions of Empire,
But for something to read in normal circumstances?
For a few pages brought down from the forked hill unsullied?

DR SYNTAX: BREATHTAKING MAGNIFICENCE, Pound, BRILLIANT PARA-PHRASES. I am delighted that you scorn to use Kelly's *Keys to the Classics.* You are, I see, DELIBERATELY DISTORTING THE STRICT SENSE IN ORDER TO BRING OUT VIVIDLY PROPERTIUS'S LATENT IRONY. I would go farther: I would say that you have expanded a facile and rather petty pair of elegiac couplets into what MUST SURELY PROVE TO BE A DURABLE ADDITION TO, AND INFLUENCE UPON, ORIGINAL POETRY IN THE ENGLISH LANGUAGE IN THIS CEN-TURY. But, pray, would you be kind enough, for the benefit of the slower-witted members of the Fourth Form, to give a literal, un-padded, word-for-word translation of the Latin, however bald? I suspect that ' CELEBRITIES FROM THE TRANS-CAUCASUS ' ARE A BRIGHT NOTION OF POUND'S OWN, SUGGESTED PERHAPS BY THE SINGLE WORD BACTRA?

POUND: O, no, Dr Syntax, Sir. Please, Sir, it goes like this. *Multi tuas laudes,* many of your praises, *Roma,* O Rome, *addent annalibus,* will be added by annalists, *qui,* who, *Bactra futura,* being Bactrians of the future (this is a bit like Macaulay's New Zealander, isn't it, Sir?), *canent,* will sing, *fines imperii,* about your fine empire. *Sed,* but, *quod,* what about, *legas,* reading matter, *pace hos opus,* when all this work is at peace? And then in apposition, Sir: *via,* a few, *intacta paginâ,* unsullied pages, *detulit,* brought down, *de monte Sororum,* from the hill of Soritis (I looked it out, Sir, and it means ' a forked complex of logical sophisms ').

DR SYNTAX: Great! This MAY SET THE ACADEMIC CRITICS ALL AGOG, but it will certainly earn you a four-column eulogy in *The Times Literary Supplement.* The anonymous reviewer will compare you with Marlowe, and say even kinder things about your genius than I have dared.

(*Dreamily.*) Talking of Dog-Latin, my boys, you all doubtless re-call Virgil's immortal lines beginning:

> *Vere novo gelidus canis sub montibus umor*
> *Liquitur . . .*

Unlike good Citizen Pound, I claim no talent for free verse, but I think I can knock up a pretty fair Shakespearean line: *Vere novo,* Strange yet how true, *gelidus canis,* the dog with chills and fevers, *sub montibus liquitur,* makes water at the lofty mountain's foot, *umor,* for a mere jest. Silence, boys, or I shall give you a hundred lines apiece! And while I am on the subject of discipline, my Poundling, let me remind you to visit my study tonight after school prayers; and mind you, *fili dilectissime,* no padding—ha, ha!

POUND (*mutters vindictively*): Pedant, Jew, pluto-democratic usurer!

THE COMMON ASPHODEL

LOVING MAD TOM[1]

(1927)

The first occurrence of the ballad *Loving Mad Tom* or *Tom o'Bed-lam's Song* is in a collection of manuscript songs and verses (British Museum, Additional MSS. 24, 665), called *Giles Earle his booke*, 1615; Earle was a friend of Thomas Campion's. It was first printed in *Wit and Drollery* (1656), next in an appendix to *Le Prince d'Amour* (1660), next in *Westminster Drollery* (1672). Disraeli popularized it in his *Curiosities of Literature* (1859).

1

From ye hagg & hungry Goblin,
y^t into raggs would rend yee,
& ye spirit y^t stand's by ye naked man,
in ye booke of moones defend yee
That of your fiue sounde sences,
you neuer be forsaken,
Nor wander from your selues with Tom,
abroad to begg your bacon
    while I doe sing any foode any feeding,
    feedinge—drinke or clothing,
    Come dame or maid, be not afraid,
    poore Tom will iniure nothing.

2

Of thirty bare yeares haue I
twice twenty bin enraged,
& of forty bin three tymes fifteene
in durance soundlie caged,

[1] My acknowledgments are due to Mr Jack Lindsay for textual research.

On ye lordlie loftes of Bedlam
with stubble softe & dainty,
braue braceletts strong, sweet whips ding dong
with wholesome hunger plenty,
    & nowe I sing &c:

3

With a thought I tooke for Maudline
& a cruse of cockle pottage.
with a thing thus tall, skie blesse you all:
I befell into this dotage.
I slept not since the Conquest
till then I neuer waked,
Till ye rogysh boy of loue where I lay
mee found & strip't mee naked.
    & nowe I sing &c:

4

When I short haue shorne my sowce face
& swigg'd my horny barrell,
In an oaken Inne I pound my skin
as a suite of guilt apparrell,
The moon's my constant Mistresse
& the lowlie owle my morrowe.
The flaming Drake and ye Nightcrowe make
mee musicke to my sorrowe.
    while I doe sing &c:

5

The palsie plagues my pulses
when I prigg yor: piggs or pullen
your culuers take, or matchles make
your Chanticleare or sullen,
When I want prouant w^th: Humfrie
I sup, & when benighted,
I repose in Powles w^th: waking soules,
Yet neuer am affrighted.
    But I doe sing &c:

6

I knowe more then Apollo,
for oft when hee ly's sleeping
I see ye starrs att bloudie warres
in ye wounded welkin weeping,
The moone embrace her shepheard
& ye queene of loue her warryer,
while ye first doth horne, ye star of morne:
& ye next ye heauenly Farrier.
  While I doe singe &c:

7

The Gipsie snap & Pedro
are none of Toms Comradoes,
ye punck I skorne, & ye cutpurse sworn
& ye roring boyes brauadoes,
The meeke ye white the gentle,
mee handle touch, & spare not
but those y^t crosse Tom Rynosseross
doe what ye Panther dare not.
  Although I sing &c:

8

with an hoast of furious fancies
whereof I am comaunder,
with a burning speare, & a horse of aire,
to the wildernesse I wander.
By a knight of ghostes & shadowes,
I sumon'd am to Tourney.
ten leagues beyond the wide worlds end
mee thinke it is noe iourney.
  yet will I sing &c:

VARIANT READINGS

(W. here stands for *Wit and Drollery;* P. for *Prince d'Amour;* West D. for *Westminster Drollery;* Dis. for Disraeli.)

1—2. rend you, P. rend ye, W. 3. Spirits that stand, W. spirits that stand, P. Spirits that stan, West D. 9. Nor neuer sing any Food and Feeding, W. 10. Money (*for* feedinge), W. 12. For Tom, W.

II—2. O thirty, P.   5. the lovely, W. (*This version also runs lines
5–6 together: followed by Dis.*)   6. in stubble, W.   7. and whips, P.
8. And, P. and a, W.   9. Still do I sing, W. Yet did I sing, P.

III—3. thus —— tall, W.   a thing they call Skies bliss you all, P.
4. fell, W.   5. till the Conquest, W.   7. rogueing, P.   9. stript stark
naked, P.   10. And made me sing, W.

IV—1. When short I have shorn my Sows face, W.   2. Horned, W.
3. Do I pawn by Skin, W.   I pawned my skin in an Oaken Inn, P.
5. Morn (*for* moon), Dis.   6. lovely owl, W., *followed by* Dis., and
omit P.   Marrow, W. marrow, P.   7. *second* the *omit,* P.   9. While
there I sing, W.

V—1. The Palsie plague these Pounces, W.   The Palsie plagues,
these Palsies, P.   2. When I plague your pigs, P.   3. Calvers, P.   4.
Chanty clear, P.   5. *Humphy,* P., I sup *carried back from next line,*
W., *also* Dis.   7. To repose, W., walking souls, W.   I walk in *Pauls*
with wandring souls, P.   8. And never, P.

VI   1. At Mortal VVars, W.   I behold the stars at mortal wars, P.
4. And (*for* in), W.   5. Embraces, W.   6. her Farrier, P.   7. While
the first doth horn The Stars of the Morn, W., the star in the morn, P.
The starre of the morne, West D.   9. For still I do sing, W.

VII—1. The Gipsie, *Snapp,* and Pedro, W.   The *Jeepsie* snap and
Tedro, P.   3. The Baud I scorn and Cutpurse sworn, P.   5. The
Soler white and gentle, W.   The Sober white, West D.   The sober
Knight and gentle, P.   6. Me trace, or touch, W.   Me trace, and
touch, P.   7. Tom's Rhinoceros, W.   *Toms* rynoross, P.   8. the
Panders, P.

VIII—1. With a Heart of Furious Fancies, W., *same without caps.,*
West D.   3. of the ayr, P.   5. With a Knight, P., West D., W.

Francis Thompson rewrote the poem. His version, first printed in
The Dial, v., does not appear in his collected works, and I think that
the editors did right to exclude it. The original no more needed rewriting by Thompson than Shakespeare's *Anthony and Cleopatra*
needed rewriting by Dryden. But why and how he rewrote it are points
of interest. Here are four of his eight verses:

1

From the hag and hungry goblin
That into rags would rend ye,

All the spirits that stand
By the naked man,
In the book of the moons, defend ye.
Beware of the black rider
Through blasted dreams borne nightly;
From Venus Queen
Saved may you bin,
And the dead that die unrightly.

2

With a wench of wanton beauties
I came unto this ailing:
Her breast was strewn
Like a half o' the moon
With a cloud of gliding veiling.
In her snow-beds to couch me
I had so white a yearning,
Like a moon-struck man
Her pale breast 'gan
To set my wits a-turning.

6

Hate, Terror, Lust, and Frenzy,
Look in on me with faces:
And monstrous haunch
And toad-blown paunch
Do show me loathed disgraces.
I hear on imminent cities
The league-long watches armèd,
Dead cities lost
Ere the moon grew a ghost
Phantasmal, viewless, charmèd.

8

As a burst and blood-blown insect
Cleaves to the wall it dies on,
The smeared sun
Doth clot upon
A heaven without horizon.

> *I dare not but be dreadless,*
> *Because all things so dread are:*
> *With a trumpet blown*
> *Through the mists alone*
> *From a land where the lists of the dead are.*

Poor Tom is, in Thompson's handling, a Romantic Revival character, but from the decayed end of the Romantic Revival—a Poe-esque character wandering witless in a James Thomson *City of Dreadful Night*. He has entirely lost his character as an Elizabethan stage-beggar, exchanging a moon-struck innocence for shabby-genteel unwholesomeness. He has even cultivated a squeamish horror of vermin, though once, as he told King Lear, he would eat the swimming frog, the toad, the newt and the water-rat; he would even drink the green mantle from the standing pool and think nothing of it. Now the sight of a squashed bug on the wall fills him with dread. Once he was on the easiest terms with his somewhat spiteful but quite familiar spirits; now they haunt him mysteriously and ' show ' him ' loathed disgraces.' And his lady is no longer Maudline but an unnamed and mystical ' wench of wanton beauties,' a punk of the highest possible class, but a punk for all that: and punks the original Tom used to scorn. Thompson, in fact, was trying to intensify the poetic horror of the poem by releasing Tom from the squalor in which he found him— a squalor which caused Tom himself no disgust but only a gentle sorrow—and setting him to wander, adjectivally, in a cloudy no-man's land of literary fancy and literary remorse.

It was a great error in poetic judgment; as unfortunate as Robert Browning's when he provided a realistically grotesque itinerary for Childe Roland's brief, strange and sufficient journey to the Dark Tower—again improving on a furious fancy of Poor Tom's:

> *One stiff blind horse . . .*
> *With that red gaunt and colloped neck a-strain,*
> *And shut eyes underneath the rusty mane.*
> *Seldom went such grotesqueness with such woe:*
> *I never saw a brute I hated so—*
> *He must be wicked to deserve such pain.*

' He must be wicked to deserve such pain ' is poor Thompson's verdict on his Poor Tom—because he did not understand the original poem.

His friend and protectress Alice Meynell had already purged the gold
of its dross, as she doubtless put it to herself, meaning the literary
part of the unliterary, by printing a severely cut and emended version
in her anthology *The Flower of the Mind*. It consists merely of five
four-line stanzas:

1. The morn's my lovely mistress . . .
2. I know more than Apollo . . .
3. The moon embraces her shepherd . . .
4. With a heart of furious fancies . . .
5. With a knight of ghosts and shadows . . .

Thompson embellished this refined version with enamel and filigree
work.

Other poets have also picked and chosen. Edgar Allan Poe, Rud-
yard Kipling, Walter De La Mare have all used the last verse ' With a
heart of furious fancies ' as an introductory motto to a piece of
romantic narrative (*The Unparalleled Adventure of Hans Pfaal;* chapter xv of *The Light that Failed;* and *Henry Brocken*) and Mr De La
Mare has used ' the gold ' again, after much the same refinement as
Thompson's and Miss Meynell's, in his *Memoirs of a Midget*. The
only case I know of a poet using a bit of the ' dross ' for preference is
Sir Walter Scott, who quotes a snatch of the ballad in *The Heart of
Midlothian:*

> *In the bonny cells of Bedlam,*
> *Ere I was ane and twenty,*
> *I had hempen bracelets strong,*
> *And merry whips, ding-dong,*
> *And prayer and fasting plenty.*

But it is at least possible that Scott was repeating a verse of the ballad
which had survived independently on the Scottish Border, a ballad
that was originally, as I hope to show, all ' dross ' and no ' gold.'

There are many obvious errors in the Giles Earle text (which we
may call, for short, E) suggesting the unintelligent copying of a manuscript now lost (which may be guessed at as Q). We may be sure that
Q was written in a double stanza like E, and not in a single stanza
like all the other songs which go to the *Tom o'Bedlam* tune; and this
is important, for when we come to examine the double stanzas in E
we find that the ' gold,' as opposed to the ' dross,' is either present

throughout each whole stanza, which holds together as a unit of thought, or else is confined to the second half of a stanza which does not so hold together. In no case does 'gold' begin the stanza and 'dross' close it. The poem is obviously the work of two authors: the 'dross' has a simplicity and brutality which suggest a popular origin, while the 'gold' is certainly the work of an educated writer. The first halves of the third and fourth stanzas:

> *With a thought I took for Maudline . . .*

and

> *When I short have shorn my sow's face*

could not have been conceived by the mind which added to the former:

> *I slept not since the Conquest . . .*

and to the latter:

> *The moon's my constant Mistress.*

The only tenable theory is that a cultivated writer took a poem which was 'dross'—a professional Bedlamite song, which we may call P, written in single stanza form with a refrain, like all the other songs that went to the same tune—and gilded it for use as a stage song that would appeal to gallants as well as groundlings. Then if we are to reconstruct P from E by an omission of all the work by the educated author of Q, we must omit not only the conventionally chosen 'gold,' but also any whole stanzas or second half-stanzas which have been used to bridge the literary and unliterary styles. This gives a poem (with the refrain as in E), consisting of the first half of stanza 1 (which Miss Meynell did not regard as 'gold' and which Thompson included only by a misunderstanding of its meaning); the whole of stanza 2, but split up into two independent verses (following the hint in *The Heart of Midlothian*); the first halves of stanzas 3 and 4; the first half of stanza 5—not the second, because the reference to Duke Humphry is a local one which would be appreciated by the Bankside audience, but which would hardly be understood in the country villages where the Bedlamites did most of their trade; the first half of stanza 7—not the second half, which is too magnificent. But some-

thing is missing. The appeal to pity is incomplete: there is no sum-
ming up, such as one expects at the end of a canting song. The missing element, which is the explanation of Poor Tom's madness in terms
of his love for Maudline, may be supplied from a hint in the first half
of stanza 3, ' With a thought I took for Maudline,' and from the second half of the same stanza with its reference to the roguish boy of
Love and to the Conquest; it is also suggested by the later-printed song
Loving Mad Tom from *Wit and Drollery* (1683), and by *To Find my
Tom of Bedlam,* from *Wit and Mirth* (1699), which is ascribed to
Mad Maudline herself. The first four verses of *To Find my Tom of
Bedlam* run:

To find my *Tom* of *Bedlam,* Ten Thousand Years I'll Travel;
Mad *Maudlin* goes with dirty Toes to save her Shooes From Gravel.
   *Yet will I sing Bonny Boys, bonny Mad Boys, Bedlam Boys are
      Bonny;*
   *They still go bare and live by the Air, and want no Drink, nor
      Money.*

I now repent that ever poor Tom was so Disdain'd,
My wits are lost since him I crost, which makes me go thus Chained.
   Yet will I, &c.

My Staff hath Murder'd Gyants, My Bag a long Knife carries,
To Cut Mince-Pyes from Childrens Thighs, with which I feast the
   Faries,
   Yet, &c.

My Horn is made of Thunder, I stole it out of Heav'n,
The Rain-bow there is this I wear, for which I thence was driv'n.
   Yet, &c.

It is unlikely that this song was sung in the villages by pretended
female Bedlamites (Maudline may be a reference to another hospital
for lunatics, St Mary Magdalene's, corresponding with the Bethlehem
Hospital from which Tom o'Bedlam took his name) though clearly P
was so sung. It is merely a specimen of *Wit and Mirth* made for singing on festive occasions, and probably hawked as a ballad, like *The
Aukreman* from *Westminster Drollery* (1661), and *The Vagabond*
from *Wit and Drollery* (1662)—all sung to the *Tom o'Bedlam* tune.

And it is unlikely that *Loving Mad Tom* (which we may call **L**) was sung professionally either, though it seems to contain lines borrowed from **P**. This poem runs as follows:

1

I'le bark against the Dog-Star,
And crow away the Morning;
  I'le chase the Moon
  Till it be Noon,
And I'll make her leave her Horning.
But I will find Bonny Maud, *Merry Mad* Maud,
  And seek what e'er betides her,
    Yet I will love
    Beneath or above,
  That dirty Earth that hides her.

2

I'le crack the Poles asunder,
  Strange things I will devise on.
I'le beat my Brain against *Charles's* Wain,
  And I'le grasp the round Horizon.
But I will find, &c.

3

I'le search the Caves of Slumber,
  And please her in a Night Dream;
I'le tumble her into *Lawrences* Fenn,
  And hang my self in a Sun Beam;
But I will, &c.

4

I'le Sayl upon a Milstone,
  And make the Sea-Gods wonder,
I'le plunge in the Deep, till I wake asleep,
  And I'le tear the Rocks in sunder.
But I will find Bonny Maud, *Merry Mad* Maud,
  And seek what e'er betides her,
    Yet I will love
    Beneath or above,
  The dirty Earth that hides her.

To Find my Tom of Bedlam reads like a companion piece to a *Loving Mad Tom* song in which the love element plainly occurs, though not necessarily to L. Another pair of companion pictures, *Forth from my Sad and Darksome Cel,* from *Wit and Mirth* (1699), and *Mad Maudline is Come,* from *Wit and Drollery* (1661), though printed earlier than L and *To Find my Tom of Bedlam,* are not of much interest except as confirming the love association of Tom and Maudline in a setting resembling that of E. *Forth from my Sad and Darksome Cel* recalls E in many points, particularly in a reference to the horning of the Heavenly Farrier.

Here, then, is my reconstruction of P, the professional song of the Abraham-men. The first verse is the sad soliloquy in explanation of insanity (supplied by analogy from *To Find my Tom of Bedlam*); the second verse is the salutation, recalling the customary ' lunatic bans ' of which Edgar speaks in *King Lear;* the remaining verses, except for the last, are proof of harmless insanity; the last is the appeal for lovers' sympathy. The poem contains no mythological references: the Book of Moons is merely, I think, an astrological almanack carried by the ' Moon-men ' (the gipsies):

P

1

In search of merry Maudline
Ten thousand years I'll travel.
Here's poor Tom goes with dirty toes
To save his shoes from gravel.
While he does sing ' any food, any feeding,
Feeding, drink or clothing?
Come dame or maid, be not afraid;
Poor Tom will injure nothing.'

2

From the hag² and hungry goblin
That into rags would rend ye

---

² 'The Hag' was the mediaeval reminiscence of the Bronze Age Goddess ' Black Annis ' or ' Anna.' She had a blue-black face and devoured young children.

The spirit that stands by the naked man
In the Book of Moons defend ye!
While I do sing, etc.

3

Of thirty bare years have I
Twice twenty been enragèd
And of forty been three times fifteen
In durance soundly cagèd.
Now I do sing, etc.

4

In the bonny cells of Bedlam
Ere I was one-and-twenty
I had bracelets strong, sweet whips ding-dong
And prayer and fasting plenty.
Now I do sing, etc.

5

A thought I took for Maudline
In a cruse of cockle-pottage:
With a thing thus tall—God³ bless you all!—
I befell into this dotage.⁴
So now I sing, etc.

6

When I short have shorn my sow's face
And snigged my hairy barrel,
At an oaken inn I'll 'pound my skin
In a suit of gilt apparel.⁵
But now I sing, etc.

---

³ The substitution in E of 'Sky' for 'God' in this obscene passage—a common evasion of the Puritanical stage-censorship—proves that E was written for theatrical use.

⁴ i.e. he thought about Maudline when he drank cockle-soup (shell-fish have a world-wide aphrodisiac reputation) which had a priapic effect upon him. 'Cockle-bread' was also an aphrodisiac.

⁵ *swigged* for *snigged* and *horny* for *hairy* in E suggest that Giles Earle copied from a badly written manuscript. The passage means that when he shaved off his bristles and roughly clipped the shaggy hair off his body ('barrel' is the belly of a horse or ass) he lies down under an oak in the moonlight. 'Thou'rt brutish, shave thyself' was a contemporary Spanish catch-word.

7

The palsie plague my pulses
If I prig your pigs or pullen.[6]
Your culvers take, or matchless make[7]
Your Chanty-clear or Solan![8]
Yet do I sing, etc.

8

The gipsies Snap and Pedro
Are none of Tom's camradoes:
The punk[9] *I scorn and the cutpurse sworn*
And the roaring-boy's[10] *bravadoes.*
I do but sing, etc.

9

But I'll find merry mad Maudline
And seek whate'er betides her,
And I will love beneath or above
The dirty earth that hides her.
Till then I sing, etc.

I get the same feeling from L as from *To Find my Tom of Bedlam:*
one of conscious ' Wit and Drollery.' With the exception of the first
verse, there is a strained, ranting tone which occurs nowhere in E,
and I believe that this first verse is the final verse of Q, the first
theatrical version of the poem, omitted by Giles Earle from his manuscript version with the same carelessness as allowed him to omit the
music for the song after ruling the lines for it; but that the author of
L happened to remember it and expanded it into a separate song by
using the second half of the stanza as a refrain and devising fresh con-
ceits in the style of *To Find my Tom of Bedlam.*

If this is so, Q can be restored as a poem by amending the obvious
corruptions of E and completing it with the first stanza of L. A young
Australian poet who is obsessed with the idea of making the theory of

[6] if I steal your pigs or chickens.
[7] take your pigeons or make a widower of.
[8] your cock or gander.
[9] whore.
[10] old soldier who blackmailed citizens into charity with oaths and threats.

la poésie pure apply to English poetry both in prospect and retrospect
recently praised the ' magic ' of *Tom o'Bedlam,* as he knew it in E, for
its very meaninglessness. When I suggested to him that ' and the lowlie
owle my morrowe ' should read ' and the lovely owl my marrow ' he
was very angry indeed. If he had been consistent he would have
adopted as more poetic the still more corrupt variant readings of later
texts, given above—e.g. ' Toms rynoross ' for *Tom* Rynosseross, and
' the Panders ' for Panther. His view seems to be widespread; for nobody has hitherto taken the trouble to make sense of ' swigged my
horny barrel ' or ' cruse of cockle pottage.'

My conclusion that the first verse of L is the missing last verse of Q
is supported by the way it picks up the various loose threads of former
verses. It carries on the figure of the tourney, disposes of the moon
for her ' horning ' the star of the morn (as mentioned in stanza 6),
and puts the necessary emotional emphasis on Maudline, the heroine
of the poem, who is scantily treated in E. So the poem ends with fierce
force as it began, not with the gentle and inconclusive ' Methinks it is
no journey.' So here is my tentative reconstruction of Q. It may have
lost other verses, but not many, because a theatrical song of this sort
was only a convenience for the scene-shifters; and scene-shifting on
the Elizabethan stage would not have taken longer than the time
needed to sing these nine stanzas.

Q

1

From the hag and hungry goblin
   That into rags would rend ye,
The spirit that stands by the naked man
   In the Book of Moons defend ye,
That of your five sound senses
   You never be forsaken
Nor wander from yourselves, with Tom,
   Abroad to beg your bacon.
While I do sing ' any food, any feeding,
   Feeding, drink or clothing? '
Come dame or maid, be not afraid:
   Poor Tom will injure nothing.

2

Of thirty bare years have I
  Twice twenty been enragèd,
And of forty been three times fifteen
  In durance soundly cagèd,
On the lordly lofts of Bedlam
  With stubble soft and dainty,
Brave bracelets strong, sweet whips ding-dong,
  And wholesome hunger plenty.
And now I sing, etc.

3

A thought I took for Maudline
  In a cruse of cockle pottage:
With a thing thus tall—God bless you all!—
  I befell into this dotage.
I've slept not since the Conquest,
  Ere then I never waked
Till the roguish fay of love where I lay
  Me found and stripped me naked.
And now I sing, etc.

4

When I short have shorn my sow's-face
  And snigged my hairy barrel
At an oaken inn I 'pound my skin
  In a suit of gilt apparel.
The Moon's my constant mistress
  And the lovely owl my marrow.[11]
The flaming drake[12] *and the night-crow make*
  Me music to my sorrow.
While I do sing, etc.

5

The palsy plague my pulses
  If I prig your pigs or pullen,

---

[11] dear companion.
[12] dragon.

Your culvers take, or matchless make
*   Your Chanty-clear or Solan!*
When I want provant,[13] *with Humphry*
*   I sup,*[14] *and when benighted*
I repose in Paul's with walking souls
*   Yet never am affrighted.*
But I do sing, etc.

6

I know more than Apollo,
*   For oft when he lies sleeping*
I see the stars at bloody wars
*   And the wounded welkin weeping,*
The moon embrace her shepherd[15]
*   And the Queen of Love her warrior,*
When the first doth horn the Star of the Morn
*   And the next, the Heavenly Farrier.*[16]
While I do sing, etc.

7

The gipsies, Snap and Pedro,
*   Are none of Tom's camradoes;*
The punk I scorn and the cut-purse sworn
*   And the roaring-boy's bravadoes:*
The meek, the white, the gentle
*   Me handle, touch and spare not,*
But those that cross Tom Rhinoceros
*   Do what the Panther dare not.*
Though I do sing, etc.

8

With an host of furious fancies
*   Whereof I am commander,*
With a burning spear and a horse of air
*   To the wilderness I wander.*

---

[13] need food.

[14] i.e. go to sleep supperless in Duke Humphry's Walk at St Paul's.

[15] Endymion.

[16] i.e. the Moon cuckolds Lucifer, and Venus cuckolds Vulcan.

> *By a knight of ghosts and shadows*
> *I summoned am to tourney,*
> *Ten leagues beyond the wide world's end—*
> *Methinks it is no journey.*
> *Yet will I sing etc.*

9

> *I'll bark against the Dog-Star,*
> *I'll crow away the morning,*
> *I'll chase the moon till it be noon*
> *And make her leave her horning,*
> *But I'll find merry mad Maudline,*
> *And seek whate'er betides her,*
> *And I will love beneath or above*
> *The dirty earth that hides her.*
> *Till then I sing, etc.*

I suppose, in fact, that the author of Q discarded the introductory stanza of P in favour of the more dramatic start ' From the hag and hungry goblin,' fitted an explanatory second half to this stanza, and retained the final stanza as the final half-stanza of a song made by doubling the existing stanzas and inserting two entirely new ones. It was important to leave Tom with both feet on the earth at the end of the poem, after his visionary trip among the clouds.

As for the author of Q, he was a poet of the first rank and either the author of, or a collaborator in, a play in which rogues and vagabonds occur. Were it not such an invidious undertaking to ascribe even a very good poem to a writer of Shakespeare's majesty, I should immediately suggest that it was sung by Edgar at the close of the third scene of the second act of *King Lear,* as an interlude to give the scene-shifters time to prepare the arrangement ' Before Gloucester's Castle; Kent in the stocks.' Edgar has just announced his intention of becoming one

> *Of Bedlam beggers, who with roaring voices,*
> *Strike in their num'd and mortified Armes,*
> *Pins, Wodden-prickes, Nayles, Sprigs of Rosemarie:*
> *And with this horrible obiect, from low Farmes,*
> *Poore pelting Villages, Sheeps-Coates, and Milles,*

Sometimes with Lunaticke bans, sometime with Praiers
Inforce their charitie: poore Turlygod, *poore* Tom,
That's something yet: Edgar *I nothing am.*

Must I play for safety instead and suggest Jonson's *Bartholomew Fair*, the song to be sung by Nightingale; or Middleton's *Roaring Girl*, the song to be sung by Trapdoor? These are the only two other possible dramatic contexts, but neither is anything like so suitable to the ballad as *King Lear*, where the outlawed Edgar plays Tom o'Bedlam and overlays the original dross of the beggars' ballad with the gold of courtly poetry. Indeed, if scholars are loth to accept Q as of Shakespeare's authorship they must assume a lost play by another hand in which the same unusual situation occurs; which would be silly. It will be recalled that Edgar attributes the loss of his wits to love. He warns Lear: 'Let not the creaking of shooes, nor the rustling of silkes, betray thy poore heart to woman.'

I NIETZSCHE

The homogeneity of the Germans has been a matter of remark since the first histories of them were written—as Tacitus writes: ' A race with a distinct character: a family likeness pervades the whole, though their numbers are so great.' It is noteworthy that the four chief names of the race—*Deutsch, Allemand, Teuton, German*—convey this sense of congenital relatedness. *Deutsch* and *Teuton* are derived from the same word—meaning ' the people ' in a corporate human sense. The Roman name for the race, as distinct from particular tribes, was *Germani,* which means ' the related ones '; it was a mishearing of *Wehrmann* (warrior), but the Germans accepted it as apposite. *Allemands* or *Alemanni* is *alle Männer* or ' all man.' Tacitus relates that their principal gods were Tuisto (the same as Teut) and his son Mannus (man), and that they sprang from the earth. That is, from the beginning Germans made a generic identity between the divine and the human.

Nietzsche was not only a German, he was increasingly conscious of what it was to be a German. *Ecce Homo,* his last book, is the most violent statement of Germanism on record; it was to him the most wonderful book, apart from his *Zarathustra,* ever written. Germans have a way of protecting themselves from an awareness of their own incoherence by telling themselves lies. Nietzsche piled lie on lie, but in the writing of *Ecce Homo* he must have come to understand himself, for the sequel was the madness which he had so long deferred: he allowed himself to disintegrate mentally and spent the rest of his life in an insane asylum. Tacitus observed how anxious Germans were, even when sober, to submit themselves to risks: they would stake their lives and liberties on a dice-bout. And reading Nietzsche —a man who, by pursuing Germanism to a desperate extreme, broke down in insanity—is for Germans an excitingly dangerous thing. Did not Nietzsche himself give warning that he who breathes the rare air of his lofty mountain-heights must beware? ' The ice is near, the loneliness is terrible.' Such cold and loneliness are metaphorical of loss of the comfortable sense of family warmth. Nietzsche is tempting the Germans to the abnormal; and they enjoy the temptation.

Ecce Homo was written in a condition medically interpretable as *euphoria,* which means to feel the highest well-being and capacity just before a complete breakdown. To begin with the physical background of this book is critically apt: Nietzsche himself was careful to explain his bodily condition by a running clinical commentary on the state of his health during the various periods of composition. The first chapter, ' Why I am so wise,' is largely an assertion of his own physical soundness and of the identity of physical soundness with spiritual well-being.

> My circulation is slow. No one has ever been able to detect fever in me. A doctor who treated me for some time as a nerve patient finally declared: ' No! there is nothing wrong with your nerves, it is simply I who am nervous.' It has been absolutely impossible to ascertain any local degeneration in me, nor any organic stomach trouble, however much I may have suffered from profound weakness of the gastric system as the result of general exhaustion. Even my eye trouble, which sometimes approached so parlously near to blindness, was only an effect and not a cause; for, whenever my general vital condition improved, my power of vision also increased.

He blames the original physical exhaustion on the German climate and the German habits of over-eating, over-drinking, gathering round stuffy stoves, and on his own sedentary habits as a philological bookworm—from all of which he has long freed himself by escaping South. He makes no reference to his real ailment, a deep-seated venereal taint, though he must have been aware of it. ' I placed myself in my own hands, I restored myself to health . . . out of my will to Health and Life I made my philosophy.'

Ecce Homo is one long diatribe against spiritual and physical uncleanness.

> I am gifted with a sense of cleanliness the keenness of which is phenomenal . . . I would die in unclean surroundings—I swim, bathe and splash about, as it were, incessantly in water, in any kind of perfectly transparent and shining element.

This bathing and swimming metaphor for spirituality is common to Nietzsche's writings; as all Germans give a spiritual significance to bathing and swimming. (Tacitus remarked on how much bathing the Germans did.) The Germans are also mountain-mad. By climbing they metaphorically express hatred of themselves for living in what Nietzsche, speaking in spiritual terms, calls the Flatland of Europe. Nietzsche's supreme praise for his *Zarathustra* is ' the loftiest book on earth, literally the book of mountain air.' Swimming and mountain-climbing take a high yearly death-toll of Germans: the number of bathers drowned in the Rhine, and of climbers killed in the Alps, is excessive. It is characteristic of the Germans, too, that once one of them gets drowned in a foreign river or killed on a foreign mountain his example is always followed by others: they do not intend to get killed, only to tempt a danger which the death of one of them has Germanized. Nietzsche knew the falsity of the climbing urge. He addressed the Germans in his *Dionysus-Dithyrambs:*

> *Ye mount?*
> *Is it true that ye mount,*
> *Ye loftier men?*
> *Are ye not, pray,*
> *Like to a ball*
> *Sped to the heights*
> *By the lowest that's in you?*
> *Do ye not flee from yourselves, O ye climbers?*

In the same poem he also writes:

> *Only the poet who can lie*
> *Willfully, skillfully*
> *Can tell the truth.*

The wish to arouse universal pity for suffering bravely borne is a characteristic of Germans for which Nietzsche had nothing but scorn and of which he wrote at length; yet he could not avoid the national idiosyncrasy himself. The year, he recorded, contained for him two hundred days of pure pain. Fear of physical indisposition makes the Germans of all people the most conscious of dietetic problems; and Nietzsche has not written twenty pages of this spiritual biography of himself as superman (the chapter heading is ' Why I am so clever '), before he feels himself obliged to note: ' In an enervating climate tea is not a good beverage with which to start the day: an hour before taking it an excellent thing is to drink a cup of thick cocoa, freed from oil.' In this strain he presses the double sense of the German word *Heiland,* which means both ' healer ' and ' spiritual saviour,' one who makes whole.

Nietzsche felt strongly in himself the German dietetic dilemma: the choice between the two extremes of ' bestial ' meat-gorging and drink-guzzling and the ' nonsense ' of vegetarianism, to which he lent himself for a time. The guzzling and sousing is the natural German habit —Tacitus commented on it—and Nietzsche rightly linked it with German intellectual barbarity. Vegetarianism is the unnatural reaction, and Nietzsche rightly linked it with the ' beautiful soul ' movement which he equally hated. Yet on the one hand he boasts of his own youthful prowess as a student-drinker at Pforta University, and on the other hand praises his *Dawn of Day,* written shortly after his severance from German cookery and drinking, for

> . . . that sweetness and spirituality which is almost inseparable from extreme poverty of blood and muscle . . . The perfect lucidity and cheerfulness, the intellectual exuberance even, that this work reflects, coincides, in my case, not only with the most profound physiological weakness, but also with an excess of suffering. In the midst of the agony of a headache which lasted three days, accompanied by violent nausea, I was possessed of most singular dialectical clearness, and in absolutely cold blood I then thought out things for which, in my more healthy moments, I am not enough of a climber, not sufficiently subtle, not sufficiently cold.

Nietzsche blamed vegetarianism, or malnutrition, for the spread of the enervating Buddhist creed; and in modern Germany there has been a sympathetic affiliation between Tagore, Gandhi and Krishnamurti cults and the *Rohkost* cult. The ' beautiful soul ' movement is apparently no modernism: the Germans have always been susceptible to Oriental religions. Tacitus was surprised by the presence of Isis rites in barbarous Germany—Isis, he said, was symbolized by a galley to denote that her worship was imported.[1] He also remarked on the German desire to be thought well of by the outside world: 'They are peculiarly pleased with presents from neighbouring nations.'

Nietzsche loathed himself for being a German, and yet the immoderacy and self-contradiction of his loathing was characteristically German. He took refuge in the lies that he was really a Pole: 'My ancestors were Polish noblemen.' But his mother was pure German, and his father, a Lutheran pastor connected with a petty Court, had a pure German mother; the Polish strain was remote. He found comfort in the thought that when he travelled abroad he was never taken for a German, but usually for a Pole. Culturally he declared himself French. 'The Poles are the French among the Slavs.' 'I believe only in French culture and regard as a misunderstanding everything else in Europe that calls itself culture.' Referring to the *National Zeitung,* he says, ' a Prussian newspaper (this explanation is for the benefit of my foreign readers: for my own part, I beg to state, I only read *Le Journal des Débats*).' Again, in one of his poems he describes himself as Genoese (by residence of a year or two), linking himself with Columbus. His Polish blood made it easy for him, he said, to be ' a good European.' Yet he was hungry and lonely for Germany and constantly slipped back in his writings into ' We Germans.' One of his poems, *In Lonesomeness,* is the most ingenuous admission of this hunger:

> *The cawing crows*
> *Townwards on whirring pinions roam;*
> *Soon come the snows—*
> *Thrice happy now who hath a home!*

---

[1] I have since come to the conclusion that Isis's galley was a moon-boat, such as was used in the cult of her counterpart Brizo of Delos, apparently the same goddess who was introduced into the British Isles in the second millennium B.C. as Brigit or Bride. This ' Isis ' cult must have been brought into Germany by Bronze Age immigrants from the Northern Aegeans. I now explain the schizophrenia in the German soul in terms of an unresolved conflict between their patriarchal Aryan strain and their matriarchal Mediterranean strain, which though recessive is attested by physical traits and numerous folk-customs.

> *Fast-rooted there,*
>   *Thou gazest backwards—oh, how long!*
> *Thou fool, why dare*
>   *Ere winter come, this world of wrong?*
>
> *Now stand'st thou pale,*
>   *A frozen pilgrimage thy doom,*
> *Like smoke whose trail*
>   *Cold and still colder skies consume.*

Nietzsche supplemented the poem with *My Answer,* as if the stanzas
had been addressed not to himself by himself, but to himself by some
critic in Germany:

> *The man presumes—*
>   *Good Lord!—to think that I'd return*
> *To those warm rooms*
>   *Where snug the German ovens burn.*
>
> *My friend, you see*
>   *'Tis but thy folly drives me far,—*
> *Pity for* thee
>   *And all that German blockheads are!*

In *Ecce Homo* he makes another accidental confession, at the end
of a passage about his Polish blood and ' *this* side of the Alps ' and
the German inability to understand music: ' I do not know how to
think either of joy or of the South without a shudder of fear.' And in
spite of his passionate invective against everything German he continued to award the highest praise to German individuals. By the time
he came to write *Ecce Homo* he had dropped most of his previous
admirations—Wagner, Schopenhauer, Goethe; but he could still
applaud Heine, Handel, Bach, von Ranke, Ritschl, Schultz, explain-
ing them as either of foreign extraction or as belonging to a race of
strong Germans now vanished. He accounts for his former adoration
of Wagner by saying that Wagner's music was ' the counter-poison
to everything German ': it was all wrong, a German drug, but if one
lived in Germany, as he himself had done, one needed it to keep alive
at all. ' If a man wishes to get rid of a feeling of insufferable oppression he takes to hashish.' Yet he had once prospectively linked him-

self with Wagner in posthumous fame. ' When, in the summer of 1876,
I took leave of Wagner in my soul . . . I took up arms, not without anger, *against myself* and on behalf of all that hurt me and fell
hard on me.' One of his chief charges against Wagner's music is that
it incites Germans not to marching or dancing, like strong old German
music, but to a falsely spiritual *swimming*.

Nietzsche could not disguise the fact that German was the language
in which he thought and felt and wrote. So he spoke of it as an
obstacle the overcoming of which made his feats still more glorious.
' Before my time people did not know what could be done with the
German language.' He boasted that he had even contrived to endow
it with wit: the famous M. Taine had spoken of his *finesses* and
audaces. Yet ' in order to cross the threshold of this noble and subtle
world one must certainly not be a German.' German dyspepsia
' utterly excludes all intercourse with my books.' He has been ' discovered in St Petersburg, Stockholm, Copenhagen, Paris, New York
—everywhere but in Germany.' This curious appreciation of his work,
in spite of the language bar, is easily explained: ' my readers are all
exceptionally intelligent men.' At this point Nietzsche cannot help
making an appeal to Germany as a poor misunderstood child cast off
by his cruel parent. He writes winningly:

> Wherever I go, here in Turin, for instance, every face brightens
> and softens at the sight of me. A thing that has flattered me more
> than anything else hitherto, is the fact that old market-women can-
> not rest until they have picked out the sweetest of their grapes for
> me.

Nietzsche was a clever tactician and knew it:

> *Deceit*
> *Is war's whole art.*
> *The foxskin*
> *Is my secret shirt of mail.*

This agrees with a statement in *Ecce Homo* about the natural de-
pravity of ' us Thuringians,' but is in flat contradiction with a neighbouring statement that he fights only honourable duels—all fair and
above-board.

His praise of everything French was well calculated. That a distinguished German classical scholar of good family and reputation

had turned King's evidence against German culture was welcome news to the French—still smarting from their defeat in the Franco-Prussian War. Nietzsche's master stroke was the declaration that France had recovered her soul in this war. He even went so far in his flattery as to put Paris at the head of the places of ' pure dry air,' followed by Athens, Provence, Florence and Jerusalem, where genius was climatically at home. French critics praised him extravagantly and the French Government eventually subsidized a translation of his collected works. Nietzsche knew that it was useless to flatter the English into accepting him as a superman; London is not among the capitals where he claims to have been discovered. He seems to have decided that the best way of attracting the interest of Englishmen was to make disparaging remarks about their *niaiserie,* in the French style: he writes of them as ' mediocre,' ' unsophisticated ' and ' benighted.' He even uses the French sneer at the size of English women's feet; and defends French classical writers—Molière, Racine, Corneille— against the claims made for Shakespeare's wild genius. But he cannot avoid the jealous, complaining intonation which the Germans inevitably fall into when talking about England. ' England's small-mindedness ' was the ' great danger now on earth ': herself and her colonies were needed for the European mastery of the world, under the spiritual leadership of a self-confident Germany.

He knew that he would get fame in Germany by repercussion: that he would be honoured as a great misunderstood German who had been honoured by the outside world, and that his apparent anti-Germanism would be understood and forgiven. A further shrewd move was his flattery of the Jews. He called the German Jews the honourable exceptions in national Philistinism; and as a result much of the impetus of the Nietzsche movement has come from Jews. The editor of the standard English translation, Dr Oscar Levy, writes in his critical notes both as a militant Jew and a militant Nietzschean. He discounts the seriousness of the Nietzsche movement in France and expresses ' the firm conviction that if we could not obtain a hearing for Nietzsche in England, his wonderful and at the same time very practical thought must be lost for ever to the world—a world that would then quickly be darkened over again by the ever-threatening clouds of obscurantism and barbarism.' The Nietzschean cult in England has been confined to a very small group, mostly consisting of

Scots; the one prominent person to champion him has been Bernard Shaw. Because of Shaw he has been accepted as a household reference, but at the price of being treated as a Shavian paradox.

Nietzsche wrote violently against Hegel, approving him only as a useful counter-poison to German sentimentality. Tragic sentimentality is another German characteristic. (The only other people in Europe to have it mixed, in the same way, with blood-thirstiness and philosophy, are the Lowland Scots.) He characterizes it:

> . . . Good-natured; incontinent in small pleasures; always ready for tears; wanting to be able to get rid of innate sobriety and strict attention to duty and exercise; a smiling, indeed a laughing indulgence; confusing goodness and sympathy and welding them into one—this is the essential characteristic of German sentimentality; rejoicing at a noble magnanimous action; thoroughly self-satisfied.

This is the natural Germanism, the Germanism of the playwright Kotzebue, he says, on which foreign elements are inappropriately engrafted. Nietzsche's prose writings are the best possible evidence of this contamination for which he blames the Goethe cult. And in evidence of uncontaminated German sentimentality there are his poems, even those composed after his flight from Germany. For example, his two hymns to Friendship; and his two poems on the subject of an Italian tombstone on which was carved a relief of a girl stroking a lamb, with the inscription: ' Pia, caritatevole, amorosissima.' In the second of these poems occur the following lines:

> *To-day, to-day alone,*
> *My soul to tears is stirred,*
> *At thee, the pictured stone,*
> *At thee, the graven word.*

> *This picture (none need wis)*
> *I kissed the other day.*
> *When there's so much to kiss*
> *Why did I kiss the—clay?*

> *Who knows the reason why?*
> *' A tombstone fool! ' you laugh:*
> *I kissed—I'll not deny—*
> *E'en the long epitaph.*

The anti-sentimental, bloodthirsty side of Nietzsche's Germanism is manifest in his glorification of war and his description of himself in *Ecce Homo* as 'the most terrible man who has ever existed,' on whose appearance follow cataclysmic world-happenings. Looking about Germany for companions in terribleness, he found them in Prussia, where there was an admixture of Slavonic blood.

> The Brandenburg nobility and the Prussian nobility in general (and the peasantry of certain North German districts) comprise the most manly natures in Europe. That the manliest shall rule, this is the only natural order of things. The future of German culture rests with the sons of Prussian officers. We require an inter-growth of the German and Slav races and we require too the cleverest financiers, the Jews, for us to become masters of the world.

Nietzsche is nowhere so inconsistent as in his alternate recommendations, as a non-German German, for the blending and for the non-blending of national races and cultures. ' Our present-day Europe, the scene of a senseless, precipitate attempt at a blending of races . . .' ' What I am concerned with—for I see it preparing itself slowly and hesitating—is the United Europe. It was the only real work, the only impulse in the souls, of all the broad-minded and deep-thinking men of this century. Only in their weaker moments did they fall back again into the national narrowness of the " Fatherlanders." ' In preaching the necessity for a consolidated European culture he either assigns the leading part to Germany or excludes Germany altogether. ' Wherever Germany extends her sway she *ruins* culture.' Now he applauds Goethe for introducing foreign culture into Germany, now he deplores the result: ' German culture is a sort of cosmopolitan aggregate.'

Nietzsche, in his attitude to women, is divided between a desperate need for their society and a fanatic desire to stand alone. One of the strongest German traits is the recourse to women in time of anxiety. Tacitus writes about the Germans' readiness to take the advice of their women—' these, too, are the most revered witnesses of each man's conduct, and his most liberal applauders '; and about the tribal marriage-ritual—the husband presenting cattle and war-like gifts to the wife, the wife presenting the husband with arms, which he must not disgrace while married to her, and thus becoming the priestess of his honour. The wilful insensitivity of Germans towards their women in everyday life has in it an element of shame—shame of their dependence on them in moments of crisis. As in the time of Tacitus, Germans still have an uncomfortable feeling that ' something of sanctity and prescience resides in the female sex.'

Nietzsche advocated the total suppression of these feelings: Germans should learn to treat their women in the Oriental fashion in the manner of strong men. Woman's first and last function was childbearing: in between, her function was to distract man and alleviate his troubles. In her distractive capacity Nietzsche insisted that she should take her cue from the man's desires, throwing prudishness to the winds: for ' love forgives all.' This is no easy task for her, he admits; man is so restless. She cannot keep his love unless she is essentially feminine, constantly whetting his sexual apetite by her fickleness. Such fickleness bars women from any part in public life or from any serious work. ' Women are so constituted that all truth disgusts them and that they try to be revenged on everyone who opens their eyes.' Yet ' the perfect woman is a higher type of humanity than the perfect man.' As for the divinatory and intuitive powers attributed to them, Nietzsche alternately pooh-poohed these powers and expressed the deep confidence in them which Tacitus mentions as a peculiar mark of Germanism. The most bitter of Nietzsche's many bitter charges against German women was that they were directly responsible for the barbarity of German culture; because they were such bad cooks, and because intellectual dyspepsia was identical with physical dyspepsia.

He gave them a complete exculpation, however, by saying that they really are not to be blamed; they are whatever man makes them. ' Man created woman—out of what? Out of a rib of his god,—of his ideal.' His own physical preference was for a majestic, contralto-voiced Germanic type—*petite* women were no women at all, he agreed with Aristotle. But this did not agree with his scorn for the size of English women's feet or with his intellectual demand for French daintness and roguishness: he hated ' placid cows ' as he hated the monogamic earnestness of German marriage which had so much impressed Tacitus. ' Bovine,' ' cows,' ' cattle,' were his strongest words of anti-German abuse. He wanted to be a bird; he had a bird-nature, he protested. And ' in order to become light and be as a bird, one must lose oneself—thus spake Zarathustra.' Nietzsche never succeeded in losing himself, only in contradicting himself; and the more self-contradictory he became, the more German—no soaring Pindaric or Napoleonic eagle, only a mad German ox entering into the spirit of the market-place by breaking loose from its herd and blundering into the booths.

II COLERIDGE AND WORDSWORTH

While ' Life went a-maying with Nature, Hope and Poesy,' Coleridge had believed that human reality and poetic reality could be reconciled. At Cambridge he had decided not to pursue metaphysical speculation, but to seek a life of practical virtue and labour in ideal surroundings and in congenial company. He was always looking for friends. The closest friends he made were also poets, though not poets in the sense that he was. They were ambitious and stupid men, but not so stupid that they failed to recognize that the very qualities which they needed to improve their own work could be borrowed from his. Southey was the first. Coleridge drew him into a scheme for forming a pantisocratic community with ten other gentlemen and twelve ladies in the back-woods of America. Coleridge wrote at the time:

> *. . . O'er the ocean swell*
> *Sublime of Hope, I seek the cottag'd dell*
> *Where virtue calm with careless step may stray,*
> *And dancing to the moonlight roundelay*
> *The wizard Passions weave a holy spell.*

Southey abandoned this colonizing scheme as impracticable, and Coleridge never recovered from the setback. It returned pantisocracy to the barren region of speculation from which he had tried to escape: moonlight and the wizard passions, failing to reconcile themselves with virtue calm and the cottag'd dell, became disconnected and unreal.

He next won the friendship of Wordsworth. Wordsworth had himself recently met with a failure, but a more complete one than Coleridge's. It is difficult at first to decide whether he was consciously aware when he was writing his poem *Nutting* of the meaning which

underlay it, or whether he was deliberately allegorizing an incident in
his life that did little credit to his social reputation. Composed in
1799, while he was on a walking tour in Germany, the poem is only
a fragment ' struck out from the *Prelude* as not being wanted there.'
It begins in the middle of a line and records a joyful holiday excursion
which he had made as a boy, dressed up in ragged clothes beside
Esthwaite Lake. He gets away all by himself to a part of the nut wood
where none of his companions has been before; there he finds a virgin
scene, a nut tree quite unravaged, ' tall and erect with milk-white
clusters hung.'

> . . . —*A little while I stood,*
> *Breathing with such suppression of the heart*
> *As joy delights in; and with wise restraint*
> *Voluptuous, fearless of a rival, eyed*
> *The banquet;—or beneath the trees I sate*
> *Among the flowers and with the flowers I played; . . .*
> *. . . a bower beneath whose leaves*
> *The violets of five seasons reappear*
> *And fade, unseen of any human eye.*

So he pauses awhile to contemplate, secure in possession, and then
beating down his sense of decency, rises up and ravages the boughs.
' But,' writes Wordsworth, ' unless I now, Confound my present feelings with the past, I felt a sense of pain when I beheld, The silent
trees, and saw the intruding sky.'

So far there is nothing remarkable in the passage, which might fit
well enough into the section of the *Prelude* celebrating childhood and
school-time and there serve as a companion picture to little William's
night adventure in the stolen boat on the lake. But three lines follow
' the intruding sky ':

> *Then, dearest Maiden, move along these shades*
> *In gentleness of heart; with gentle hand*
> *Touch—for there is a spirit in the woods.*

and we are left wondering who this dearest Maiden may be—a riddle
which in the childhood context has no answer. When we turn to the
ninth book of the *Prelude,* ' Residence in France,' we wonder afresh

what significance to the context the tale of *Vaudracour and Julia* can
have there, in which:

> . . . *Thou also, there may'st read,*
> *At leisure, how the enamoured youth was driven,*
> *To fatal crime . . .*
> *How, between heart and heart, oppression thrust*
> *Her mandates, severing whom true love had joined,*
> *Harassing both; until he sank . . . supine,*
> *Save when the stings of viperous remorse,*
> *Trying their strength, enforced him to start up,*
> *Aghast and prayerless. Into a deep wood*
> *He fled, to shun the haunts of human kind;*
> *There dwelt, weakened in spirit more and more;*
> *Nor could the voice of Freedom, which through France*
> *Full speedily resounded, public hope,*
> *Or personal memory of his own worst wrongs,*
> *Rouse him; but, hidden in those gloomy shades,*
> *His days he wasted,—an imbecile mind.*

Wordsworth's secret was revealed only a few years ago. When he
visited France in a burst of revolutionary enthusiasm in 1792 he had
met at Blois a girl named Annette Vallon, seduced her and left her
with a daughter, Caroline. His uncles deterred him from marrying
Annette, and soon war between France and England separated the
lovers, their correspondence was intercepted, and they did not meet
again until ten years later.

The ' dearest Maiden ' in *Nutting* is surely Caroline, then a child of
six; the poem amounts to an apology for the wrong done to her
mother. He asks the child to forgive his transgression, to be gentle
with these shades of the past, but for which she would not be alive
to enjoy the beauties of the forest of Blois. Wordsworth's sansculotte
enthusiasm on his arrival in France is well conveyed in the phrase
' motley accoutrement, in truth, more ragged than need was.' It is
curious that in *Nutting* the wood of latent meaning is the Forest of
Blois, where Wordsworth seduced Annette, and the wood of manifest
statement is in the Lake District; whereas in the *Prelude* passage, the
wood where Vaudracour hid from human kind is, in the latent mean-

ing, a wood of the Lake District, but in the manifest statement, a forest in France.

It is probable that Wordsworth wrote *Nutting,* with all but the ' dearest Maiden ' passage, as part of the Childhood book of the *Prelude;* and that it was only when he reached ' Residence in France ' that he suddenly recognized its symbolic reference to the Annette episode. He wanted to include it at that point as an allegory with the ' dearest Maiden ' ending, and probably an introduction sketching the story of his unhappy romance. But caution reasserted itself: he printed *Nutting* separately and inserted as much of his confession at the Blois stage of his autobiography as the story of Vaudracour and Julia could carry off. These experiences had been Wordsworth's plunge into unreality, and he set himself to destroy all incriminating evidence of them. In *Vaudracour and Julia,* though recording the closeness of the tie which bound the two lovers and the spiritual collapse of Vaudracour after he had been separated from Julia by obedience to family orders, he so distorts the actual happenings as to acquit Vaudracour of all infamy and assist the drawing of the moral of human reality: the love was too idealistic, and should have remained unconsummated.

In the third book of the *Excursion* a further confession of guilt is put in the mouth of ' The Solitary,' whose account of his blameless wedded life and subsequent poetical activities does him only credit. Yet a sense of guilt prevailed over all Wordsworth's elaborate self-excusing. The Solitary is unbalanced by his wife's death: despair drives him to revolutionary politics and to Rousseau-istic experiment. Both activities proving fallacious remedies, he retires to the countryside to commune with Nature. He tells his visitors:

> *Stripped as I am of all the golden fruit*
> *Of self-esteem; and by the cutting blasts*
> *Of self-reproach familiarly assailed;*
> *Yet would I not be of such wintry bareness*
> *But that some leaf of your regard should hang*
> *Upon my naked branches:—lively thoughts*
> *Give birth, full often, to unguarded words;*
> *I grieve that, in your presence, from my tongue*
> *Too much of frailty hath already dropped.*

Coleridge had not been base. He had not wilfully retreated; he had merely not been able to find strength to cling to poetic reality. Strength, for him, came to mean human companionship and assistance. Wordsworth assumed a righteousness proportionate to his sense of guilt; and Coleridge, aware of guilt only in himself, did not realize, when he wrote to Southey that Wordsworth was the greatest man he had met, what his righteousness hid. The failure of the revolutionary principle in France to achieve ideal results seemed an *ex post facto* justification of Wordsworth's desertion of the cause, and of Coleridge's abandonment of the American plan. Between them they made this amendment to Godwin's ethical idealism, to which they had both been committed (the words are Coleridge's):

> Those feelings and that grand ideal of Freedom . . . do not belong to men, as a society, nor can possibly be either gratified or realized under any form of human government: but belong to the individual man, so far as he is pure and inflamed with the love and adoration of God in Nature.

Instead of practising pantisocracy on an ideal shore, Coleridge decided to content himself with Wordsworth's scheme of deducing morality from Nature, as observed in the English countryside, and using this morality to soothe his spiritual dissatisfaction. Wordsworthian Nature did not, however, satisfy Coleridge; poetic reality still beckoned. So he persuaded Wordsworth to collaborate in *Lyrical Ballads,* which was to consist of poems of two sorts—those dealing with natural, and those dealing with supernatural, incidents. He made this concession to Wordsworth: that the supernatural incidents were to be put under the discipline of the natural emotions which they would excite. In Coleridge's *Ancient Mariner* the wedding-guest represents ordinary humanity, for whose benefit the mariner, a sinner redeemed from torment by the love he has suddenly felt for some beautiful water-snakes, attempts to confute poetic reality with moral counsels. But the poetic reality of his story has infinitely the greater force.

Among Coleridge's other contributions to *Lyrical Ballads* was *The Foster-Mother's Tale.* Here he tells of a youth who became very learned and ' ere his twentieth year had unlawful thoughts of many things.' He was put into a dungeon for heresy (dreaming there of green savannahs), but escaped to America; where he sailed alone in a boat up a great moonlit river, to live, a naked man, with the wild Indians: and was never seen again. In spite of the formal censure of the youth's behaviour, this is a strong plea for poetic reality. Wordsworth countered it, in the second edition of *Lyrical Ballads,* where it was reprinted, with a strong restatement of human reality—the poem *Ruth.* This is a tale about a romantic young man who, having lived in mistaken idealism among the American Indians, sang of green savannahs to an English maiden. He begged her to go back with him as his helpmeet. But he had learned the vices of the Indians, who were far from noble savages, and so betrayed her. His ship sailed without her. She went mad. Then, recovering somewhat, she lived an innocent life as a rustic tramp, playing on a hemlock pipe and communing with Nature; and Wordsworth promised her a Christian burial when she came to die. Coleridge had written the first part of *Christabel* in the same year: it was a still stronger plea for poetic reality—the ' frightful ' beauty of Geraldine, the witch who infected with her wickedness the modest dutiful Christabel of his pretended preference. Not being able, without violence, to subject the poem to the human discipline which he had introduced into the *Ancient Mariner,* he did not offer it for inclusion in *Lyrical Ballads.*

Lewti, though at first included, was cancelled at the last moment: poetic reality was idealized in it as a beautiful Circassian for whom a lover vainly sighed. For *Lewti, The Nightingale* was substituted. Here Coleridge made his most formal disavowal of the witch, whom the nightingale's song had evoked in her aspect of Melancholy, saying that Melancholy was an idle illusion—for ' as thou my friend and thou, my sister ' (William and Dorothy Wordsworth) had learned, the nightingale (poetry) was really a merry bird. To hold the other view would, he said, be to profane Nature's sweet voices, always full of love and joyance. But the poem itself, after the first three lines, which show the witch's influence, proves how far his poetic energy was sapped by such disavowals.

In Coleridge's poems the commonest symbol of the haunting presence of the witch is the moon. It occurs at the emotional peak of *The Ancient Mariner, Christabel, The Foster-Mother's Tale,* and *Lewti.* It is the main theme of *Dejection* (written four years after these poems) where he again addresses Wordsworth and tries to overbear melancholy with joy; but the moon has taken the shape of an Indian canoe and the Virtuous Lady Joy is routed. He records in this poem that he has been unable, in spite of Wordsworth's inspiration, to think of what he needs must feel.

The only poem in which he dared to find the moon good was *Frost at Midnight;* but he wrote it for his newly-born son Hartley, who might be blessed with the spiritual independence which he had failed to attain himself. In this poem he forgot all his Wordsworthianism, as he did in *The Three Graves,* written at the time that *Lyrical Ballads* was being prepared, but not included among them. In *The Three Graves* Coleridge savagely identified the sun, Wordsworth's god of joy and duty, with the mad vulgar mother who curses her two sensitive daughters and her son-in-law to perpetual unhappiness despite every virtuous endeavour on their part. In *Kubla Khan* he made his most complete recantation of human reality, indulging in a wanton luxury that came near to devilishness. *Kubla Khan* was written in the *Lyrical Ballads* period, but held back for a number of years, with the other unsuitable poems, until after his breach with Wordsworth: and then published only at the request of Byron, whom Wordsworth had taught Coleridge to regard as a representative, with Shelley, of the Satanic school of poetry. Even then he excused its composition as due to an opiate following the distress of mind produced by the calumny and ingratitude of men who had been fostered in the bosom of his confidence (Wordsworth not yet among them).

When friends failed him, Coleridge was always lost. As early as 1797, in his poem *To the Rev. George Coleridge,* published as the dedication of his *Poems,* he tells how much he has already suffered from disillusions and betrayals in his friendships:

> *. . . through life*
> *Chasing chance-started friendships. A brief while*
> *Some have preserv'd me from life's pelting ills;*
> *But, like a tree with leaves of feeble stem,*
> *If the clouds lasted, and a sudden breeze*
> *Ruffled the boughs, they on my head at once*
> *Dropped the collected shower; and some most false,*
> *False and fair-foliag'd as the Manchineel,*
> *Have tempted me to slumber in their shade*
> *E'en 'mid the storm; then breathing subtlest damps,*
> *Mix'd their own venom with the rain from Heaven,*
> *That I woke poison'd! . . .*

He then eulogizes the dedicatee as his earliest friend, whom he has loved as a brother and revered as a son. But in one copy of this book Coleridge wrote above the dedication: ' N.B. If this volume should ever be delivered according to its direction, *i.e.* to Posterity, let it be known that the Reverend George Coleridge was displeased and thought his character endangered by the Dedication.—S. T. Coleridge.'

Shortly after writing *Kubla Khan* he went with the Wordsworths to Germany. Parting from them there he took up metaphysics again, though he admitted its devilishness. On his return to England he showed a sudden surprising energy, writing vigorously on politics for the daily press. He renewed his friendship with Southey; and it was at this time that Southey gave him the first three stanzas and two further stanzas of *The Devil's Thoughts.* Allowed this license by a friend whom by the standard of his own human deficiencies he could regard as a model human being, Coleridge let himself go as a devil, throwing the responsibility for his elaborations of the theme on the blameless origin of the nucleus. This poem and the later *Two Round Spaces on the Tombstone,* and *The Rash Conjurer,* all have a vigour which directly belies his pious affectations of childish innocence in *Something Childish but Very Natural, My Baptismal Birthday, A Child's Evening Prayer, Answer to a Child's Question*—with which they are contemporaneous. The child poems were written in momentary reaction against metaphysics and in sycophantic imitation of Wordsworth's childishness, which was more proper to Wordsworth's narrow-minded obedience to authority. This vigorous mood did not last long. He lost his concentrating force and wrote less and less. He even had to depend on Southey for the support of his family— Southey who had abandoned his idealistic principles and become an industrious hack-writer, and was about to accept a pension from the Government for political services; and who held, moreover, an unfavourable opinion of Coleridge's work and habits. Coleridge and Southey were married to sisters; it was Southey who had forced Coleridge into marriage, and with a woman who proved to be chiefly interested, as Southey was, in worldly success.

Coleridge's inevitable break with Wordsworth was long delayed. At first there had been a fair exchange. In return for Wordsworth's friendship and moral stimulation, Coleridge had given him not merely

a scholarly background to work against, but constant critical help in
the use of language. (At the time of the breach Coleridge complained: ' I have loved with enthusiastic self-oblivion those who have
been well pleased that I should, year after year, flow with a hundred
nameless rills into their main stream.') But, like Southey, who had
practically given up poetry for the journalistic successes of prose,
Wordsworth now looked down on Coleridge. The Napoleonic wars
had made a patriot of him: he portrayed an ideal England where
duty and liberty met, a symbol of an unbanely poetical human reality.
Coleridge had followed suit, but timidly. Patriotism and nature-wor-
ship in Wordsworth turned to preaching; preaching ended in eccle-
siasticism. In 1802, for final self-justification, he had paid a brief visit
to Annette at Calais, in company with his sister Dorothy, explained
himself, and then returned to marry a Lake Country neighbour who
made him a devoted wife.

   In the complacent *Prelude,* addressed to Coleridge who had by
then fallen far behind Wordsworth in popular success, the affection
and gratitude expressed are little more than what he might have
granted a wise old family servant, now in decay, who would be interested in the record of his young master's rise to eminence. Only at
the end does he give Coleridge credit for being a poet too, playfully
reminding him of the days when, before turning their minds to more
serious tasks, they had ' wantoned together in wild Poesy '—he links
Coleridge's *Ancient Mariner* and *Christabel* with his own *The Idiot
Boy* and *The Thorn*—and encouraging him to spend the few remaining years of his life in raising a monument of glory to himself. He
claims to have shown him the way and trusts that together they will
instruct posterity:

> *Prophets of Nature, we to them shall speak*
> *A lasting inspiration.*

Coleridge, aware that since those wanton days he had written practically nothing, and impressed by Wordsworth's huge output, replied
with *To William Wordsworth,* in the decayed family-servant style,
humbly grateful for mention in a work that seemed a classic as soon
as written. He said that on first hearing it read he burst into tears,
realizing how he had wasted his own life; but that the tribute had
given him some hope again and he now apologized for scattering

poison-flowers of self-depreciation among the triumphal wreaths which were the author's due. He made a reference to Wordsworth's revolutionary visit to France, encouraging the legend that Wordsworth, glorious in his performances there, had left only because the revolutionary cause seemed hopeless, and was

> *. . . thenceforth calm and sure*
> *From the dread watch-tower of man's absolute self.*

A few years after the publication of *The Prelude* came the breach, subsequently repaired for good manners' sake, but in reality a final breach. Coleridge had lost confidence in Wordsworth and in himself; Wordsworth only in Coleridge. Coleridge continued to lament his own idleness; particularly he wished that he could have finished *Christabel*. But the second part, completed on his return from Germany, had turned out tedious and discouraged a third part.

> *Work without Hope draws nectar in a sieve,*
> *And Hope without an object cannot live.*

He was a 'Delinquent Traveller' and, no longer fit for 'America' (for true poetic experience, he meant), thought himself fit only to be enrolled among the criminal 'founders of Australian races.' But in *The Delinquent Travellers,* one of his best poems, he claimed for his unregenerate aberrancy, or delinquency, a higher poetic merit than for Wordsworth's social self-improvement. And he reasserted, however cynically, what he had expressed many years before in *Frost at Midnight*—a confidence in himself as the destined father of poets, successful where he failed:

> *—The Rogues! I see it in their faces!*
> *Receive me, Lads. I'll go with you,*
> *Hunt the black swan and kangaroo,*
> *And that new Holland we'll presume*
> *Old England with some elbow-room.*
> *Across the mountains we will roam*
> *And each man make himself a home:*
> *Or, if old habits ne'er forsaking,*
> *Like clock-work of the Devil's making,*
> *Ourselves inveterate rogues should be,*
> *We'll have a virtuous progeny;*

> *And on the dunghill of our vices*
> *Raise human pine-apples and spices.*

He still clung by habit to the idea of friendship and virtue.

> *Old friends burn dim, like lamps in noisome air.*
> *Love them for what they are: nor love them less*
> *Because to thee they are not what they were.*

But he knew that he was for his fellows only a devil now—a cast-off,
boring devil. In a piece called *Luther—de daemonibus* he wrote:

> '*The Angel's like a flea,*
> *The devil is a bore———*'
> '*No matter for that,*' quoth S.T.C.
> '*I love him the better therefore.*'

As for the progeny of the first travellers to Australia: they have
indeed turned out so virtuous that a few years ago the City Council
of one of the State Capitals burnt all its early archives. ' Human pine-
apples and spices ' could not be bettered as a characterization of the
pantisocratic modern Australian. Coleridge's son Hartley did become
a poet, but repeated his father's failures. Coleridge's sons of the spirit
were the pre-Raphaelites, headed by Dante Gabriel Rossetti. Of these
only William Morris had the healthy energy for carrying the group's
idealistic principles into orderly practice. But his Coleridge-like poetic
beginnings—*The Defence of Guinevere*—were soon lost in his growing success as an importer of practical beauty into Victorian everyday
life—his printing, furniture, fabrics, etc. He continued to write, but
what was not social-propaganda prose was interior-decorator verse applauded by the same ' liberal ' public which had applauded the hard-
working Southey.

III   KEATS AND SHELLEY

Keats' chief interest was the poet's relations with poetry, and the
imagery he chose was predominantly sexual. Poetry for him was not
a philosophical theory, as it was with Shelley, but a moment of phys-

ical delirium. The figure which Laura Riding has used[1] in character-
izing Keats ('He . . . disposed himself . . . toward spiritual rape by
a vigorous poetic personhead imagined as in pursuit of conquests ') is
one which occurs constantly in his poems. The first occasion is in
Sleep and Poetry:

> *O Poesy! for thee I grasp my pen*
> *That am not yet a glorious denizen*
> *Of thy wide heaven; yet, to my ardent prayer,*
> *Yield from thy sanctuary some clean air,*
> *Smooth'd for intoxication by the breath*
> *Of flowery bays, that I may die a death*
> *Of luxury, and my young spirit follow*
> *The morning sunbeams to the great Apollo*
> *Like a fresh sacrifice; or, if I can bear*
> *The o'erwhelming sweets, 'twill bring to me the fair*
> *Visions of all places . . .*

Keats' contemporaries found in this sort of writing a quality which
they interpreted as moral perversity. The slamming reviews which
depressed him so much, because postponing the moment of poetic
ecstasy which he identified with the moment of poetic fame, resulted
rather from the critics' recognition of his perversity than from their
obtuseness about his craftsmanship, or their prejudice against him as
Leigh Hunt's protégé. Perversity, to the English mind, means any confusion of the usual functions and prerogatives of the two sexes, and
Keats never seemed to be playing a *manly* role in his poems. Although
he was male-minded enough in ordinary sexual business, as his letters
to Fanny Brawne, and his song ' Give me women, wine and snuff,'
show, the critics were right: he did mix the sexes in his poems. This
resulted from his personalization of Poetry as an active female figure,
and from his disavowal of the rape which the intellectual poet, as
male, makes of Poetry—poems, in classical imagery, being the poet's
children begotten of the Muse. He rejected traditional poetic psychology because the ecstasies it provided were banal and repetitious:
not because he knew the nature of poetic experience, but because he
had a greed of it and felt that it could not occur within the known, ex-

---

[1] *Poems and Poets, Epilogue II* (1936).

hausted poetic conventions. So he reversed the traditional metaphor by making Poetry, as a dominant female, pursue the shrinking, womanish poet with masculine lustfulness.

Endymion was the stock classical figure of human youth and beauty lying asleep, secretly beloved by the watchful deity—the Moon. Keats, who had said that if poetry did not come to a poet as naturally as leaves to a tree it had better not come at all, used Endymion as the figure of a poet who, by putting himself into a recipient attitude, won without further effort ' the o'erwhelming sweets ' for which his soul longed. (Keats used to court poetical inspiration by dressing up in traditional poetic robes and laurel crown.) Endymion first learns the technique of attracting goddesses by a study of Adonis in his bower; a heavenly guide conveys him there and, as if to give him a foretaste of amorous delights, cossets him with sweets—always associated in Keats' poems with poetic seduction—wine alive with sparkles, juicy pears, cream sweeter than nurse Amalthea skimmed for the boy Jupiter, and a bunch of blooming plums, ready to melt within an infant's gums. From Adonis' bower it was no long journey, by eagle-ride part of the way (to point the connexion with the seduced Ganymede), to a mossy bed where Endymion could fling himself on his back and presently clasp a naked waist above him. It was Dian, and he whispered to her:

> *O known Unknown! From where my being sips*
> *Such darling essence, wherefore may I not*
> *Be ever in these arms?*

The reviewers called *Endymion* ' indecent.' They wrote as classicists, and they were right in calling the poem indecent from a classical point of view: Diana should never have been equated in her sexual technique with Venus.

Hyperion started in a more ' manly ' fashion. Hyperion was the Sun-Titan, an inexperienced youth, not yet converted into Apollo, the god of Poetry; the poem gives an account of this metamorphosis. Keats is said to have interrupted the writing of *Hyperion* because of the unfavourable reception of *Endymion*. *Endymion* was disliked because it did not reveal the author as a normal male being: critics did not analyse the nature of the abnormality, but decided that he was conceited in some unusual way. In a letter to his publishers, the more conventionally conceited, over-manly Byron wrote, for God's sake to send him no more Keats: and added abuse so indecent that his editors have deleted all but *manicon*, ' catamite,' which they print as ' manni-kin.' Keats was aware that *Hyperion* was more spiritually ambitious than *Endymion,* and may have argued that it would be still less favour-ably received, for in *Hyperion* he was identifying himself with the god of Poetry. (The reaction of shame is recorded in his poem of apology to Delphic Apollo for having assumed his laurel-garland.) He did not understand that it was the mawkish quality of his ambition which critics disliked rather than the fact of his ambition. Hyperion is, in the end, not much more of a man than Endymion. He does not become the god of Poetry except by quasi-sexual relations with a female prin-ciple of reality described as Mnemosyne or Memory. She is an awful goddess, a supreme shape, and comes on him while he is half-asleep. He gazes into her eyes and:

> *Soon wild commotions shook him, and made flush*
> *All the immortal fairness of his limbs,*
> *Into a hue more roseate than sweet pain*
> *Gives to a ravish'd nymph when her warm tears*
> *Gush luscious with no sob . . .*
> > *. . . So young Apollo anguish'd.*
> *His very hair, his golden tresses famed,*
> *Kept undulation round his eager neck.*
> *During the pain Mnemosyne upheld*
> *Her arms as one who prophesied.—At length*
> *Apollo shriek'd—and lo he was the God.*

Keats toned down this passage when he eventually published it, leav-ing out the orgiastic pleasure of the ravished nymph, and making the climax less final:

> *Apollo shriek'd—and lo from all his limbs*
> *Celestial . . .*

At ' Celestial ' the printed version broke off politically, as if he had cast his pen down in despair on reading the notices in the *Quarterly* and *Blackwood's.*

In *Sleep and Poetry* Keats had already begun this technique of sexual counter-changing; it is shown most clearly in his confused

identity of the spirit of Poetry, which should have been female, with
the slumbering Endymion and Apollo the mighty:

> *A drainless shower*
> *Of light is poesy; 'tis the supreme of power;*
> *'Tis might half-slumbering on its own right arm.*
> *The very archings of her eye-lids charm*
> *A thousand willing agents to obey.*

His second volume, *Lamia, Isabella, The Eve of St. Agnes and
Other Poems,* was given more favourable notices because he had disguised the indecency by taking the sexual figure one stage further.
The conventional imagery had been of the male poet ravishing the
Muse; his perverse improvement on this had been woman, a mannish
Muse, ravishing the womanish poet. He now showed a definitely
female figure inviting rape by a definitely male figure; but he told the
story from the female point of view. By doing this he avoided the
charge of perversity: he showed himself yielding to temptation as an
apparently normal sexual adventurer, though to change his Muse into
a conventionally feminine one he had to invest her with all his own
sexual coyness. (In *The Eve of St. Agnes* Madeline lies asleep but
amorously expectant, while Porphyro at her bedside heaps up the extravagant jellies and candied fruits and syrops and spiced cakes in gold
and silver vessels.) Then she listens to his serenade of *La Belle Dame
sans Merci* and finally allows him to throb like a star among her
dreams. The sweetmeats in these rape-scenes stand for the ' beauties '
of poetry on which Keats laid more stress than on poetry itself. The
' beauties ' were ' verisimilitudes,' or the ore with which every rift
should be loaded: the poetic object was an illusion of glory in which
the Muse was expected to indulge the passive poet. *The Eve of St.
Mark* (not included in this volume) was written in the same vein.
Bertha sat alone in her room in the Minster Square at Canterbury.
Everyone was at church, and the streets were deserted. The stage was
set for the lover to come along with his sweetmeats, soft drinks and
musical instrument; to which blandishments Bertha could not but
yield. She kept her virginity only because of Keats' failure to finish
the poem.

Isabella and *Lamia* are both poems of self-pity. Isabella is the spirit
of poetry luxuriously grieving for the poet who has been murdered by

the ' ledger-men '—i.e. the materialists, the rationalists, the critics. They even rob her of the sweet-basil which grows from his dead head. Lamia, who in classical legend was a frightful demon-succubus, Keats treated as ' poor Lamia,' the Spirit of Poetry whom old Apollonius, the philosopher, stares at, sees as a snake and banishes from sight.

> *Philosophy will clip an Angel's wings,*
> *Conquer all mysteries by rule and line,*
> *Empty the haunted air, and gnomèd mine—*
> *Unweave a rainbow, as it erewhile made*
> *The tender-person'd Lamia melt into a shade.*

Lamia is the morbid figure of poetry made dismal by neglect—by the want of such honeyed flattery as Keats imagined fitting tribute from the poet. For all his absorption in romances of chivalry he never made Poetry into a Fairy Queen who demanded from her knightly poet active proof of his valour and devotion.

Keats wrote in a letter to Woodhouse that a poet was functionally irresponsible and had no identity, only yearning and fondness—allowing himself to be pressed upon and annihilated by stronger identities with whom he came into contact. In a letter to his brothers he glorified Shakespeare, in the same strain, as possessing the supreme poetic quality—' *Negative Capability, that is, when a man is capable of being in uncertainties, mysteries, doubts, without any irritable reaching after fact and reason.'* Keats felt himself torn between two demands: the demand of the critics and the sweeping demand of poetry itself. Between them he equivocated with that fluttering complaisance which he calls ' Negative Capability.'

In the same letter Keats writes:

> Coleridge, for instance, would let go by a fine isolated verisimilitude caught from the Penetralium of mystery from being incapable of remaining content with half knowledge. This pursued through volumes would perhaps take us no further than this, that with a great poet the sense of Beauty overcomes every consideration, or rather obliterates all consideration.

Keats rightly felt that Coleridge had a poetic conscience which would not let him be content with random ecstasies. He wrote, further:

> As to the poetic character itself (I mean that sort of which, if I am anything, I am a member: that sort distinguished from the

Wordsworthian or egotistic Sublime: which is a thing per se, and stands alone) it is not itself—it has no self, it is everything and nothing—it has no character.

He was here distinguishing between Wordsworth's self-protective insensitivity to the pleasures of poetry and his own cultivation of poetry as the science of hedonics.

Shelley, who championed Keats as a victim of critical cruelty and saw him as performing something like his own philosophical arbitration between the human audience and poetry itself, displeased contemporary critics for reasons opposite to those for which they damned Keats.

It was not his professed atheism and Jacobinism which outraged popular feeling, so much as his spiritual hermaphroditism. Laura Riding in the essay quoted above shows how he tried to reconcile the opposite sympathies to which the poet is exposed: by a compromise in which judgment was evaded by a philosophical equating of the human with the poetic. At one time, indeed, he debated whether he should make philosophy or poetry his profession; and though he chose poetry, he tried to combine the philosopher and the poet in a Satanic character of superior physical and mental powers. In his *Defence of Poetry* he sets Bacon among the great poets and Shakespeare, Milton and Dante among the philosophers of the very loftiest power. Queen Mab is his first Queen of Poetry: but she does not have love-relations either with Oberon or with a mortal youth. She merely imbues the soul of a girl called Ianthe (Harriet Shelley) with a righteous, philosophical view of human affairs; the verses are annotated with astronomical data, recommendations for a vegetarian diet, and thoughts on the nature of time. She appears later as The Witch of Atlas, an energetic spirit who flies about with a winged monster of her own creation, called Hermaphrodite. Hermaphrodite is the poet-compromiser:

> *A sexless thing it was, and in its growth*
> *It seemed to have developed no defect*
> *Of either sex, yet all the grace of both,—*
> *In gentleness and strength its limbs were decked;*
> *The bosom swelled lightly with its full youth,*
> *The countenance was such as might select*

> *Some artist that his skill should never die,*
> *Imaging forth such perfect purity.*

Towards the close of the poem Shelley gently rebukes Keats for conceiving the Spirit of Poetry as sexed and therefore unpropitious for
the harmonious levelling of things which should be the poet's end:

> *'Tis said in after times her spirit free*
> *Knew what love was, and felt itself alone—*
> *But holy Dian could not chaster be*
> *Before she stooped to kiss Endymion,*
> *Than now this lady—like a sexless bee*
> *Tasting all blossoms, and confined to none,*
> *Among these mortal forms, the wizard-maiden*
> *Passed with an eye serene and heart unladen.*

But the Witch is only a fanciful presentation of the Spirit of Poetry.
The poem closes:

> *These were the pranks she played among the cities*
> *Of mortal men, and what she did to Sprites*
> *And Gods, entangling them in her sweet ditties*
> *To do her will, and show their subtle sleights,*
> *I will declare another time; for it is*
> *A tale more fit for the weird winter nights*
> *Than for these garish summer days, when we*
> *Scarcely believe much more than we can see.*

First must come the serious business of smoothing out troubles of a
more immediate sort. Mary Shelley criticized the poem as having no
human interest; and he replied with some joking verses, acknowledging the ineffectiveness of his vision:

> *How, my dear Mary,—are you critic-bitten*
> *(For vipers kill, though dead) by some review,*
> *That you condemn these verses I have written*
> *Because they tell no story, false or true?*
> *What, though no mice are caught by a young kitten,*
> *May it not leap and play as grown cats do,*
> *Till its claws come? Prithee, for this one time,*
> *Content thee with a visionary rhyme.*

But he never managed to synthetize into a single figure the poet, and the philosopher, and the Promethean man of action on whose strategy the miracle of human salvation seemed to depend.

IV   LUCRETIUS AND JEANS

Lucretius records a philosophic excitement in the strangeness of the material universe: a state of consciousness above the immediately physical but below consciousness of reality itself. The comfortable range of human thought reaches as far as the familiar strangeness of one's own being, and Lucretius could make a voyage of exploration outside his body without breaking its spell over his mind. Much the same sort of psychological adventuring has since been undertaken by Rimbaud and his successors, to whom the apparent impossibility of pursuing sensations beyond the limits of physical consciousness has implied the cruel inadequacy of the human mind to define truth; but Lucretius' work has a more direct connexion with the fanciful scientific cosmogony of Sir James Jeans than with the mental struggles of poets who have turned aside, from the straight path towards doom or resurrection, into a cerebral cul-de-sac. Science is concerned with isolating a minimum incident of certain duration—duration so certain that it need not be thought of as future, but only as the inevitable extension, by repetition, of the shortest, most instantaneous immediacy that can be conceived. Both Lucretius and Jeans, who demonstrates better than any other modern scientist the inevitable sentimentality of the scientific view, somehow manage to coax happiness out of the notion that some time, though not now, the universe must end. The outer immensity of space—since the practical realm of sensation lies within relatively meagre boundaries—is employed by both as a field for respectable scientific Corybantics. And they find in the littleness of earth, and in the littleness of the individual, the source of a more workaday optimism: they make terrestrialism the capacity to isolate the particular local incident, or reality, from the general way of things—to perpetuate it in despite of the finality which lies at the end of the road. A still more striking resemblance between Lucretius' Epicurean science and modern scientific thought is their common impatience with causality, so that they even omit the demonstration of cause, as something in itself evil, or fatally governing. Lucretius was interested in causality only as the stimulus of effects; he did not much care what causes he ascribed to things—how ostensibly fallacious they were—so long as in ascribing a cause he clarified the effect which it perhaps precipitated.

A textual comparison of Lucretius' *De Rerum Natura* and Jeans' shortest and most poetical work *Eos: or the Wider Aspects of Cosmogony* strengthens this resemblance. As a popular historian Jeans is as unreliable as Lucretius—their first similarity. He asserts, for instance, that only in the past ten generations has the Earth ceased to be regarded as the centre of the universe. But Lucretius in the first century B.C. had explicitly stated that there could be no centre of the universe, because it was infinite; and this was not his own peculiar view but an Epicurean commonplace. Jeans also speaks of the atomic theory as the property of ' our scientific ancestors of half-a-century ago ': unaware that John Dalton only revived ' scientifically ' another Epicurean commonplace familiar to every classically educated Englishman. Jeans is excited at meeting Newton's anticipations, in his *Opticks* (1704), of present-day scientific theory; yet equally striking ones occur in Lucretius. For instance, Jeans' concept of space as being filled with wandering radiations from dead matter which contribute practically nothing to the sum of things is paralleled by Lucretius:

> *Principio hoc dico, rerum simulacra vagari*
> *Multa modis multis in cunctas undique partis*
> *Tenvia . . . multo magis haec sunt tenvia textu*
> *Quam quae percipiunt oculos visumque lacessunt*
> *. . . simulacraque eorum*
> *Quorum morte obita tellus amplectitur ossa.*

(In the first place I tell you that many images (reflections) of things wander about in many ways and in all directions, very thin . . . they are much thinner in texture than the images which strike the eyes and assail the vision . . . reflections also of those whose death is passed and whose bones are buried.)

Since this is only one of several parallels we may conclude that Jeans has not read Lucretius; yet there are numerous passages in *Eos* which would translate directly into Lucretian hexameters. For instance:

> Under the action of great heat the outermost of the atomic electrons begin to break loose from the atom and fly off at a tangent, just as, when water is heated up, the outer molecules break loose and set off on independent journeys of their own. Finally the water is wholly evaporated; the heat has transformed it into a mass of gas (steam) in which each separate molecule flies along its own individual path like the bullets on a battle-field. In precisely the same way, the application of heat to the atoms causes successive layers of electrons to break loose from their moorings, and the atoms become smaller and smaller until finally no coherent structure remains but merely a powdered *debris* of atomic constituents, each nucleus and electron going its own way regardless of the rest.

The resemblance lies in the humanistic way in which they both write about their atoms, or particles, or molecules, or ' first-beginnings,' or ' seeds of things,' or electrons, or whatever invisible tininesses they happen to be discussing. ' Set off on journeys of their own . . . flies along its own individual path . . . each nucleus and electron going its own way regardless of the rest.' So Lucretius, talking of certain of his tininesses:

> *Multaque praeterea magnum per inane vagantur*
> *Conciliis rerum quae sunt rejecta nec usquam*
> *Consociare etiam motus potuere recepta.*

> (Many of them, too, go wandering through space: they are rejected from the councils of things and have nowhere been able to ally their motions together even when admitted.)

Both Lucretius and Jeans are philosophizing in terms of infinitesimal units of matter or energy, or what-not—so insignificant that it is painfully headachy, except for scientific adepts, to bring the mind to bear on them at all, but which exist more tangibly than difficult generalizations because they answer troublesome questions ' beautifully ' (Jeans' word). These infinitesimal units represent man in his most disorganized, irresponsible state; as the beautiful answers in which they assist are the most irresponsible answers. Leucippus invented them first, but they have been constantly recharacterized since his day in a variety of senses. To Leucippus they were infinitely small and indivisible. Later they had theoretically to be given ' parts,' to distinguish one atom from another; but only qualitative parts, the atom being still admittedly indivisible—which is Lucretius' view. Dalton ' weighed ' his atoms but still forbade anyone to divide them: ' thou knowest thou canst not cut an atom.' Rutherford and Bohr, however, gave these qualitative parts separability, making a miniature solar system of each atom—which is Jeans' view. His ' atomic electrons ' are infinitesimal parts of the atomic nucleus, of which the diameter is ' only a small fraction of the millionth of a millionth of an inch.' Yet Jeans writes about these *semina rerum* as Lucretius did in the passage quoted (*Multaque praeterea . . .*)—as if they were queer little idiosyncratic creatures of his personal acquaintance. Both writers are making every effort to be at home in a common-sense way in strange reality—to create an economical means of talking about universal problems, eliminating all the difficult aspects. So Jeans:

> The infinitely great is never very far from the infinitely small in science, but it would be hard to find a more sensational illustration of the unity of science than that just given [i.e. the resemblance between atomic structure and the structure of solar systems].

In discussing the stars Jeans speaks of ' groups of bright stars moving in orderly formation through a jumble of slighter stars, like a flight of swans through a confused crowd of rooks and starlings.' So also Lucretius:

> . . . *cum lucida signa ferantur* . . .
> *Flammea per caelum pascentis corpora passim.*

> (. . . when bright constellations, with fiery bodies, go grazing here and there across the sky.)

Both are fundamentally more interested in analogy than in theory. So Jeans says, in writing of cosmogony: ' One could hardly be prosaic if one tried.' And Lucretius: ' It is pleasant to drink at virgin springs of song, and to seek an illustrious chaplet for my head from fields whence the Muses have crowned no poet before me.'

Yet Lucretius' common sense is nonsense from the present-day scientific point of view. His wandering radiations or reflections, for instance, were offered as explanations of the fancies which men get in dreams about Centaurs and Chimaeras. That the world was not the middle of things he used as a final argument against the existence of

upside-down animal life at the antipodes. His erratic stars were represented as possibly going in search of food. However, the only real
difference between him and Jeans is that, though both are fancifully,
and nonsensically, simplifying major universal problems, Jeans seems
more respectably intricate in that he has a much greater accumula-
tion of scientific hypotheses to deal with; his work is simplifying
previous simplifications. In its design of substituting simple for complicated formulas of explanation, science was bound to grow more
complicated itself, the more ambitious it became of being a completely
adequate substitute for truth. But Lucretius' task was intricate in another sense: he had no complicated scientific apparatus at his disposal.
He must constantly make the change-over from abstruse into practical
language, and fortify his own system with abstruse explanations where
it was incomplete; and he frequently complained of the inadequacy
of Latin, compared with Greek, for abstruse statement, though simple
statement was his object. Thus, Jeans' swan-flock figure is a complicated mechanistic nicety justifying a whole tradition of scientific rhetoric; while Lucretius' ' stars grazing across the sky,' though part of
the plan which he shares with Jeans of fanciful simplification (' honey
smeared round the medicinal cup of wormwood '), leave behind them
an irksome linguistic difficulty. He would have liked his figure to convey of itself the analytic notion of freewill on the part of the stars, as
well as the merely descriptive notion of erratic movement; but Latin
exacted more explicit precision. He felt obliged to complete the description with suggestions of purpose in movement that the strict,
descriptive Latin use of the word ' grazing ' could not possibly convey.

   Yet Lucretius was more devoutly scientific than Jeans and other
scientists who no longer think of themselves as fighting a lonely and
difficult battle against superstition—the superstition of those who do
not want too easy an explanation. For, as between science and religion, it is science which is the bigot, science which wants to achieve
mental peace by localized tricks of thought. Religion now indulges
science, in so far as it keeps people in comfort and good humour by its
charlatanism while the higher business is going on and in so far as it
uses such pious language as ' in the service of mankind ' to conceal
the spiritually destructive nature of the service. The scientific battle is
won and over-won. Scientists can draw what conclusions they like in
the name of science and, so long as the public is convinced that

' people well up in science ' treat these conclusions with respect, they will be accepted as pontiffs of practical truth—even when they are only improvising accounts of phenomena of which, by the nature of the analytical economies they practise, they can have none but the most arbitrary knowledge. Jeans speaks of the interior mechanism of the latest atom as confidently as if it were that of the latest aircraft engine.

Lucretius, not so comfortably placed, always emphasizes the tentative nature of his cosmogonal doctrine. Having said that one of many causes may explain the motion of stars—either that the whole sky may be driven by currents of air, or that the stars may, independently of the sky, be mechanically driven by internal force, or that they may be moved by tides in the ether, or that they may move consciously, in search of food—he ends by admitting that which of all these causes holds good in *our* universe it is difficult to say. Since there are so many various universes, as he has already shown by proving the infinity of matter in the total universe, each of these theories must hold good *somewhere;* and which one fits this particular universe, he will not rashly decide, for he must go step by step in a scientific spirit.

In present-day science such reservations have gradually dropped out, because scientists are careful to express their suppositions in mathematical formulas which, applied artistically to such problems as the structure of the atom or the inner temperatures of stars, give ' beautiful ' results. They are applied only to safe, prepared cases— though remaining unworkable in unstereotyped ones: there must be a sympathetic equivalence between formula and case.

> The mathematician need not hesitate to thrust his calculations right into the heart of the stars, and he can usually show, with something approaching very near to certainty, that at the centres of most of the stars nearly all, or perhaps quite all, of the electrons must have broken loose from their parent atoms leaving the stellar matter almost or quite pulverized into its constituent nuclei and electrons.

A beautiful result is as good as a demonstrable proof and can be superseded only by a still more beautiful result. ' Beauty is truth; truth, beauty,' wrote Keats as a chemist-contemporary of Dalton's. Lucretius, too, likes beautiful results; but he has no mathematical bludgeon at his disposal—only a store of imposing phenomenal curiosities, such as the action of a magnet on iron rings, the hurly-burly of motes in a sunbeam, the origin of forest fires in the rubbing together of twigs. He uses these as far as they will go. Unbeautiful results irritate him and in the last event he is reduced to his general reservation about the tentativeness of his doctrine. Thus, at one point he has been led to state that men once used to employ wild beasts in battle, such as lions and boars, against their enemies. He adds that this was an unbelievably foolish thing to do, because obviously the beasts would turn on their own masters with indiscriminate slaughter —but perhaps the men were reckless and did not care what happened to them, or perhaps the whole historical account which he has just given (with exciting detail) really belongs to the story of another universe altogether.

Lucretius is here doing what he always does when he stumbles against a piece of theory which seems humanly uncomfortable—he discounts its immediate applicability: such as that men were once born from wombs sprouting out of the earth, whose limbs were all wrongly placed on the trunk, so that they could not fend for themselves or reproduce their kind; or that the earth originally brought forth enormous monsters. His object is to rid men of terror, not to substitute scientific terrors for religious ones. He points out that an infinite variety of happenings and creatures obviously occur *somewhere* in the total universe, but that the natural laws current in other universes do not apply to this. A Chimaera, he says, obviously cannot occur in this world because the fixed laws which, according to our practical experience, rule the natures of lion, goat and snake (the components of a Chimaera) would be set in contradiction by such a mixture—and the final impossibility of a Chimaera is that it is held to breathe out fire, which would burn the goat-stomach of the creature.

Lucretius is no more an 'original' scientist than Jeans, though both may claim to have added their quota of interpretation and suggestion to the scientific aggregate. To avoid the charge of idiosyncratic madness they both ask authority for their work by citing previous scientists. What men have once thought—Democritus, Empedocles and Epicurus, Dr Hubble, Prof. McLennan and Prof. Millikan—it is not unnatural to think again. Jeans has a bigger body of authorities to cite and a more compact corpus of scientific facts: he is able to draw on these facts for the human comfort which it is his chief interest to give.

Thus, Jeans would be unlikely to support a scientific argument, as Lucretius does, with the fact that a leaden bullet slung from a military catapult melts when sent a long distance; he would have a mathematical formula pigeon-holed somewhere proving that the friction of the air is not great enough to make the lead anything more than somewhat hot to the touch. But his lack of historical accuracy, already referred to, suggests that, ' irreproachably scientific ' though his work may be, this is only because he is writing when he is. Had he lived in Lucretius' time he would have been equally ready to believe, on Epicurus' authority, that clouds were bladders full of wind or water or fire, and that thunder probably came from their scraping their sides together, then bursting, discharging fire in the form of lightning and water in the form of rain: for it was a theory which fitted the known facts ' beautifully.' His own electrons and protons behave very much like Lucretius' clouds:

> They are pure bottled energy; the continuous breakage of these bottles in the sun sets free the radiation which warms and lights our earth, and enough unbroken bottles remain to provide light and heat for millions of years to come.

The optimism which is the chief link between these writers is founded on extreme fear of mortal extinction. But both treat this fear as troubling only other people; for themselves, they are secure in the serene retreats of science. Jeans can write unconcernedly:

> With an ardour equalled only by that of man's longing for personal immortality, many seem to desire that the universe itself should prove in some way to be immortal.

and Lucretius:

> *Et quoniam docui cunctarum exordia rerum*
> *Qualia sint et quam variis distantia formis . . .*
> *Hasce secundum res animi natura videtur*
> *Atque animae claranda meis iam versibus esse*
> *Et metus ille foras praeceps Acheruntis agendus,*
> *Funditus humanam qui vitam turbat ab imo . . .*

(And since I have explained the beginnings of all things and how they differ in their shapes . . . I must next explain in this poem the nature of mind and spirit, so as to cast that fear of Hell headlong out which affects man's life so deeply.)

Both cast out the fear by concentrating on the relative littleness and isolation of man in the total scheme of things; also by saying that, granted that *some time* human beings must face finality, mortal extinction will fall equally on everything. Both admit that the universe is running down and will come to an end one day. Lucretius insists that the end of this universe does not matter: there are always other universes. Jeans' view is much the same, though he does not speculate on other universes because he makes this one much more inclusive. Both comfort their readers by saying that it will be so long a time before the universe ends that they need not worry about the end. But both blow hot and cold according as they wish to affect their readers emotionally one way or the other, alternately insisting on the newness and on the oldness of the world for man.

> In all probability the life in front of the human race must enormously exceed the short life behind it. *Jeans.*

> *Verum, ut opinor, habet novitatem summa recensque*
> *Naturast mundi neque pridem exordia cepit.*

> (But my belief is that the universe is new and our world is new, and that it is not long since the beginning.) *Lucretius.*

> So far as we can judge, our part of the universe has lived the more eventful part of its life already; what we are witnessing is less the rising of the curtain before the play than the burning out of candle-ends on an empty stage on which the drama is already over. *Jeans.*

> *Sed quia finem aliquam pariendi debet habere,*
> *Destitit, ut mulier spatio defessa vetusto.*

> (But because she [Mother Earth] must have some limit to her bearing, she ceased, like a woman worn-out by old age.) *Lucretius.*

Similarly they blow alternately hot and cold in the matter of fixed laws and arbitrary phenomena. Jeans disposes of the idea that an original fortuitous combination of atoms made the universe, by a mathematical pronouncement that the chances for its fortuitousness are precisely one in $10^{420,000,000}$ (this last figure being short for a sum starting with 10 and ending in four hundred and twenty thousand million zeros); yet he concedes that *how* the universe was originally set going is shrouded in impenetrable mystery. When he comes to speak of the Earth itself he says that it is quite an unusual phenomenon, an astronomical freak, and that there are ' millions of millions ' of chances to one (he does not give the precise figure) against the surface of any planet being in the same bio-chemical condition as ours to-day. So too Lucretius. He insists on the fixed laws, the decrees of fate, which govern everything. Yet he holds that the original atomic beginnings of things broke these eternal fixities by an accident; and that this resulted in the present universe, a compromise between fate (the fixed unalterable properties of things) and accident (things that come and go without prejudice to these properties).

Lucretius held that space was infinite, but that this universe (meaning as much of physical totality as people of his time could comprehend) was comfortably finite. His ' this universe ' was a much more modest one than Jeans' ' this universe ' because it did not include all matter, the infinitely greater part of which he held to lie outside in other universes. Jeans, while agreeing with Lucretius that space has no limit, and even with his contention that space and matter are co-extensive, makes ' this universe ' include all the universes outside the visible one—and still declares it to be finite. How does he evade this paradox of finite limitlessness? By a word he has learned from Einstein, which curiously enough is the very word that Lucretius learned from Epicurus; a word that Epicurus used in evading the paradox of how his originally fate-bound atoms started the hurly-burly of creation—namely, *clinamen,* or swerve. Lucretius writes:

> *Quare etiam atque etiam paulum inclinare necessest*
> *Corpora; nec plus quam minimum, ne fingere motus*
> *Obliquos videamur et id res vera refutet.*

(So I insist that the atoms must make a slight swerve; and not more than the least possible, or we shall seem to be assuming oblique movements—which is an untenable hypothesis.)

And Jeans writes that ' a general guiding principle, that of generalized relativity, fixes a limit to space.' Light does not travel straight, but with a *swerve* so slight as to have been unsuspected until only the other day when the mathematicians discovered it accidentally. This swerve denotes a curvature of space. So, if we were to go far enough, we should only ' come back on ourselves '; travelling as fast as light, we should come back on ourselves in one hundred thousand million years. Lucretius used *clinamen* to account for human free-will, too.

The swerve is, of course, the very nature of scientific thought, as well as the carefully irresponsible, disobedient nature of matter itself; and it allows of infinity, or continuous duration, so long as people think at individual random, as it also provides the comfort of finity, or individual peculiarity of being.

Both Jeans and Lucretius feel the same embarrassment in talking about divine being: and yet neither can resist mention of divinity. There is no room for divinity in their self-like intellectual universe, yet they cannot help introducing it emotionally. They both let it be understood that gods or God (Lucretius preaches with missionary zeal what by Jeans' time has become a scientific assumption) have nothing whatever to do with things as they are; yet indulge their own sentimentality and that of their readers in poetical references to the divine. So Lucretius:

> *Hunc tu, diva, tuo recubantem corpore sancto*
> *Circumfusa super, suavis ex ore loquellas*
> *Funde petens placidam Romanis, incluta, pacem.*

(Goddess Venus, as you and Mars lie twined together in a divine sexual embrace, please beg him charmingly to give us Romans peace.)

And Jeans, less naughtily:

> And we cannot say how long the stellar matter may have been in the nebular state before it formed stars. Nothing in astronomy fixes with any precision the time since
>
> ' the great morning of the world, when first God dawned on chaos.'

The strongest note which they both of them strike is optimism as the counter-weight to fear—optimism derived from the admission and exploration of fear:

> . . . we are standing at the first flush of the dawn of civilization. Each instant the vision before us changes as the rosy-fingered goddess paints a new and ever more wonderful picture in the sky . . . *Jeans.*

> *Diffugiunt animi terrores, moenia mundi*
> *Discedunt, totum video per inane geri res.*

(Terrors of the mind flee away now, the walls of the universe open out, I see action going on throughout the whole of space.) *Lucretius.*

This lyricism necessarily brings its gloomy reaction. Lucretius, in spite of his serene philosophy, comes in the course of his argument upon several uncomfortable fatalities from which he swerves away, recovering his balance with difficulty. Eventually he gets into what motor-cyclists call a ' roll '—a slight skid inducing a greater and greater skid from which there is no recovery. He is discussing the plague at Athens. Hitherto he has been able to limit his digressions on uncomfortable topics to a few lines, though the account of the wild beasts in battle lasted for fifty before he could extricate himself. But in discussing the plague he goes on and on, trying to find some way of discounting this fatal horror, or of alleviating it; but can think of none. He is fascinated against his free-will by the ulcers, the retchings, the salty yellow spittle, the black bowel-discharge, the nose-bleeding, the desperate self-castration; and after a hundred and sixty lines he collapses at a point where the terrified survivors are brawling over the stinking and loathsome corpses of their relatives. There the whole poem breaks off.

Jeans ends in nightmare too:

> In any case, our three-days-old infant cannot be very confident of any interpretation it puts on a universe which it only discovered a minute or two ago . . . And ever the old question obtrudes itself as to whether the infant has any means of knowing that it is not dreaming all the time. The picture it sees may be merely a creation of its own mind, in which nothing really exists except itself; the universe which we study with such care may be a dream, and we brain-cells in the mind of a dreamer.

HOW POETS SEE

(1939)

A poet should be aware of the way in which he looks at the world (in the most literal optical sense) and takes in what he sees; if he finds that he has contracted visual habits which prevent him from seeing things clearly or wholly, he should study to correct them. Here I record my own visual peculiarities with a mental resolve to correct them as soon as possible; and afterwards discuss the visual peculiarities of Keats, Wordsworth, Coleridge, Milton and Donne in relation to their poems.

1

In looking at any object, for example a house or a person, I concentrate my gaze on what I choose as the central point and focus it clearly, allowing the rest of the object to form a blur—of which however I apprehend the extent and general colouring. If after studying the central point I am still interested in the object, I look for other points of interest: thus, after long acquaintance with a person I know his single features by heart, but cannot recompose his face in memory. I must always have seen in the same partial way, because when thinking of the house where I spent my childhood, I remember the shapes of the different window frames, the look of particular bricks in the wall, the angle of the slate roof, but cannot recompose the general façade. In ordinary conversation I concentrate my gaze on both eyes of the person addressing me; in difficult conversation I tend to concentrate it on his right eye, and if the strain persists abnormally, I lose focus and he recedes into the distance, so that I see him whole, but small. I have, however, a perfect memory-sense by touch: I can remember the shape of any body or inanimate object I have once touched, and if I were asked to reconstruct the dimensions of a house in which I have lived for some years, I should imagine myself walking through it in the half-dark, and know just how the rooms stood in relation to one another, their size, the position of their furniture, and so on.

I never see people or objects against a clearly defined background, or separated from me by a clearly defined foreground. Background and foreground I make distinct objects: I see only with a fixed focus. (In walking, I always tend to swerve to the right of my indicated course: thus, I choose to walk on the left side of a person so that his proximity keeps me from straying.)

I never have clear visions of objects except in half-sleep or slight fever or great emotional stress.

In apprehending objects with no outstanding features which can be used as a central point—for instance, a haystack or an upturned packing-case—I tend to use as my arbitrary central point a position two-thirds of the way down the side to the left of me.

In visualizing a room, I walk across and around it in my imagination, unless there is someone in it, already moving, whom I can watch —in which case, I remain still.

I see well in the half-dark; by an effort to see all that there is, as well as by an abnormal expansion of the iris. The reaction of my eyes to light is very slow and I take more than the normal time to focus.

2

Keats was short-sighted. He did not see landscapes as such, so he treated them as painted cabinets filled with interesting objects. In *I stood tip-toe upon a little Hill,* one of his earliest poems, he explains his habit of seeing—or of not seeing. He did not look at the sky, but started from the farthest horizon, standing on tip-toe to survey as much earth as possible lying between him and it. Then, gloatingly, he let his eye travel up some small inviting path, in search of objects surmised to be there, though beyond the visual range of even the most long-sighted eye. His habit was to allow his eye to be seduced from entire vision by particular objects. He wrote, in *Calidore,* another early poem, that no healthy man could lightly pass by objects which looked out invitingly on either side of a boat as it progressed through beautiful scenery.

He saw little but what moved: the curving, the wreathing, the slanting, the waving—and even then, it seems, not the whole object in motion but only its edge, or high-light. To remedy this ghostliness of vision he invariably drew on his memory of how the objects felt, tasted, sounded or smelt. In *The Eve of St. Agnes,* for example:

> *. . . her vespers done,*
> *Of all its wreathèd pearls her hair she frees;*
> *Unclasps her warmèd jewels one by one;*
> *Loosens her fragrant boddice; by degrees*
> *Her rich attire creeps rustling to her knees . . .*

All that he has seen here is the twisted pattern of a seed-pearl hair ornament, and the moving neckline of a woman's shift as it exposed her body in falling.

He did not see faces as faces, but allowed himself to be held by the glitter of the eyes. He once wrote about a portrait of Spenser which had impressed him; here there was no glitter of eyes, so his attention was held by the arch of the eyebrows, and he records nothing else.

The first impression conveyed by his ballad *Meg Merrilies* is that he has given a detailed account of her looks; but in fact he has seen nothing except the glitter of her eyes in the moonlight, the movement of her brown hands as she plaits rushes, and her tallness. Similarly with the ' lady seen for a few moments at Vauxhall ': he remembers the shine of her eyes against the evening illuminations and the rouged point of one cheekbone. Not having noted her lips, he tries to re-create them in sensuous memory by pressing his ear against them in his imagination; but what lives in his visual memory is the moving line of the wrist edge of her glove as she peeled it off her hand. In *La Belle Dame sans Merci* he gives a general description of her face as ' full beautiful,' but the only particularity recorded is the wildness of her eyes; of the rest of her nothing is seen except the light movement of her foot through the grass, and the swaying length of her hair.

His eye could be readily caught by what moved suddenly or freakishly or with emotional effect:

> *Scarce can his clear and nimble eye-sight follow*
> *The freaks and dartings of the black-winged swallow.*

But for the most part his sight was turned inwards, to a mind-sight built up by the other senses, as in men who have gone blind early in life and can remember only in flashes what sight is.

> *A lance . . . reflected clearly in a lake*
> *With the young ashen boughs, 'gainst which it rests*
> *And the half-seen mossiness of linnets' nests.*

He even deliberately externalizes colours that appear on the retina when the eye is shut:

> *Lo, I must tell a tale of chivalry*
> *For large white plumes are dancing in mine eye—*
> *Not like the formal crest of latter days*
> *But bending in a thousand graceful ways . . .*

3

Though Wordsworth tried to make accuracy and completeness of visual description, reinforced with religious or philosophical dogma, a substitute for poetic inspiration, he did at least look at the external shapes of things, and their relation one to another, and note them down conscientiously. He set out with the deliberation of a landscape painter. He records in *The Recluse* that as a boy he would choose, if possible, a look-out station which was aerial, though not giddy, with a depth of vale below and a height of hills above, and make it yield the most extensive possible field of vision. Thence he would gaze:

> *From high to low, from low to high, yet still*
> *Within the bound of this huge concave.*

In his early *Evening Walk* this habitual searching sweep of the eye is proved in action. It starts from the sky, rests on the hill-top, sweeps down the cliffs to the scree at the bottom, then up again by another line, and down again until the entire view is covered.

Every contributory object is seen against the background, the play of light and shadow is precisely recorded and nothing intruded (as with Keats) that is not visibly present. One downward sweep of the eye:

> *While, near the midway cliff, the silvered kite*
> *In many a whistling circle wheels her flight;*
> *Slant watery lights, from parting clouds, apace*
> *Travel along the precipices base;*
> *Cheering its naked waste of scattered stone,*
> *By lichens grey, and scanty moss, o'ergrown;*
> *Where scarce the foxglove peeps, or thistle's beard* . . .

Sixty years later he was still looking and recording in the same way. In *Musings near Aquapendente* he wrote:

> . . . *remembrance holds*
> *As a selected treasure thy one cliff,*
> *That, while it wore for melancholy crest*
> *A shattered convent, yet rose proud to have*
> *Clinging to its steep sides a thousand herbs*
> *And shrubs* . . . *behold, how far and near*
> *Garden and field all decked with orange bloom,*
> *And peach and citron, in Spring's mildest breeze*
> *Expanding; and along the smooth shore curved*
> *Into a natural port, a tideless sea* . . .

Then back again:

> . . . *while on the brink*
> *Of that high convent-crested cliff I stood* . . .

Against Keats' *Meg Merrilies* might be set Wordsworth's *Old Cumberland Beggar*. Wordsworth saw him entire and studied him against various backgrounds, noting precisely how he walked, sat, ate, what was the colour of his face and hair; how he looked in the company of villagers and fellow-travellers, even what his field of vision was:

> . . . *on the ground*
> *His eyes are turned, and, as he moves along*
> *They move along the ground; and, evermore,*
> *Instead of common and habitual sight*
> *Of field with rural works, of hill and dale,*
> *And the blue sky, one little span of earth*

> *Is all his prospect . . . seeing still*
> *And seldom knowing that he sees, some straw,*
> *Some scattered leaf, or marks which, in one track,*
> *The nails of cart or chariot wheel have left*
> *Impressed on the white road—in the same line*
> *At distance still the same.*

But he could describe the beggar so carefully only because he found him a picturesque subject for visual portraiture in the style of David Wilkie, not a friend or a live person. When emotion interrupted his visual habits, as in the *Lucy* poems, his descriptive power failed and he resorted to stock phrases: ' fresh as a rose in June,' ' fair as a star,' ' sportive as the fawn.' He gives us no hint of how Lucy looked, or walked, or sat or ate—only of how he himself felt about her before and after her death.

4

Coleridge's vision was of equal range and attention, but with a less studied choice of station than Wordsworth's, and his feelings were always derived from the sight; with Wordsworth it was a prepared feeling which determined the sight. Coleridge's anticipations of what he would see were often corrected by looking. In an early poem, *Reflections on Having Left a Place of Retirement,* he wrote:

> *. . . steep up the stony Mount*
> *I climbed with perilous toil and reached the top.*
> *Oh! what a goodly scene! Here the bleak mount,*
> *The bare bleak mountain speckled thin with sheep;*
> *Grey clouds, that shadowing spot the sunny fields;*
> *And river, now with bushy rocks o'er-browed,*
> *Now winding bright and full, with naked banks;*
> *And seats, and lawns, the Abbey and the wood,*
> *And cots, and hamlets, and faint city-spire;*
> *The Channel there, the Islands and white sails,*
> *Dim coasts, and cloud-like hills, and shoreless Ocean—*
> *It seemed like Omnipresence!*

He saw with his heart as well as with his eyes, and before long

learned to eliminate the merely descriptive from his poems. His letters
are full of such passages as this:

> We drank tea the night before I left Grasmere, on the Island in
> that lovely lake, our kettle swung over the fire hanging from the
> branch of a Fir-tree, and I lay and saw the woods, and mountains,
> and lake all trembling, and as it were *idealized* through the subtle
> smoke which rose up from the clear red embers of the fir-apples,
> which we had collected; afterwards we made a glorious Bonfire on
> the margin, by some elder bushes, whose twigs heaved and sobbed
> in the up-rushing column of smoke—and the Image of the Bonfire,
> and of us that danced round it—ruddy laughing faces in the twi-
> light . . .

He wrote that it was a ' well-known fact ' that what most impresses
the eye and stays the longest in memory is ' bright colours in motion.'
With Wordsworth, colour was seen not as an effect of changing light,
but as a condition or category—as the ' red ' in red-currants is an
adjective of category, or the ' red ' in red blackberries is one of condition. Blue sky or water to him meant calm weather; white road
meant drought; grey lichens were a different variety from the yellow.
The only critical use of colour I have discovered in Wordsworth's
poems is the adjective ' grain-tinctured ' applied to a cloudy sky. This
anomaly has a grotesque possible explanation: an accidental punning
transposition of Milton's ' skie-tinctured grain ' (*Paradise Lost,* V,
280), applied to the Phoenix's lowest set of wings. Wordsworth was a
draughtsman, who saw tone rather than colour and form rather than
tone and composition.

Comparing Snowdon with the Peaks, Coleridge wrote (1800):

> We have no mountains in the North equal to Snowdon, but then
> we have an encampment of huge mountains, in no harmony perhaps
> to the eye of the mere painter, but always interesting, various and
> as it were nutritive.

In a letter from Ratzeburg (1799) he had described at great length
the effects of light on a frozen lake covered with mist.

> When the sun peeped over the hills, the mist broke in the middle,
> and at last stood as the waters of the Red Sea are said to have done
> when the Israelites passed; and between the two walls of mist the
> sunlight burst upon the ice in a straight road of golden fire . . .
> intolerably bright, and the walls of mist partaking of the light in a
> *multitude* of colours. About a month ago the vehemence of the

wind had shattered the ice; part of it, quite shattered, was driven to
shore and had frozen anew; this was of a deep blue, and represented
an agitated sea—the water that ran up between the great islands of
ice shone of a yellow-green (it was at sunset), and all the scattered
islands of *smooth* ice were *blood,* intensely bright *blood* . . . In
skating there are three pleasing circumstances—firstly, the infinitely
subtle particles of ice which the skate cuts up, and which creep and
run before the skater like low mists, and in sunrise or sunset become
coloured; second, the shadow of the skater in the water seen through
the transparent ice; and thirdly, the melancholy undulating sound
from the skate.

He was perhaps the first English poet who saw colour as colour:
transient colour was a phenomenon which the ordinary eye was
hitherto trained to disregard as idle, change of colour being seen only
as it indicated what seemed material difference—colour of hair in
youth and age, of the sky at dawn or dusk, of fruits as they ripened,
of grass or leaves as they flourished or withered. For the rest, colour
was emblematic, as purple for royalty, green for jealousy, white for
purity; or distinctive, as ' my blue bowl, my russet nag, my red jerkin.'

Coleridge saw people not with the portraitist's eye but with the eye
of feeling tempered with judgment. Here is his description of the poet
Klopstock, whom he visited ' in a neat little parlour in a little commonplace summerhouse, one of a row.'

> The poet entered. I was much disappointed in his countenance,
> and recognized in it no likeness to the bust. There was no compre-
> hension in the forehead, no weight over the eyebrows, no expression
> of peculiarity, moral or intellectual, in the eyes, no massiveness in
> the general countenance. He is, if anything, rather below the middle
> size. He wore very large half-boots, which his legs filled, so fearfully
> were they swoln . . . His enunciation was not in the least affected
> by the entire want of his upper teeth . . . I looked at him with
> much emotion—I considered him as the venerable father of German
> poetry; as a good man; as a Christian; seventy-four years old; with
> legs enormously swoln, yet active, lively, cheerful and kind, and
> communicative. My eyes felt as if a tear were swelling into them.
> In the portrait of Lessing there was a toupee periwig, which enor-
> mously injured the effect of his physiognomy—Klopstock wore the
> same, powdered and frizzled. By the bye, old men ought never to
> wear powder—the contrast between a large snow-white wig and the
> colour of an old man's skin is disgusting, and wrinkles in such a
> neighborhood appear only channels for dirt . . . It is an honour to
> poets and great men that you think of them as parts of nature; and

anything of trick and fashion wounds you in them, as much as when you see venerable yews clipped into miserable peacocks. The author of the ' Messiah ' should have worn his own hair.

5

Sight to Milton was painful; he loved light, but it hurt him. The only colour that he saw happily was green, which he dwelt on for its human comfort, especially the green of an arbour or grove shading the eyes from the sun, which spelt for him either natural innocence or an occasion for acts of mortal lust. The sentiment of *Il Penseroso* constantly recurs in his poems.

> *And when the Sun begins to fling*
> *His flaring beams, me Goddess bring*
> *To arched walks of twilight groves . . .*
> *There in close covert by som Brook,*
> *Where no profaner eye may look,*
> *Hide me from Day's garish eie . . .*

But, as a change from mere green and the ' shadows brown ' of groves, he saw with pleasure the pale yellows, blues and pinks of Spring flowers.

In his *Comus* there is a famous debate in terms of sight on the subject of temperance, Comus arguing with the Lady against the waste of beauty in the Puritan-Stoic system of values. He holds that if all the world should in petulance feed on pulse, drink water, and wear only frieze, mankind would be strangled by the unused fertility of Nature:

> *Th'earth cumber'd, and the wing'd air dark't with plumes . . .*
> *The Sea o'refraught would swell, and th'unsought diamonds*
> *Would so emblaze the forehead of the Deep,*
> *And so bestudd with Stars, that they below*
> *Would grow inur'd to light, and come at last*
> *To gaze upon the Sun with shameless brows.*

But though he is here making a virtue of his photophobic weakness, interpreting it as humility and temperance, his secret ambition was to gaze on the Sun direct. While he had sight, twilight was the most ' genial ' time of day for him; and it was only in his blindness that he

gave way to his desire for the insufferable effulgence of sunlight on
diamonds, beryl, polished gold or whatever else would shine. In
Samson Agonistes, Samson does not long for colour and familiar
sights—he longs only for light. Milton desired to be, in relation to the
Sun or to solar truth, what the Son was to the Father. (*Paradise Lost,*
VI, 719.)

> *He said, and on his Son with Rayes direct*
> *Shon full, he all his Father full exprest*
> *Ineffably into his face received.*

His eye was seduced by ringlets, mazes, curious knots, Gordian
twines and quaint curves, which he intellectually rejected as wanton.
From descriptions in his poems it is clear that the first thing that he
saw in a woman was not her bright love-darting eye (as it was to
practically all his contemporaries), but her hair. He was, in fact, a
trichomaniac and if there was one passage in Classical literature which
disturbed him emotionally more than any other, it must have been
Apuleius' account of the same obsession in himself. (*Metamorphoses*
II, 8.—*Cum semper mihi unica cura fuerit . . .*)

> I have an obsession about hair. Whenever I meet a pretty woman,
> the first thing that catches my eye is her hair; I make a careful
> mental picture of it to carry home and brood over in private. This
> habit of mine I justify on a sound logical principle: that the hair is
> the most important and conspicuous feature of the body, and that its
> natural brilliance does for the head what gaily coloured clothes do
> for the trunk. In fact, it does a great deal more. You know how
> women, when they want to display their beauty to the full, shed
> their embroidered wraps and step out of their expensive dresses,
> and proudly reveal themselves with nothing on at all, aware that
> even the brightest gold tissue has less effect on a man than the deli-
> cate tints of a woman's naked body . . .
> What joy it is to see hair of a beautiful colour caught in the full
> rays of the sun, or shining with a milder lustre and constantly vary-
> ing its shade as the light shifts. Golden at one moment, at the next
> honey-coloured; or black as a raven's wing, but suddenly taking on
> the pale bluish tints of a dove's neck-feathers. Give it a gloss with
> spikenard lotion, part it neatly with a finely toothed comb, catch it
> up with a ribbon behind—and the lover will make it a sort of mirror
> to reflect his own delighted looks. And oh, when hair is bunched up
> thick in a luxurious mass on a woman's head, or, better still, allowed
> to flow rippling down her neck in profuse curls! I must content my-

self by saying briefly that such is the glory of a woman's hair that though she may be wearing the most exquisite clothes and the most expensive jewellery in existence, with everything else in keeping, she cannot look even moderately well dressed unless she has done her hair in proper style.

Fotis, I grant, needed no advanced knowledge of hairdressing: she could even indulge an apparent neglect of the art. Her way was to let her long, thick hair hang loosely down her neck, braiding the ends together and catching them up again with a broad ribbon to the top of her head; which was the exact spot where, unable to restrain myself a moment longer, I now printed a long passionate kiss . . .

If the woman's hair which Milton saw was bright and curled and dishevelled, like Fotis', he lusted; if it was smoothly braided he dared to love. It was only then that he noted the curve of her lips, and next the curves of her body. Vine-tendrils allured him so strongly that he seemed to see them in motion—' the gadding Vine,' ' the mantling vine that crawls '; and in *Comus,* the Genius of the wood claimed the power

> . . . *to curl the grove*
> *With Ringlets quaint, and wanton windings wove.*

With a man he first saw the brow, then the eyes beneath, then the hair. His descriptions of Adam and Eve are:

> *His fair large Front and Eye sublime declar'd*
> *Absolute rule; and Hyacinthin Locks*
> *Round from his parted forelock manly hung*
> *Clustering, but not beneath his shoulders broad:*
> *She as a veil down to the slender waste*
> *Her unadorned golden tresses wore*
> *Disheveled, but in wanton ringlets wav'd*
> *As the Vine curls her tendrils . . .*

At Cambridge he wore very long hair and had the reputation of being narcissistic: ' Our Lady of Christ's ' was his nickname. He cherished the recollection of his former good looks in his gouty old age and made blind Samson lament:

> . . . *these redundant locks*
> *Robustious to no purpose clustering down.*

In looking at scenery he seems to have started with his eye on the ground and raised it gradually upward to the tree-tops or wooded hills, and then lowered it as the light hurt his eyes, then looked ' from side to side in bredth.'

6

Donne, in his amatory poems, saw no more than the reflection of his own hopes and fears:

> *I fixe mine eye on thine, and there*
> *Pitty my picture burning in thine eye.*

He involved his mistress in this seeing:

> *Our eye-beames twisted, and did thred*
> *Our eyes, upon one double string . . .*
> *And pictures in our eyes to get*
> *Was all our propagation.*

And then blamed her for what had happened because of his own habit of self-looking:

> *Send home my long strayed eyes to me,*
> *Which too long have dwelt on thee.*

though in another poem he had begged the God of Love:

> *Give me thy weaknesse, make me blinde*
> *. . . In eyes and minde.*

He mistrusted the eye as seeing only the outward loveliness of a woman:

> *For he who colour loves, and skinne*
> *Loves but their oldest clothes.*

and:

> *I never stoop'd so low, as they*
> *Which on an eye, cheeke, lip can prey,*
> *Seldome to them, which soare no higher*
> *Than vertue or the minde t'admire . . .*

Every sight he saw was either negligible or unpoetic unless it could be compressed into a striking image: as lead pouring in a stream from the roof of a burning church, or the young preacher in his first sermon singling out for violent harangue a lady whom he has wronged. For the most part he borrowed his images either from popular literature —the sick turquoise, the pregnant woman ready to travail at the sight of some food she loathes—or from science: such images as celestial and terrestrial globes, meridians, parallels, the Antipodes, appealed to his inner sight for their regularity and comprehensiveness. His outward eye he seems to have kept deliberately blinkered.

'MAD MR. SWINBURNE'

(1945)

Many waters cannot quench love,
Neither can the floods drown it.
Who shall snare or slay the white dove,
Faith, whose very dreams crown it,
Gird it round with grace and peace, deep,
Warm, and pure, and soft as sweet sleep?
Many waters cannot quench love,
Neither can the floods drown it.

Set me as seal upon thine heart,
As a seal upon thine arm,
How should we behold the days depart,
And the nights resign their charm?
Love is as the soul: though hate and fear
Waste and overthrow, they strike not here.
Set me as a seal upon thine heart,
As a seal upon thine arm.

This poem touches me in a peculiar way, for ' Mad Mr. Swinburne '
is inextricably mixed in my childhood memories with such mythological figures of terror as the Ogre of Beanstalk Castle, the Bogy Man,
the hosts of Midian prowling and prowling around, and Charlie
Peace, the murderer who used to hide in his victims' houses, spread-
eagled under a dining-room table-top. My parents lived on the fringe
of Wimbledon Common over which in the late 'nineties my sisters
and I used to be taken out most mornings by our nurse. Usually we

went past Rushmere Pond and across to the Putney Road, which had a tall avenue of trees lining the Common side, with long wooden benches provided at intervals. This was Nurses' Walk and along crowded Nurses' Walk every morning at the same hour from his lair at ' The Pines,' Putney, came ' Mad Mr. Swinburne ' rattling the two-pence in his pocket which was the daily allowance made him by his friend Theodore Watts-Dunton for a pint of beer at the near-by Rose and Crown Inn.

' Mad Mr. Swinburne ' was said by some nurses to be ' Wicked Mr. Swinburne '—I suppose because he had once written some shocking poems, though this was not explained to me at the time—and many of them used to gather up their charges and hurry away at his ap-proach. My picture of him is of a nimble and shrill-voiced gnome dressed in a biscuit-coloured suit with tails and talking insistently and shrilly at the top of his voice. He had wispy white locks and a tall hat perched at the back of his head; but this part is perhaps confused by a memory of Tenniel's Mad Hatter in *Alice in Wonderland*. His mad-ness consisted chiefly in his addressing respectable nurses without an introduction and gazing ecstatically into their perambulators.

On one occasion ' Mad Mr. Swinburne ' succeeded in catching me, having appeared suddenly from behind a tree near the Jubilee foun-tain, and bestowed some sort of blessing on me—I was too frightened to know what—but it had great literary virtue, as I afterwards learned, because Swinburne as a young man had received the blessing of Wal-ter Savage Landor, and Landor as a child, the blessing of Dr Samuel Johnson.

The rhythm in this poem is extraordinarily powerful and resurrects deep-sunken memories, but with a corrective vision of a little nimble old man no longer wicked, or ogreish, or mad, but drunk with uni-versal love—the unhappy excesses of his youth and middle-age for-gotten—and joyfully welcoming the Kingdom of Heaven in the persons of certain overdressed, overfed, priggish little late-Victorian children. I can still discern the insistent shrillness in the assonantal play of ' slay . . . faith '; ' peace, deep '; ' sweet sleep '; ' nights re-sign '; ' hate . . . waste '—at which technicians of the Miltonic and Tennysonian schools would virtuously shudder. For myself, I would not have the poem otherwise, though Swinburne of course had not the least idea of the meaning of the verses in the *Canticles,* out of

which he has built it. It is the May-bride of Shunem, a well-watered
village of Lower Galilee, who is addressing her lover of the year:
' Set me like an amulet on your right arm, the satchel (containing the
Divine Name), turned towards your heart.' The Jewish editors of the
Scriptures, unwilling to suppress this ancient collection of marriage
songs, made them symbolic of the love of Israel for Jehovah; the
Christian Church followed suit shamelessly by making them symbolic
of the love of the Church for her Redeemer.

THE GHOST OF MILTON

(1947)

In 1942 while I was writing *Wife to Mr. Milton,* a historical novel about Milton's life with Marie Powell, his first wife, I felt his ghost haunting my writing-table with glowering eyes and minatory whispers; but refused to be daunted. The ghost has walked England in times of national crises ever since Wordsworth conjured it up during the Napoleonic wars:

> *Milton! thou shouldst be living at this hour:*
> *England hath need of thee: she is a fen*
> *Of stagnant waters: altar, sword, and pen,*
> *Fireside, the heroic wealth of hall and bower,*
> *Have forfeited their ancient English dower*
> *Of inward happiness. We are selfish men;*
> *Oh! raise us up, return to us again;*
> *And give us manners, virtue, freedom, power.*
> *Thy soul was like a Star, and dwelt apart;*
> *Thou hadst a voice whose sound was like the sea:*
> *Pure as the naked heavens, majestic, free,*
> *So didst thou travel on life's common way,*
> *In cheerful godliness; and yet thy heart*
> *The lowliest duties on herself did lay.*

But the final effect of a year spent in reading Milton's works in bulk and detail, together with all the available historical evidence about his life, was a thankfulness that he was *not* living at that hour.

When my novel was published, the reviewers, both British and American, were inspired to righteous indignation. They accused me

of ' guying Milton in preposterous fashion, in disregard of contemporary evidence, and reducing him to the stock figure of the ranting,
long-nosed Puritan of farce '; of maliciously giving Marie, the supposed authoress of the story, a lively and charming character whereas,
as all the world knew, she was a ' clod ' and a ' manacle '; and of out-
raging history by my suggestion that Milton sent her home after a
wedding-night fiasco and a month of unconsummated marriage,
whereas, they said, the marriage was unquestionably consummated
and it was Marie who deserted him. Worse, I had not allowed him to
speak a single word of great poetry from the first chapter to the last.
Two or three of them took their stand on *Lycidas:* nobody, they declared, could have written so perfect a poem and treated his wife as
badly as I made out. One wrote:

> Where is the ' sweet and affable deportment ' recorded by the
> anonymous biographer who was probably his younger Phillips
> nephew; the ' delightful company, the life of the conversation, the
> unaffected cheerfulness and civility ' remembered by his daughter
> Deborah; the courteous scholar, ' extreme pleasant in his conversa-
> tion, and at dinner, supper, etc.,' described by Aubrey, Richardson,
> Edward Phillips and the rest? Where is the Milton who made such a
> tremendous social success with the polite Italians during his tour
> of 1638 and 1639? This vulgar bully and churl is not he. Nor is
> Mary credible. Far from being the dull girl, the ' mute and spiritless
> mate,' the ' image of earth and phlegm,' only good for physical inter-
> course, of the divorce pamphlets, here is a clever, lively, highly
> educated young woman, holding her own in conversation with
> Milton himself.

This reaction interested me as a proof of the extraordinary power
still exercised by Milton's ghost, which on a plea of blindness has
secured a charitable conspiracy of silence about his true character and
actions. I had thought it only fair, since Milton's prejudiced account
of Marie had so long held the field, to let her borrow my pen and
say her say as the spirited daughter of a Royalist father—Richard
Powell, J.P., lessee of the Manor House at Forest Hill, Oxford, a village within easy walk of Magdalen Bridge. But she wrote of Milton
as a renegade Arminian and renegade Royalist, not as the prick-eared
Puritan of farce: and if he ranted in her account, he ranted in pure
Miltonic, not in Hudibrastic, style.

Since Marie was the writer, no ' contemporary evidence ' as to

events after her death was relevant, and it is certain that between
Whitsun 1642 when, at the age of thirty-three, Milton went on a visit
to Forest Hill to collect a large debt and astounded his household by
bringing back not the money but the debtor's sixteen-year-old daughter, and May 6, 1652, when she died, having borne him four children,
he wrote no poems at all. Apart from official correspondence, some
occasional verse and a few rudimentary works of scholarship, his
writing was wholly polemical and much of it vituperative and obscene.
It would have been absurd for me to bring him on the stage spouting
great poetry.

Jonathan Richardson, a sincere admirer of *Paradise Lost,* has given
us the domestic background (*Explanatory Notes and Remarks on
Milton's Paradise Lost* [1734]):

> He had other domestic vexations, particularly that uncommon
> and severe one of the affront and scorn of a wife he loved and the
> continuance of it for some years, and this without allowing him time
> to know what conjugal happiness was. Many of his choicest years
> of life were employed in wrangling, and receiving and racquetting
> back reproach, accusation and sarcasm. Which though he had an
> arm and dexterity fitted for, 'twas an exercise of his abilities very
> disagreeable to him; as it must be to one accustomed to praise, as
> he was in his younger years . . .

No ' mute and spiritless mate ' she! His ill-temper seems to have been
partly due to constipation, for Edward Phillips goes out of his way to
report the name of his favourite laxative. It is possible that later, after
having known ' what conjugal happiness was ' by marriages to Kath-
erine Woodstock (' my late espoused saint ') and to Elizabeth Min-
shull, and abandoned polemics in favour of religious epics, Milton
may have become more cheerful, and behaved affably and civilly to
guests, so long as they admired his genius and sympathized with his
blindness and his crippling gout. But only to his guests, not to his
three daughters by Marie.

Wordsworth's eulogy of Milton's inward happiness as he travelled
on life's common way majestic and free as a Star is flatly contra-
dicted by Richardson, who records that after the Restoration he was:

> . . . in perpetual terror of being assassinated. Though he had
> escaped the talons of the law he knew he had made himself enemies
> in abundance. He was so dejected he would lie awake whole nights.

As for Wordsworth's view of his unselfishness and virtue, it does not bear even a casual scrutiny. He was egotistical, unscrupulous and grasping. Fundamentally he was interested in nothing but his own career; in hacking his way to the Temple of Fame over the dead bodies of his enemies, rivals and friends. Granted, he was a loyal servant of God, but he made God a shield and buckler for his own murderous campaign. Even in his Latin *Lament for Damon* (Charles Diodati), grief for his friend's death does not prevent the intrusion of a long passage about his own epical ambitions. He paid the price of blindness not so much for the defence of the Commonwealth as for the conquest of Salmasius: 'Conquering kings their titles take . . .' and he hoped that if he completely confounded Salmasius in his own field, he would succeed to the title of First Scholar of Europe. His austerities were not a gauge of his virtue: they were founded on a mystical belief in the magical power of chastity as a means to immortality. But his ambitions proved his undoing. When the Civil War threatened and dramatic poetry went out of fashion he decided to win public fame by polemical writing, and this insensibly drew him into dishonesty. By the time he had been made Secretary for the Foreign Tongues to the Council of State (a proto-Fascist institution) and incidentally Assistant Press Censor—why is this fact kept out of the textbooks when so much stress is laid on the *Areopagitica?*—he had smudged his moral copybook so badly that he had even become a 'crony' of Marchmont Needham, the disreputable turncoat journalist. The evidence that he arranged for the interpolation of an extra prayer into one of the many early editions of *Eikon Basilike* and then made it the subject of a scurrilous attack, in *Eikonoclastes,* on the memory of Charles I is fairly conclusive; and that he suspected that the book was itself a forgery does not make the action any less disgraceful. When the Commonwealth collapsed, he naturally returned to his early poetic ambitions.

The temporary hospitality he gave to Richard Powell when he brought his hungry and down-at-heels family to London after the capitulation of Oxford is often presented as an act of generosity; but the legal documents in the case tell a different story. That Powell had twice cheated him, first by borrowing money on worthless security and then by contracting to pay him a £1,000 dowry on the day he married Marie, but without any hope of doing so, does not exculpate

Milton from the charge of moral baseness: he profited from Powell's helplessness—he was a dying man—to secure moneys from his estate to which a certain ' widow Ashcroft ' had a prior claim; and he later defrauded Ann Powell of her ' widow's thirds.'

The Italian tour, quoted by the reviewer in evidence of Milton's social qualities, was undertaken before his marriage; and he evidently then felt that he was treading on classical holy ground and must put his best foot forward. He was anxious to show the Italians that a ' frozen Hyperborean ' could be a man of charm, sensibility and erudition. The Italians have always been pleased to welcome distinguished Northerners who talk fluent Italian, know their Virgil, and write fairly correct little Italian love-poems. However, it is on record that Milton offended the religious susceptibilities of some of his hosts by tactless disputation, and that others found him uncomfortably strait-laced.

As for the early days of the marriage, Milton's nephew and pupil, Edward Phillips, who was a child of eleven in 1643, recorded his impression forty-three years later that a few weeks after the marriage Marie went home to Oxford on a visit but did not return to London when summoned, her family being staunch Cavaliers and Oxford being the Royalist headquarters. The impression of his brother John Phillips, who was nine at the time, also recorded about forty-three years later, was that Marie did not like the ' reserved ' life in Milton's Aldgate Street house and was encouraged by her mother to desert him. Earlier evidence, not easy to set aside, is Ann Powell's plea, July 16, 1651, to the Commissioners of Sequestration at Haberdashers' Hall, that she could not prosecute Milton for a debt he owed her because he was:

> . . . a harsh and chollericke man, and married to Mrs. Powell's daughter, who would be undone if any such course were taken against him by Mrs. Powell, he having turned away his wife heretofore for a long space upon some other occasion.

Believing that each of these accounts had some truth in it, I did my best to reconcile them in the light of the military and political situation, the financial relations of Milton and his father-in-law, and the state of the divorce laws in 1643.

The marriage-night fiasco can be deduced negatively from the ideal account of Adam and Eve's honeymoon in *Paradise Lost* and positively from a variety of lesser sources. It is nowhere stated by Milton or any contemporary that the marriage was consummated but the reviewers considered this proved because, as one of them wrote, ' the whole gravamen of Milton's complaint was of the baseness and horror of a merely physical union between those whose minds are so far apart that the higher purposes of matrimony, cheerful society and intelligent and affectionate intercourse, are impossible.' He quoted from *Tetrachordon:*

> What courts of concupiscence are these, wherein fleshly appetite is heard before right reason, lust before love or devotion?

But this quotation was irrelevant since it refers only to the question whether a wife's misconduct is a better cause for *divorce* than incompatibility of temperament. The difference between dissolution and divorce under Canon Law, the authority of which Milton did not challenge, was that after a dissolution either spouse was at liberty to marry again; but after a divorce (for which a wife's adultery was a valid plea) the husband was entitled to separation only and would be committing bigamy if he married again. The violence of the four divorce pamphlets irresistibly suggests the effect on a chaste, sensuous, thirty-four-year-old he-virgin of frustrated consummation of marriage. Had there been consummation, Milton would never have found it in his conscience to attempt, in 1645, a technically bigamous marriage to ' Dr. Davis's daughter.' Clearly, he considered that since he had not been paid the marriage dowry; and since he had temporarily returned Marie to her father with her maidenhead intact; and since she had afterwards refused to come back to him; and since because of the Civil War there were no bishops available to dissolve the marriage, he had a right to consider himself free. It was fortunate for him that Marie came back in time: had bigamy been proved against him at the Restoration, as well as political crimes, neither *Paradise Lost* nor *Samson Agonistes* would have been written.

As for Richardson's story, related at second-hand, of the party of gentlemen, admirers of Milton's poems, who visited his youngest daughter Deborah (then married to a poor Irish artisan) early in the reign of George I, and asked for memories of her late father—surely it was only natural for her to tell them what they cared to hear? Addison, one of the visitors, made her a handsome present. But we have sworn evidence in the Canterbury Prerogative Court case, in which she and her sisters had overturned his nuncupative will, which shows their life with him to have been hateful. The will is shocking. Milton makes the non-payment of Marie's dowry the excuse for disinheriting his daughters by her:

> The portion due to me from Mr. Powell, my former wife's father, I leave to the unkind children[1] I had by her, having received no part of it; but my meaning is, they shall have no other benefit of my estate than the said portion and what I have besides done for them, they having been very undutiful to me. All the rest of my estate I leave to disposal of Elizabeth, my wife.

My attitude to Milton must not be misunderstood. A man may rebel against the current morality of his age and still be a true poet, because a higher morality than the current is entailed on all poets whenever and wherever they live: the morality of love. Though the quality of love in a painter's work, or a musician's, will endear him to his public, he can be a true painter or musician even if his incapacity for love has turned him into a devil. But without love he cannot be a poet in the final sense. Shakespeare sinned greatly against current morality, but he loved greatly. Milton's sins were petty by comparison, but his lack of love, for all his rhetorical championship of love against lust, makes him detestable.

With all possible deference to his admirers, Milton was not a great poet, in the sense in which Shakespeare was great. He was a minor poet with a remarkable ear for music, before diabolic ambition impelled him to renounce the true Muse and bloat himself up, like Virgil (another minor poet with the same musical gift) into a towering,

---

[1] The reason of their unkindness is not far to seek. John Phillips records that:

' . . . excusing only the eldest daughter by reason of her bodily infirmity and difficult utterance of speech (which to say truth I doubt was the principal cause of excusing her) the other two were condemn'd to the performance of Reading, and exactly pronouncing of all the Languages of whatever Book he should at one time or other think fit to peruse. Viz. the Hebrew (and I think the Syriac), the Greek, the Latin, the Italian, Spanish and French. All which sorts of Books to be confined to Read, without understanding one word must needs be a Tryal of patience, almost beyond endurance; but it was endured by both for a long time, but broke out more and more into expressions of uneasiness.'

Deborah, ' his favourite,' escaped to Ireland three or four years before his death, as a lady's companion.

rugged major poet. There is strong evidence that he consciously composed only a part of *Paradise Lost;* the rest was communicated to him by what he regarded as a supernatural agency.

The effect of *Paradise Lost* on sensitive readers is, of course, overpowering. But is the function of poetry to overpower? To be overpowered is to accept spiritual defeat. Shakespeare never overpowers: he raises up. To put the matter in simple terms, so as not to get involved in the language of the morbid psychologist: it was not the Holy Ghost that dictated *Paradise Lost*—the poem which has caused more unhappiness, to the young especially, than any other in the language —but Satan the protagonist, demon of pride. The majesty of certain passages is superhuman, but their effect is finally depressing and therefore evil. Parts of the poem, as for example his accounts of the rebel angels' military tactics with concealed artillery, and of the architecture of Hell, are downright vulgar: vulgarity and classical vapidity are characteristic of the passages which intervene between the high flights, the communicated diabolisms.

The very familiarity of *Lycidas* discourages critical comment and it is usually assumed—though I disagree with this—that Dr Johnson showed a lack of poetic feeling when he criticized the falsity of its sentiments and imagery:

> It is not to be considered as the effusion of real passion: for passion runs not after remote allusions and obscure opinions. Passion plucks no berries from the myrtle and ivy, nor calls upon Arethuse and Mincius, nor tells of tough satyr and fauns with cloven hoof. Where there is leisure for fiction there is little grief.

Milton's effusion was certainly not spontaneous; in 1637 he had been invited to collaborate in a projected memorial anthology in honour of Edward King, his late fellow-student at King's College, Cambridge, and was apparently the last to send in his piece. It is unlikely that his grief for King was any more sincere than the admiration he had expressed for Shakespeare seven years previously when similarly invited to compose a commendatory sonnet for a new edition of the Plays (the first of his poems to be printed[2]); and young King's

---

[2] In the 1645 edition of his *Poems,* Milton is careful to date the sonnet ' 1630,' as if to show that the humble admiration for Shakespeare which he professes there should be discounted as youthful modesty. The only other reference he

appointment by Royal mandate to a vacant College Fellowship seems to have so embittered Milton, who considered that he had the first claim to it himself, as to turn him into an anti-monarchist. There is authentic emotion in *Lycidas,* but it springs, as in his *Lament for Damon,* from the realization that young intellectuals of his generation are as liable as anyone else to die suddenly;[3] Fate's latest victim might well have been John Milton, not Edward King; which would have been a far more serious literary disaster. It also springs, but more obscurely, from the Fellowship grudge—apparently the irrelevant attack, in the second part of the poem, on Bishops who are unfaithful to their flocks, was aimed at William Chappell, his hated former College tutor, recently promoted Bishop of Ross, as being the enemy who had secured King his Fellowship. Dr Johnson was rightly scandalized by the sudden change at this point in the poem from ' the vulgar pastoral . . . in which appear the heathen deities Jove and Phoebus,

---

ever makes to Shakespeare is a patronizing mention in *L'Allegro* of (apparently) *As You Like It:*

> Or sweetest *Shakespear* fancies childe,
> Warble his native wood-note wilde.

The English poet for whom he felt the strongest antipathy was John Skelton, in whom poetic love was instinctive, whose conscience never made a coward of him and who openly repudiated all unnatural austerities while in the service of the Muse Calliope. Here I suspect retrospective jealousy in Milton, masked as virtuous scorn, for a man who had won degrees at three, not merely two, universities; whom Erasmus had described as ' the light and glory of English letters '; and whom Henry VIII, a poet himself, had crowned with laurel. It is not generally realized that Milton is referring to Skelton in his *Areopagitica:*

' I name not him for posterity's sake, whom Henry the 8th named in merriment his vicar of hell.'

Milton has deliberately obscured the point of Henry's joke, which conveyed no moral censure: Skelton was Rector of Diss in Norfork, and *Dis* was the Roman Underworld, or Hell.

[3] It was a silly death. The ship in which King was returning to Ireland fouled a sunken rock close to the Anglesey coast only a short distance from land and began to sink. The sea was calm but (like the Knave of Hearts and Blackbeard the Pirate) King had never learned to swim. There was no lifeboat handy, and the crew had apparently grabbed all the available empty casks. So he knelt praying quietly on the deck until he went down with the ship. The moral seems to have been lost on Milton: in his treatise *Of Education,* he recommends weapon-training, dancing, wrestling, riding and visits to the Navy as recreations that should supplement a young gentleman's study of theology and the liberal sciences, but makes no mention of swimming.

Neptune and Aeolus . . .' to a satire on contemporary Church Government. He writes:

> The shepherd is now a feeder of sheep and afterwards an ecclesiastical pastor, a superintendent of a Christian flock. Such equivocations are always unskilful; but here they are indecent.

When he adds that *Lycidas* ' has no art,' this is true only in the sense that it is a poem strangled by art. Johnson sturdily resisted the musical spell which the opening lines cast on more sensitive readers:

> *Yet once more, O ye Laurels, and once more*
> *Ye Myrtles brown, with Ivy never-sear,*
> *I com to pluck your Berries harsh and crude,*
> *And with forc'd fingers rude,*
> *Shatter your leaves before the mellowing year.*

and did not trouble to examine carefully the principles on which they were written.

So far as I know, nobody has ever pointed out that in the extravagantly artful interlacing of alliteration throughout this passage Milton is adapting to English metrical use the device of *cynghanedd,* or recurrent consonantal sequences, used by the Welsh bards whom he mentions appreciatively early in the poem. It may well be that he learned of the device when he visited the Court of the President of Wales, for whom he had written *Comus,* in 1634.

The initial consonants of the first lines are an alliterative interlace of Y.M.L. which is interrupted by the harshness of the alliterative pairs B.B., C.C., and F.F., and which, after *Shatter,* reappears to decorate the ' dying close.' The interlace of C.S.D. in the next two lines is linked to the foregoing with another B.B.:

> *. . . leaves before the mellowing year.*
> *Bitter constraint, and sad occasion dear,*
> *Compels me to disturb your season due . . .*

Then follows a more complicated interlace: a P.H.N.L. sequence connected to the C.S.D. sequence by a bridge of D's, and followed by a watery succession of W's to close the stanza.

> *For* Lycidas *is dead, dead ere his prime*
> *Young* Lycidas, *and hath not left his peer:*

Who would not sing for Lycidas? *he knew*
Himself to sing, and build the lofty rhyme.
He must not flote upon his watry bear
Unwept, and welter to the parching wind,
Without the meed of som melodious tear.

It was naughty of Johnson to pretend that ' the diction is harsh, the rhymes uncertain, the numbers unpleasing ': the sound of the poem is magnificent; only the sense is deficient. In the opening lines *Brown,* introduced for its resonance and as an alliterative partner to *Berries,* suggests a false contrast between myrtle leaves which go brown and ivy leaves that stay green; whereas both sorts of leaf go brown in old age and fall off after younger leaves have taken their place. Laurel is sacred to Apollo, the god of poetry; ivy to Dionysus-Osiris, the god of resurrection; myrtle to Venus, goddess of love. But ivy and myrtle drop out of the poem immediately and seem to have been introduced only for the melodious sound of their names; and though it is clear from the next lines that Lycidas' death, in August before the year has mellowed, has unseasonably forced Milton's hand, he does not explain why he has to shatter the leaves of these trees while plucking the un-ripe berries. If he needs the berries, though of these three sorts only myrtle berries are edible, when they ripen in mid-winter, he does not have to disturb the leaves; if he needs a wreath he can cut a young shoot and shatter neither berries nor leaves. Clearly *Shatter* is used merely for its violence of sound; the presumed sense is ' I have come to pluck your berries and leaves before the year has mellowed,' but this is not conveyed.

And if he needs a wreath, for whom is it intended? For himself, later to converse with Apollo and have his ears encouragingly touched, or for the laureate hearse of his fellow-poet? The exigencies of his complicated metrical scheme have blurred the logic of the stanza—*parching* and *melodious* are further examples of words chosen for their sound at the expense of meaning—but his musical craftsmanship has lulled successive generations of readers into de-lighted acquiescence, and in Johnson's words ' driven away the eye from nice examination.' It is enough for them to catch the general drift: that a poet has died before his time, shattering the hopes of his friends, and that a fellow-poet, suddenly aware that he is human too, is fumbling broken-heartedly among the evergreens with a confused notion that he ought to weave someone—but whom?—a garland of some sort or other; and that he feels vaguely (but is too downhearted to work the theory out) that the Bishops are to blame for everything.

THE COMMON ASPHODEL

(1949)

The poetic education given in the modern English literature class is meagre and wholly unpractical: it does not include a course in primitive religion, without a grounding in which such poems as *La Belle Dame sans Merci, The Ancient Mariner* and *Tom o'Bedlam's Song* yield only a small part of their sense; or even in elementary nature study. One could, for example, get full marks by answering the classroom question ' What is Asphodel? ' with ' A yellow flower mentioned by Homer as growing in Elysium, on soft beds of which the souls of the just were believed, in his time, to rest their weary limbs.'

But this answer would be inaccurate as well as insufficient. Pope who wrote in his *St. Cecilia's Day:*

> . . . *Happy souls who dwell*
> *In yellow meads of asphodel*

and Tennyson who wrote in his *Lotos-Eaters:*

> . . . *Some, 'tis whispered, down in Hell*
> *Suffer endless anguish, others in Elysian valleys dwell,*
> *Resting weary limbs at last on beds of asphodel.*

were seldom poets enough to check their botanical facts, and here they have blundered badly. Asphodel meads are not yellow and even ghosts would find asphodel beds extremely uncomfortable for lying about on.

The asphodel is a tall, tough-stemmed, handsome whitish flower, known in England as ' king's spear,' with bunchy leaves not unlike a daffodil's. (' Daffodil,' by the way, derives its name from ' asphodel ';

and it may have been king's spear otherwise known as ' affodel ', not the narcissus-like daffodil, which Milton ordered to fill its cup with tears at Lycidas' funeral. But the ' nectared lavers strewed with asphodel,' of *Comus,* are nonsensical whichever flower he meant.) It grows wild on the poorest soil in most parts of the Mediterranean countries, and the asphodel meadow through which, in the *Odyssey,* the dead walked should be pictured as rocky and waterless waste-ground with clumps of caper, spurge and lentiscus. Nor was Elysium even in Homer's time a place where the souls of the just were sent; it was where the souls of kings were privileged to go, irrespective of moral qualities. Their vassals and subjects, however virtuous, were not so blessed and had to descend to darker and less pleasant places underground. Elysium—the word is apparently pre-Greek—seems to have been originally a river-mouth islet to which the king's corpse was brought for burial, like King Arthur's to Avalon, and where he became an oracular hero. When this custom was discontinued in Mycenaean times ' the islands of the blessed ' became a mere figure of speech and in the *Odyssey* they are vaguely located in the far West ' beyond the streams of Ocean, the White Rock, the Gates of the Sun and the Land of Dreams.' The White Rock was perhaps the Dover cliff-line.

Asphodelos as a flower name occurs nowhere in Homer; but four times as an adjective qualifying *leimon,* a meadow. It probably there-fore stands for: *a,* not; *spod,* ashes (*spod* could become *sphod* in Attic Greek); *elos,* valley. If so, the *asphodelos leimon* is really ' the meadow in the valley of what escapes unburned,' namely of the king's soul which survives the funeral pyre; and *leimon* (formed from *leibo,* ' pour ') may mean, rather, ' libation-place.' The connexion between these sepulchral islands and the asphodel, or king's spear, which is first mentioned by the early poet Hesiod, seems to be that it was a food plant. Although in Classical times asphodel and mallow were, prover-bially, eaten only by the very poor, they must once, before corn was grown in Greece on a large scale, have been the staple diet even of kings. The asphodel has potato-like tubers, often as many as eighty to a single plant, which when baked in wood ash and eaten with salt and oil are said to be nourishing; Hesiod mentions an appetizing dish of baked asphodel beaten up with figs, but I do not know that anyone has sampled it in modern times. The seeds were also parched and

eaten like corn, and even made into bread. Mallows are still popular
in the south of France but asphodel has everywhere been ousted from
the poor man's table by the potato; even the recent famine in the
Greek islands failed to repopularize it. And the leaves are no fodder
for sheep or goats, though pigs will eat the tubers if they are hungry
enough.

Since the asphodel must have been the only food plant which the
souls of heroes would find growing in profusion on their sepulchral
islands, ' the dead,' as Sir Thomas Browne records in his *Urn-Burial,*
' are made to eat Asphodels about the Elysian meadows.' And since
the tubers, like the souls, rose blessedly from the ashes of their wood-
fire, the plant is likely to have taken its Greek name from the place,
' the valley of what escapes unburned,' rather than the place from the
plant.

The later Greeks in defiance of the laws of etymology explained
the word as formed from *aspis,* a viper, and *deilos,* terrible; which
amounted to calling it ' snake's bane.' It was said that snakes could be
kept at a distance by scattering its seeds on the ground; and the
physician Nicander recommended the juice of the stems as a cure for
snake-bite. These were guesses only and could easily have been disproved by experiment; but guesses based on primitive homoeopathic
logic. Since the young stems closely resemble snakes; and since their
royal flowers appear at the Spring Equinox when the Sun-god cele-
brates his victory over the Great Snake of winter; and since asphodels
grow in Elysium where the blessed heroes walk; and since heroes are
embodied in oracular snakes—therefore asphodel must be good
against snakes. And since snakes were poetically connected with generation long before Freud exploited the symbolism, asphodel must
also be a powerful aphrodisiac—as Pliny says it is. (This can also be
easily disproved by experiment.) Pliny records that the stalks were
hung up outside Italian farm-houses to keep off noxious spells: the
theory probably being that common ghosts and demons, conjured up
by witches to harm the inmates, would mistake the place for the
asphodel meadows in the Islands of the Blessed, where they had no
right to go.

Brockhaus' Konversations-Lexikon (1925) says that sugar and
alcohol are now extracted from asphodel tubers, especially in the
Languedoc. But the yield does not seem to be very high; an asphodel

factory started five or six years ago in Majorca (where I live) during a sugar famine failed dismally, though the raw material is plentiful here and may be had for the carting.

I think that this is quite enough about asphodel.

Date Due

SEP 9 '57